Heroic Fraternities

Heroic Fraternities

How College Men Can Save Universities and America

Anthony B. Bradley

WIPF & STOCK · Eugene, Oregon

HEROIC FRATERNITIES
How College Men Can Save Universities and America

Wipf & Stock
An Imprint of Wipf and Stock Publishers
199 W. 8th Ave., Suite 3
Eugene, OR 97401

www.wipfandstock.com

PAPERBACK ISBN: 978-1-6667-1553-8
HARDCOVER ISBN: 978-1-6667-1554-5
EBOOK ISBN: 978-1-6667-1555-2

02/27/23

To my Clemson University Pi Alpha brothers of Alpha Phi Alpha, Inc.
who first taught me what fraternity means
and
to Nick Fischer and the men of Sigma Phi Society at UVA
who helped me see that a heroic future for fraternities was possible.

Contents

Acknowledgments

This is a book about human flourishing and early research for this project overlapped with grant support I received from the Acton Institute. I am forever grateful for their dedication to supporting scholars who advocate for a free and virtuous society. This book would not exist were it not for the work of my research assistant Jackson Kane, a former student at The King's College. He did a significant amount of research, helped provide the framework for more than one chapter, and he personally conducted student interviews. Jackson's ideas, questions, and insight provided critical direction for the book. Noah Ebel, a student at The King's College at the time of the writing of this book, provided essential framing for the chapter on fraternity history, based on an independent study "Religion, Fraternity, and Sports in American Society," which informed his work with the book. I also like to thank Isaac White for his work in managing the fraternity president interviews. I am fortunate to have worked with very gifted students and alumni.

During the writing of this book, I had the opportunity to test these ideas out in front of fraternity audiences at the University of Virginia and the University of Mississippi. At UVA, I'd like to thank Nick Fischer and Sigma Phi for the invitation to come and address the men on grounds about heroic masculinity. At the University of Mississippi, I'd like to thank Brian Sorgenfrei for getting me connected with former Sigma Nu president Reed Peets. Additionally, I'd like to thank Andrew Meyer, who was president of the Interfraternity Council at The University of Mississippi during the writing of this book, for making the arrangements to present heroic masculinity to fraternity men on his campus. Those campus visits played a massive role in redirecting much of the content of the book.

McIver Wood from Birmingham, AL helped me understand the Latin roots of the word "fraternity" and deepened my appreciation of the etymology of the word. As I brought the book to a close, students at the University of Virginia, Clemson University, and Mercer University offered critical feedback. I'd like to especially thank UVA's Nick Fischer, the 2021–2022 president of the Sigma Phi and Kayvon Samadani, the 2022 president of UVA's Inter-Fraternity Council. I'd also like to thank Clemson's Chad Frick, the 2020–2021 president of Alpha Sigma Phi. These three men represent the kind of heroic cadre of men that any college president would want leading their university's Greek community. Jake Fraley, of Phi Delta Theta at Mercer University, provided outstanding contextual and grammatical analysis. Taken together, these four men provided expert quality control for the book.

As always, I'm grateful for the great team at Wipf and Stock, including Matthew Wimer and others, who were willing to take the risk of publishing yet another of my controversial projects. I am very thankful for Mark Hijleh who was Provost at The King's College during the writing of this book for providing initial office space and resources to make this project happen. Additionally, I'd like to thank Brig. Gen. Tim Gibson (retired), who served as president of The King's College during the writing of this book. I am incredibly grateful for his support of faculty publishing projects like this one.

Lastly, I am forever indebted to the copyeditor for this book, Lydia Zabarsky. Lydia single-handedly took the draft that I gave her, and elevated the quality of entire book to a level I could not have accomplished on my own. Her coaching, feedback, recommendations, sequencing, and attention to detail made this book exponentially better. I am so glad I found her. She can be found at www.gothamscribe.com.

Part 1

Models of Manhood

1

The Benefits of Brotherhood

"For the guys who are in here, this is their bedrock involvement at the university. We do all kinds of stuff. We have club athletes. We have guys who run philanthropy organizations. We have people doing really serious research in class, but this fraternity is their foundation. It's their support network."

—NICK FISCHER, UNIVERSITY OF VIRGINIA

Fraternities are under threat. Nationally, the Abolish Greek Life movement is gaining momentum. The media is regularly calling for fraternities to be abolished. Many university presidents are rightly ambivalent about fraternities because of the occasional story of a reckless fraternity going too far, and causing real harm. There are calls for more accountability and punitive sanctions.

I believe we can end fraternity suspensions forever without making Greek life more punitive. Fraternities too often defend their existence by pointing to their philanthropic work, community service, or alumni donor support. I believe this is the wrong approach. What makes a fraternity great is not how much money brothers can raise for charity, the volunteer hours they accrue landscaping or cleaning highways, or how much money their alumni donate to the university. What makes a fraternity great is the character of each man in a chapter committed to self-improvement and dedicated to the pursuit of honor, virtue, and excellence. Accountability is reactionary and passive. Fraternities need to be positioned to form virtues. Virtuous men are motivated by that which is good. A fraternity's best defense and greatest asset is the character of its brothers. In fact, whenever I stand in front of a fraternity to speak to them about transitioning a chapter from mundanity to greatness, I see a room of untapped potential. I believe that fraternities are the most overlooked value-adding men's organization on college campuses today. I believe they have to the potential to add more value to the overall college experience than sports teams at Power Five universities. This is a book about why fraternities are great and how they can sustain a culture of excellence devoted to bettering campus life for students, faculty, staff, and themselves.

As of December 2021, the North American Interfraternity Conference (NIC) had fifty-six member organizations with four thousand chapters, located on over eight hundred campuses in the United States and Canada, with approximately three hundred and fifty thousand undergraduate members. If we can unlock the untapped potential in each of these chapters, it could change college campuses and redirect America's future. College campuses are desperate for a generation of men willing to pursue "the heroic," and college fraternities are logical organizations to cultivate. For chapters rebellious enough to forge a countercultural path, they have a once-in-a-generation opportunity to foster unprecedented greatness at scale.

"Heroic masculinity" refers to men who use their presence, power, strengths, and creativity to benefit those around them. They recognize that making the lives of other people better is one of the most fulfilling and rewarding things a man can do. It gives a man a sense of purpose and direction in life. Everything about him makes other people better. When he leaves a room people are better off for having him around. His friends are better students because of his help and encouragement. His fraternity brothers are more virtuous when they hang out with him. Heroic masculinity has massive implications for friendships, family life, the workplace, recreation, and beyond. Men join fraternities because they want to be great men, and they seek a community of like-minded men in the pursuit of excellence. Men join fraternities because they want to be around men who are going to push them to better themselves. Men join fraternities because they want to see good men transformed into great men who leave their mark on the world.

A small number of reckless fraternities have obscured the potential for greatness embedded in the very structure of fraternity culture. They have reduced Greek life to self-seeking rather than value-adding lifestyles. These are the fraternities we read about in the news: The ones responsible for clear cases of sexual assault; the ones who caused outsized physical and emotional harm amongst its members; the ones that that foster racist beliefs; the ones who encourage a culture that abuses drugs and alcohol—even if it kills someone. I followed over two thousand and three hundred fraternity chapters on Instagram while I was researching this book, and I was overwhelmed by the death notices. Many of them were drug overdoses. Drugs laced with fentanyl are wreaking havoc and taking the lives of brothers all over the country.

Self-seeking fraternities that harbor selfishly underdeveloped males resistant to adulthood tarnish the reputation of *all* fraternities. They are the focus of the Abolish Greek Life movement. They are the ones that make the headlines. They are the ones depicted in movies targeting schoolboys who think their behavior is "sick." Unfortunately, it literally is. Reckless fraternities are "Peter Pan" fraternities, brimming with men who don't want to grow up, and it is these irresponsible and immature boys who make it a regular practice to recruit terrible men into their brotherhoods. Fraternities do not make men terrible—we know that—but terrible men often seek them out. Peter Pan fraternities are characterized by "disordered masculinity," rather than heroic masculinity. The brothers in them usually have some combination of traits of three types of men: self-serving, self-centered, and self-preserving.[1]

The self-serving man focuses his relationships on what other people can do for him. He's primarily concerned with how other people can add value to his life, and uses people to that end. Everything he does is for the service of self. His own advantage leads his pursuit of relations, and dictates his choice of major, friends, and so on. "What's in this for me?" is the question driving his decisions.

A self-centered man is a man who puts his needs and interests above the needs of others. He is obsessed with himself, and excessively determined to put himself at the center of everything. If a discussion, an event, or plans are not about him, he will either become disinterested, or will force others to bend to his preferences or desires. He is in love with himself, and thinks everyone else should be, too. He believes that he is entitled to having people put him at center. "What does this have to do with me? is the question driving his decisions.

The self-preserving man focuses his life on *not* serving the needs of others. He is primarily concerned with avoiding anything that might require him to sacrifice his time, his expertise, or his money for the benefit of others. He will lie, cheat, steal, and turn a blind-eye to those who do if it preserves his advantage, comfort, or ease. The self-preserving man is driven to ask: "How does this keep me from experiencing any discomfort?" Self-preserving men believe they deserve to not be inconvenienced, even if

1. Hemmer, *Man Up*, 49–55.

it means inconveniencing others. If a fraternity recruits self-serving, self-centered, and self-preserving men it's just a matter of time before they get suspended for sexual assault violations, alcohol or substance abuse, or causing emotional or physical harm to those around them.

Heroic men are driven by questions of "How can I help?" and "What can I learn?" They seek reciprocal relationships, but are confident enough not to keep score. They do not keep a record of wrongs against them. They protect the reputation of others. They are patient and kind. They do not assume their preferences or desires are central to every arrangement, and they take a genuine interest in experiences they have not had, knowledge they have not yet acquired, and opinions other than their own. They are also not afraid of discomfort or a little drudgery. They do not take revenge. They recognize that a small inconvenience often reaps its own reward.

Fraternities that initiate men who are committed to heroic masculinity have a braver, more generous vision of the world. They welcome newcomers, cultivate interests, bridge divides, and foster creative ways to engage in fun, and provide entertainment for others, while treating new pledges, women, their brothers, and themselves with the utmost respect. They know that the best fraternity events are the ones where people wake up the next day with better lives: They have made new friends, invented new games, organized new sports teams, learned something from an unexpected conversation. They do not need to drink to alleviate discomfort or numb pain, push until they violate, or boast until they bore. That is not who they aspire to be, which is why that is not who they are.

I believe that universities and alumni should increase their investment in fraternities, rather than abolish them. Fraternities do not need more accountability so much as they need men who aspire to be men of virtue, honor, and service to their immediate communities. Much can be gained from improving a structure that already provides benefit. Despite the bad press, research proves that fraternities foster positive mental health, serve as a success accelerator for students, and engender tremendous loyalty and connection among alumni to support their alma mater.[2]

While college men are experiencing loneliness and depression at increasing rates, fraternities empower students to create a strong support system.[3] This family—this home—that fraternities offer can provide help and guidance when a member needs it most.

Research shows that this connection can create a strong sense of belonging, leading members to have more positive mental health and less

2. NIC Research, "Findings."
3. NIC Research, "Findings."

anxiety and depression than other students.[4] Brothers feel comfortable having tough conversations and learning from each other, and when they seek help, research shows members are twice as likely to reach out to a fraternity brother than anyone else.[5]

The proof:

- Fraternity members report higher levels of positive mental health, and less depression or anxiety than unaffiliated members.[6]

- Nearly 80 percent of fraternity men report excellent to good mental health and wellbeing.[7]

- When members seek help, they are twice as likely to turn to a brother than anyone else.[8]

- Fraternity and sorority members believe that good support systems exist on campus for students going through a tough time.[9]

- Fraternity and sorority members are more likely to seek therapy or counseling at some point in their lives.[10]

- Fraternities provide an environment where members can have tough conversations, especially about personal issues like relationships, family and mental health struggles.[11]

Fraternities are an accelerator for success, in college and beyond. Students spend 90 percent of their time outside the classroom. Fraternities capitalize on those hours by preparing men for success in college and in their futures far beyond what their peers experience. A study of thousands of alumni of diverse backgrounds shows this holds true regardless of an individual's background or socioeconomic status entering college.[12]

Because of higher expectations, as well as the support and network fraternities provide, members experience greater gains in learning and graduate at higher rates than their peers.[13] Nearly 75 percent of chapters offer focused

4. NIC Research, "Findings."
5. NIC Research, "Findings."
6. Assalone, "Mental Health Study."
7. UT-PERC, "Single Sex Fraternities."
8. UT-PERC, "Benefits of Single Sex Fraternities."
9. Assalone, "Mental Health Study."
10. Assalone, "Mental Health Study."
11. UT-PERC, "Benefits of Single Sex Fraternities."
12. NIC Research, "Findings."
13. NIC Research, "Findings."

leadership development programming at least monthly, and 83 percent of members say their confidence in their leadership skills increased because of their membership.[14] Fraternity and sorority members also report higher levels of interaction with people different from themselves, lending to members being more prepared than their peers to join a diverse workforce and community.[15] So, it is no surprise that fraternity alumni are twice as likely to believe their college experience prepared them well for life after college.

Fraternity members can tap built-in alumni networks, finding jobs more quickly than their peers. Research shows almost half of members had a brother helped them find an internship or job, and provided them with career advice.[16] Fraternity alumni report being more fulfilled in their careers and lives in every aspect of wellbeing measured, from career to community and financial to physical, because of the relationships and resources they can leverage.

So, while research shows that one in five students considers joining a fraternity but don't because of concerns around academics or finances, studies show membership is a worthwhile investment.

The proof:

- Eighty-three percent of members indicate stronger leadership confidence as a result of their fraternity membership.[17]

- Fraternity members show significantly higher learning gains than their peers in their first year of college.[18]

- Despite being less diverse than students in general, fraternity/sorority members reported higher levels of interaction with people different from themselves than did other students.[19]

- Fraternity alumni are twice as likely to feel that their alma maters prepared them well for life after college and that they gained important job-related skills.[20]

- Fraternity alumni find jobs more quickly after graduation, and are more engaged in the workplace.[21]

14. NIC Research, "Findings."
15. NIC Research, "Findings."
16. NIC Research, "Findings."
17. UT-PERC, "Single Sex Fraternities."
18. Pike, "Greek Experience."
19. Pike, "Greek Experience."
20. Gallup, "Fraternities."
21. Gallup, "Fraternities."

- They're more likely to thrive in every aspect of wellbeing—career, community, financial, physical and social wellbeing.[22]

- Fraternity members leverage their networks, with almost half stating that another member helped them find an internship or job, and provided them with career advice.[23]

- One in five students considers joining a fraternity or sorority, but ultimately decides not to because they're "too busy with academics" or have financial concerns.[24]

- Fraternity members experience stronger retention and persistence to graduation.[25]

Fraternities create lifelong connection to the campus, community, and their peers. Fraternity men love their collegiate experience—as students and as alumni. In fact, more than eight out of ten fraternity members say they would re-join their organizations.[26]

Research shows, fraternity membership connects men to the university in a way that nonmembers simply don't experience. They're more satisfied as students and as alumni are more likely to recommend and give back to their alma maters.

Members are more engaged inside and outside of the classroom than their peers—they report feeling more supported by their faculty and nearly half serve in leadership roles across campus. They're also more connected to their local communities, with research showing they spend significantly more time volunteering than nonaffiliated students.[27]

The proof:

- Seventy-five percent of fraternity members demonstrate strong satisfaction with their overall student experience.[28]

- Seventy-eight percent of fraternity members feel a strong connection to campus and are more satisfied with their experience.[29]

22. Gallup, "Fraternities."
23. Gallup, "Fraternities."
24. Burkhard and Timpf, "Fraternity Life."
25. Baier and Whipple, "Greek Values."
26. NIC Research, "Findings."
27. NIC Research, "Findings."
28. UT-PERC, "Single Sex Fraternities."
29. Pike, "Greek Experience."

- Nearly half of fraternity members serve in other campus leadership roles.[30]

- Fraternity members are more involved in co-curricular activities, and membership promotes student leadership and development, as well as satisfaction with the collegiate experience.[31]

- Fraternity members have stronger interaction with faculty than their peers, with higher numbers feeling like their professors cared about them as a person or made them excited about learning.[32]

- Fraternity members spend significantly more time volunteering, mentoring and doing other types of service work, and they feel like they belong in their communities.[33]

- Fraternity members feel a stronger connection to, and are more engaged in, their communities.[34]

- Fraternity alumni feel a deeper sense of loyalty with their alma mater because of their positive college experiences, and they are more likely recommend their school to others and donate after graduation.[35]

- If they had to do college over again, more than eight out of ten fraternity members would re-join their organizations.[36]

I know this is all true because I pledged Alpha Phi Alpha at Clemson University and doing so set me up for a lifetime of success.

30. UT-PERC, "Single Sex Fraternities."
31. Pike, "Greek Experience."
32. Pike, "Greek Experience."
33. Burkhard and Timpf, "Fraternity Life."
34. Burkhard and Timpf, "Fraternity Life."
35. Gallup, "Fraternities."
36. NIC Research, "Findings."

2

Men On Campus

"There have been a lot of tears shed here. There's been a lot of
arguments. There's been a lot of reconciliations. It is a master class
in human relationships and going through it with people. There are
relationships that have started here at the bottom, guys who didn't like
each other, who now are quite good friends, and who trust each other
a lot. The richness of human relationships here is above average."

—NICK FISCHER, THE UNIVERSITY OF VIRGINIA

By the Numbers

Men and boys in America are struggling, and if we do not provide
steps to offer them more support, we will see the disintegration of
institutions like the family and the marketplace that allow for sustainable
human flourishing.[1] We see reports of their struggles on the news, and we
see it on campus where many college-age men arrive with a decided limp.
Depression, anxiety, suicidal ideation, loneliness, and poor self-esteem were
all a normative part of their high school experience, especially for students
who missed a year or more of in-class time during the early days of COVID-
19.[2] The typical modern "frat boy" is therefore not rowdy, reckless, and ir-

1. Chira, "Crisis of Men," 2016; Farrell, "'Boy Crisis.'"
2. Vestal, "COVID Harmed Kids' Mental Health."

responsible. Instead, he is more often a young man who has experienced an immense amount of pain. That background makes him particularly receptive to fraternities, which position themselves as easy places for young men to get their emotional needs met. Many young men join fraternities seeking hope and healing in a world that has neglected their needs. Fraternities are in an uniquely strong position to help. Their living structure and social organization provide young men with multiple opportunities to form friendships, forge connections, and give and receive support. This provides young men with a crucial opportunity to actualize a positive mental health experience, which so many young men need—and so few get. One in ten men experience depression and anxiety.[3] They are collectively disappearing from colleges and the labor force. According to recent data by Emsi, a labor-market data firm, between 1980 and 2009 declines in prime-age male workforce participation "jumped off a cliff," from 94 percent to 89 percent.[4] That drop represents nearly three million prime-age men no longer actively working or seeking work. In America's colleges and universities, women now account for 61 percent of new enrollees, while men's numbers have sunk.[5] Men in America die by suicide at 3.5 times the rate of women.[6] *City Journal*'s Patrick Brown recently reported on the spike in men overdosing on drugs:

> The latest CDC data shows that 35,419 single and divorced prime-age (twenty-five- to fifty-four-year-old) men died of drug-related causes, a 35 percent increase from the year before.[7] The never-married make up about one-third of the prime-age male population, but compose two-thirds of that demographic's drug-related deaths. Similarly, the share of prime-age divorced men who succumbed to drug overdoses was nearly twice their share of the population at large.[8]

The American College Health Association (ACHA) National College Health Assessment (NCHA) Executive Summary from spring 2019 shows that over the past twelve months men reported experiencing the following:

- 47.9 percent felt things were hopeless,
- 76 percent reported feeling exhausted (not from physical activity),

3. United Press International, "CDC: Men with Depression."
4. Emsi, "Demographic Drought."
5. *Inside Higher Ed*, "Fewer Men Are Attending College."
6. United Press International, "CDC: Men with Depression."
7. NCHS, "CDC: Vital Statistics."
8. Brown, "Opioids and the Unattached Male."

- 78.4 percent reported feeling overwhelmed by all they had to do,

- 58.0 percent reported feeling very lonely,

- 60.7 percent reported feeling sad,

- 50.7 percent reported feeling overwhelming anxiety,

- 37.1 reported feeling so depressed that is was difficult to function,

- 37.3 reported feeling overwhelmed with anger,

- 13.0 percent reported seeking professional help for anxiety, and

- 11.7 percent reported seeking professional help for depression.

Those that sought professional help also listed the following as "traumatic" or "very difficult to handle:"

- academics (42.5 percent),

- career (26.3 percent),

- intimate relationships (28.2 percent),

- finances (29.5 percent), and

- sleep difficulties (29.7 percent).

Men are dropping out of the labor force, not attending college, dying of addiction, and experiencing extremely high rates of anxiety, depression, and despair. We may need to accept the fact that we are not providing enough support for them, or adequately addressing issues that impact them. Suicide is the second leading cause of death for men fifteen to twenty-four years old. Men account for six out of every ten college-age suicide.[9]

Arriving on Campus with an Emotional Hole

Sixty-nine percent of high school students who graduated in 2018 ended up in college.[10] The Higher Education Research Institute (HERI) at UCLA found the three most common "very important" reasons students choose to attend college are: getting a better job (86 percent), learning more about their interests (82 percent), and getting training for a specific career (77 percent).[11] What this misses, though, is what so many have come to expect from and recognize about the college experience: It is where the typical

9. NAMI, "Mental Health in College-Age Men."
10. U.S. Bureau of Labor Statistics. "College Enrollment and Work."
11. HERI-CIRP, "2014 Freshmen Survey."

eighteen-year-old goes to begin the process of establishing their identity in the world—and fraternity men are no exception. The university system and its fraternities foster identity development and self-definition by providing young men with rites of passage, replacement "families," and the freedom to use these tools to develop an independent self-reliant fully adult "self." With all the possibilities these tools afford, it makes sense as to why young men look forward to initiations, new families, and adult responsibilities in fraternities even put themselves in harm's way by those who are self-serving, self-centered, and self-preserving.

Warren Farrell diagnoses this hole in his book, *The Boy Crisis*.[12] This parenting book describes why it is that a significant number of college men are putting themselves in contexts of disordered masculinity where self-serving, self-centered, and self-preserving men are so much more likely to drink, haze, rape, discriminate, and destroy. Farrell explains that while we have prepared girls well for the "crisis of missing fathers" and the shifts in the workplace and gender roles that grew out of the women's movement, boys—and the men they become—have been left behind. He argues that although gender roles for girls and women have evolved, they haven't for boys and men. We continue to treat them as future expendable soldiers and breadwinners, just as we have historically, even while their access to their fathers has become markedly more limited, and provides them with ever fewer mentors.[13]

We see the evidence for this all around us. Young men need initiation into the heroic by other men and when this does not happen, the consequences are usually dire. The United States suffers from massive problems with violence, in no small part because of the behavior of our young men. This is why 93 percent of America's prison inmates are male in a system filled with violent offenders.[14] This is why virtually all mass shooters are male. This is why men make up 75 percent of those who commit suicide.[15] Farrell explains these tragedies by attributing them to a "purpose void."[16] The purpose void leads to resignation and carelessness about the needs of others.

This purpose void exists because, as Farrell points out, the young men of the past had a built-in purpose for the greater part of human history: They were raised to protect and provide, as soldiers and providers, in service and

---

12. Farrell and Gray, *Boy Crisis*, 15–39.

13. Farrell and Gray, *Boy Crisis*, 15–39.

14. Federal Bureau of Prisons, "BOP Statistics: Inmate Gender."

15. Farrell and Gray, *Boy Crisis*, 15–39.

16. Farrell and Gray, *Boy Crisis*, 15–39.

sacrifice to their countries and families.[17] Since the late twentieth century, however, there has been far less need for men to be the unique providers of protection and sustenance to their families and nations; not every man in the United States has to, or can, enlist in the military and—as a result of shifting gender roles and responsibilities—women are now more commonly accepted as capable breadwinners. It is also a net positive that young girls can now mostly self-determine some worldly impact beyond that of a homemaker, if they so desire. But Farrell reminds us that we never sent an equivalent message to boys: They no longer need to provide and protect. Traditional roles have changed for men, as well. Too many young men have no idea why their life matters beyond getting a job and making money.

In a world with fewer wars, only a small minority of the nation's men derive a sense of purpose from military service, but our parenting styles do not reflect that reality. Farrell points out that the traditional way of raising boys was largely bereft of physical touch, and otherwise resisted forming overt emotional attachments. That may have made sense in an era when war and other dangerous occupations made men more likely to die young, but there is no practical justification for our emotional callousness today. Our antiquated practice of raising boys to fulfill a manly purpose in mostly nonexistent roles is compounded by the rise in dad-derprived homes, which means boys end up with even fewer consistent male role models to guide and understand them. As a result, young men are more likely to become violent, aimless, and suicidal than their female counterparts.[18]

Aimless violence is, of course, at the heart of self-serving, self-centered, and self-preserving misconduct, and we will only eradicate it if we find a solution to the problems of disordered fraternities that frees those involved, rather than restricts them. The fraternities themselves—and the men who join them—need a sense of purpose that makes the self-serving, self-centered, and self-preserving values endemic to hazing and sexual assault irrelevant. A freeing solution always trumps a restrictive one. Without question, there is a purpose void and fraternities as the preeminent, college-aged young men's clubs of America an outstanding opportunity to provide a realistic solution. We ought to call young men to heroic masculinity as quickly and thoroughly as we can—and all evidence suggests we should. The resentment and victimization of the "other"—freshmen, rival fraternities, women, and minorities—that we so often see in self-serving, self-centered, and self-preserving fraternities is a direct result of some level of insecurity and purposelessness in their own position in life and on campus.

17. Farrell and Gray, Boy Crisis, 274.
18. Farrell and Gray, Boy Crisis, 15–39.

If we look around and see purposeless young men who have been deprived of touch—especially from their fathers—we ought to use fraternities to give young men the new family they are looking for. A fraternity system filled with purposeful and heroic men will never be a danger to themselves or their peers on any college campus.

In many cultures, boys demonstrate their attainment of adulthood—and released to establish their purpose, successful or not—through a rite of passage. History shows us this and the psychological data we have on men confirm it.[19] The current vision of masculinity that pervades self-serving, self-centered, and self-preserving masculinity, and much of popular American culture, requires that men prove their manliness by demonstrating their ability to hold their liquor, make conquests out of women, and otherwise triumph over other men. A number of our boys want these things, but it is asked of all of them, and that is what leads to such significant numbers falling into a disordered brand of masculinity, and perpetuating it in those who follow. The rites of passage of old (or perhaps more recently than that) that uplifted the self-confident, gentler, healthier, wise, strong, self-aware, and more leadership-oriented aspects of manhood have been replaced by rites of passage that land too many fraternities in trouble with their universities as a result of alcohol abuse, drugs, hazing, sexual assault, and racism, and they now mark an increasing number of suspensions. The alluring nature of these new rites is not necessarily rooted in a desire to do wrong. Instead, with their stress on alcoholic, drug-related, sexual, and hazing domination they reveal a desire to practice virtue, but in a disordered way. It's the way self-serving, self-centered, and self-preserving men achieve respect and status from other disordered men. There are positive ways to "dominate" in each of these arenas: Temperance and self-control with substances is one example. Respect (and more self-control) with women is another. Devising meaningful, uplifting, and demanding trials of initiation for freshmen and minorities into fraternities is yet another show of strength. The goal ought to be to retain fraternities as the mass brotherhoods built on loyalty and exclusivity that young men so crave (and need), and to reconstitute toward the heroic those that offend and violate the values we want to instill in their members. We rely on the institutions that help all of our children—boys and girls alike—to become the citizens and participants of tomorrow's world, and right now there are a considerable number of boys who are not being taught prudence, justice, courage, and self-control during their formative years. Fraternities have historically prided themselves on doing just that. The Greek brotherhoods in our university system have always asked to be

19. Farrell and Gray, *Boy Crisis*, 15–39.

judged by the character and achievements of their members, but a handful are routinely failing that test across the country because too many brothers have a purpose void and are incarcerated to being self-serving, self-centered, and self-preserving. It is time to pay on making sure young men have an opportunity to be a great as we know they truly want to be.

Fear of Being Left Out

There are often two key types of high school students who go to college and get involved in intense party scenes with the potential to do harm. They are most easily described as "winners" and "outsiders." Winners went through high school getting their way socially: They were athletes, they were socially dominant, they may have even been bullies, though that stereotype seems to be dying out in many places. In Todd Phillips' *Frat House*, an unreleased HBO documentary from 1998, numerous unsavory partying and hazing practices are displayed at two fraternities, mostly focusing on those of an Alpha Tau Omega chapter at Muhlenberg College in Pennsylvania. During one interview early in the film, one brother in a high-tier, dangerous fraternity explains his exceptional social station at the college and how it stemmed from his high school success:

> We were the kids in high school who ran the fuckin' school, that's all it is. We played the sports, we ran the school, we ran the parties. This is where I belong, this is what I should be doing. This is what I was doing in junior high, high school, and now into college. I hang out with a bunch of guys, and I have a great social life.[20]

This interview came on the heels of several scenes of rush week where those "kids . . . who ran the fuckin' school"—upperclassman and freshmen alike—are seen partying at bars, in houses, and on the street to a point of danger to themselves and the women with them, all taking advantage of each other and the opportunity to drink with seeming impunity.[21] Teenage invincibility with adult freedom and infantile responsibility is frightening. The year 1998 was, however, long before the #MeToo movement, so conversations about consent were still underdeveloped, and the prolific role of alcohol throughout the film's interviews put the fraternity men in a place where they were strikingly honest about their reasons for attending parties,

20. Phillips, *Frat House*.
21. Phillips, *Frat House*.

and making the mistakes. Simply stated, they wanted fun, acceptance, family and, at least, the appearance of sexual dominance and conquest.

These winners got a taste of what it meant to be in control of friend groups at the top of a social ladder. They had their first experience with alcohol or drugs as early as their preteen years. They, like many boys, saw porn for the first time between eight and eleven years old. The appetite for all that the worst-behaving frats have to offer is cultivated in these boys from their earliest formative years.[22] On the other side of the spectrum, there are those who did not taste these perks of athletic, social, or popular prowess: outsiders. These outsiders, voluntarily or not, were on the outside looking in on, or were even oblivious to, the partying that went on during their teenage years. Some outsiders become jealous, as a result. Others took from their experience the expectation that this was what they were meant to be doing in order to be men. So, when they got to college, they received a social fresh start that allowed many to re-create themselves, without the reputation, moral consideration, parental control, physique, or sexual inexperience that may have prevented them from participating in their high school party scene. These students decided to apply to their state college with plans to blend in with those who they looked up to, ignored, or even resented in high school, just to have fun in college.

When these outsiders join fraternities, they look like Will from the film *Goat* (2016). Daniel Flaherty's character begins the pledge process with the main character of the film, Brad Land. As they pledge Clemson University's Kappa Sigma, the hazing intensifies to a point where Brad and Will are commiserating and Brad suggests dropping out. Will refuses, confiding, "I'm having sex for the first time in my life."[23] He wants the frat for something he feels he could not attain on his own and, given the monopoly most fraternities have over alcohol, drugs, social prestige, and sex on campus, he is likely right. As yet another reminder of why this kind of fraternity power is so harmful, it does not feel like creative license when Will dies of a heart attack that the film attributes to stress caused by Kappa Sigma's Hell Week.

Thanks to the "frat film" genre *Animal House* invented, both winners and outsiders know the promise and peril of fraternities long before they decide on a college. Films in the frat genre are so profoundly easy to sell that Todd Phillips, the director of the *Frat House* documentary, spent the next two decades remaking dramatized versions of it, many set in a fraternity house, including *Road Trip, Old School, The Hangover* trilogy, and *Project X*. Collectively, these films amplify and monetize the dangerous allure of

22. Fight the New Drug, "Kid's First Porn?"
23. Neel, *Goat.*

binge-drinking, sexual harassment, and "going crazy," as the pinnacle of all-American adult male fun. If our more problematic frats had continued to resemble *Animal House*—apart from some of the more ridiculously unrealistic moments, of course, such as driving a custom-made tank down Main Street—they would likely be considerably safer. Unfortunately, since that film reimagined college as four years of partying, it has been a vicious downward cycle where movies promote alcohol, sex, and hazing, boys bring it to fruition when they go to college, and then demand more alcohol, sex, and hazing in their lives. As fantasies, these depictions of manly fun are self-fulfilling prophecies given how easy they are to imitate. What is dangerous about them is that young men who identify as winners, outsiders, and everything in between are putting lives at risk to enjoy what fraternities offer. Let us lower the stakes, negotiate their offer, keep campuses safe, and nurture better men into adulthood.

It is crucial, however, that we fully recognize that the twisted appeal of the most fractious fraternities is largely built on a distorted vision of virtue, rather than an impulse to do wrong. Alcohol and drug abuse, hazing, sexual assault, racism, and property damage are the corrupted gates to the acceptance, friendship, social status, fun, and professional network in communities of self-serving, self-centered, and self-preserving men. The desperation to enjoy these things is fortified by the expectation that these are the "best four years of your life," and voracious appetites stoked by film fantasies and the complexities of high school experience, good or bad. Freshmen join fraternities because they want to be happy, and there is no fault in that. But together, these factors, create toxic college environments. A recent graduate of Furman University explained to us why he joined his fraternity:

> It was all socially motivated. . . . The only people who can have parties are Greek organizations. . . . [T]he only Greek organizations that can have houses off campus are fraternities. So if you want this more stereotypical college life, like, if you want to go to a party on a Saturday night, you're going to have to join a frat . . . The guys from my pledge class are the guys I'm still friends with . . . Friends, activities during the week, parties on the weekend. That's what I wanted to do.[24]

On many campuses Greek organizations seem to have a monopoly on so much of what freshmen want out of college life that even those who have not been totally convinced of "going Greek" to the extreme join up for their shot at friendship and fun. Another Furman graduate told us a similar story about how he lacked male companionship before pledging:

24. Graduate B, Furman interview.

> When I realized I had to work for it halfway through my fresh-
> men year, that I don't have that group of guys to fall back on, this
> one guy took me to a rush event. [He] introduced me to all of
> his friends who would be my five closest friends from Furman.
> I immediately meshed with them, and I now had a reliable way
> to drink, and a really close-knit group of guys who seemed like
> what I needed.

Self-serving, self-centered, and self-preserving men are aware of the longing and desire to form bonds with a group of men to drink and have fun. They are also aware that the opportunity is often restricted to those who join fraternities. One senior at Cornell University found this out the hard way when he did not join a fraternity after enjoying a fun rush week with all of his friends: "I got kind of panicked like, 'Wait a minute, *all* of my friends are doing this, they're all going to go somewhere.'"[25] And when they did, "I lost my community from rush . . . I had no real community."[26] As a Greek-heavy school, the situation at Cornell is probably more drastic when your friends all join fraternities without you. This student was able to establish community by joining the school's competitive club system, but the fear of this loss of connection is ever-present in most freshman boys on college campuses. Few are willing to take their chances on the less party-centric experience of being what Greek slang labels a GDI: a "goddamn independent."

When asked about the impact that leaving his fraternity had on meeting women, one of the Furman graduates said that, since Greek houses are the only places on campus where drinking is permitted, and the sororities do not have houses, "[I]f your goal is to hook up with girls, you really have to be in a fraternity. That's where girls go to have fun. . . . Fraternities are the only outlet for that."[27] Yes, of course, we would prefer that students not make hookups with women a goal, the reality for self-serving, self-centered, and self-preserving men. To change that, we need to work on, and within, the fraternity system to expand the good of human co-educational relationships beyond hooking up. We need to call them to heroic relationships with their female peers because that is what the large majority of men in fraternities actually want even if they do not always know how. Even in situations where a student may not be interested in hooking up with random sorority women, fraternities have been known to stress hookups as a mark of manhood. Contrary to popular belief, college men want to take things slow and test out their skills at romance. Most college men respect their own bodies

---

25. Senior, Cornell interview.
26. Senior, Cornell interview.
27. Graduate B, Furman interview.

and the dignity of women and do not want to see women harmed but that is not what is usually modeled or depicted as aspirational. Consider *Frat Star* (2017), which takes place during Hell Week, and includes a night devoted to a scavenger hunt of illicit exploits. Most are straight up hazing and drinking, but one requires Nick, the main character, to sneak into a sorority, wake up a specific girl, and perform a sexual act with her. Nick is reluctant because he is interested in another girl in that sorority, but he does it. This starts him on a path of randomly hooking up with women at parties, not because he wants to, but because it helps him establish a reputation among his peers as someone who sleeps around often and well.[28] People are often concerned about the objectification and self-objectification of sorority women, but we ought to wake up to the fact that fraternity men are similarly pressured into sexual encounters they otherwise would have refused or not sought out if not for the social pressures—and rewards. For many young men, sex is more often than not a cover charge, a proxy for the acceptance and social status they seek. This calls to mind the Fort Valley State case of the sorority house advisor "instructing" sisters to perform sexual favors for local businessmen and politicians to cover their dues.[29] If the majority of Greeks—male and female—do not want to participate in the hookup culture that they actively engage in, rescuing them from this spectator sport of sex and shame will be a welcome reprieve for those who suffer from it. Fraternities should regularly protest the on-going Hollywood mischaracterization of fraternity culture as communities of self-serving, self-centered, and self-preserving men. Yes, some are like that but not all and the disordered ones get too much airtime.

Exploring Male Friendship

It is important to recognize that although the popularity of fraternities has waxed and waned over their two-hundred-year history, the things men seek from them are permanent staples of the human experience. Jungian psychology points out that what men find most fulfilling are activities enjoyed in the context of a hierarchical, exclusive group. Hierarchies provide them with a ladder to climb, which is why the exclusivity of a group that can reject them is also appealing. When they succeed, they can say, "I was accepted because I am superior to other men who were not accepted." Such harsh competition may seem unattractive, or even unhealthy to, but, again, there may be an opportunity to use exclusivity for heroic ends if we apply different standards. Certainly, we want to avoid groupthink and the over-empowerment of the early

28. Johnson and Serbu, *Frat Star.*
29. Brown, "AKA Sorority."

twenty-somethings who run them but competition is not bad and perhaps the problem is that fraternities have not been invited enough to compete and sharpen each other for pro-social outcomes. To the degree we lean into fraternities, our most effective solutions will likely be grounded in the framework of providing group relationships to men that so many young men naturally and innocently want. We ought to use that fact to our advantage, or at least factor it into our calculations for how to improve fraternities. The fact is hierarchies are useful and fulfilling in myriad ways: They create positive stress, known as "eustress," for its membership, allowing them to recognize where they are on the ladder and why, allowing them to see a clear and consistent way to progress, if they so desire. What is broken now is how that path has been constructed. To become a fraternity man—a "star," for the most successful—many current systems reward the massive intake of drugs and alcohol, the ability to sexually conquer at will, and a level of dominance over younger members and nonmembers. When you combine this with the fact that many male friendships are "instrumental," in the sense that men prefer to make use out of their friendships, a fraternity with poorly directed aims will ask pledges and brothers to "make use" of themselves by degrading themselves and others. It is this path which can be made far more virtuous, lifting those brothers up who can moderate their use of substances, exercise self-control and wisdom with women, welcome "lesser" members, and have only the healthiest competition with other men. This will create a fraternity hierarchy into one of harmonious, virtuous instruments, rather than one of discord.

Male friendships within a fraternity setting are nuanced. They are also certainly not all equal, even though all are essential to the function of a fraternity hierarchy, and each individual within it. Dr. Geoffrey Greif, an author and educator, who has spent a career examining relationships, including those between men, developed a typology to describe varying kinds of friendship, based on notions of "must," "trust," "just," and "rust."

"Must" friendships occur between men who are closer to each other than anyone else. They describe relationships where men are able, even compelled, to share the best and worst moments in their lives with each other. It describes the one or two guys in the fraternity that a young man becomes extremely close to, beyond the level of any of the other members. "Must" friends show us that men need someone whom they can talk to freely, without judgment, and feel supported, and be of vital service to in return.

"Trust" friendships are similarly close, but do not have the same level of relational and emotional intimacy as "musts." These relationships include friendships made close due to specific circumstances: All or part of a pledge class that got particularly close, for example, even though they do not share as much with each other as "must" friends do. "Trust" friends show us the value of casual, yet meaningful, closeness that does not reveal all, but still requires openness and trust within a certain tier of a larger hierarchy.

"Just" friends are exactly that, *merely* friends, or "casual acquaintances, which is probably indicative of most of the relationships within a fraternity among both different classes, including alumni classes. "Just" friends, as well as "rust" friends (below) show how there is, yet again, a need for dependability and fallback friendship, without the more extended investment in time and energy of closer friendships.

Finally, "rust" friends are those that have known each other for a long time, but "drift in and out of each other's lives, essentially picking up where they left off."[30] These are men that young men meet in their early years in the fraternity, and they struggle to keep very constant contact with, but are nevertheless able to maintain the closeness they had the last time they saw each other at a homecoming, reunion, or some chance encounter. "Rust" friends, in particular, seem to be unique to men, as there may be years of little or no contact, but a sudden meeting can rekindle a relationship, which resumes where they last left off, allowing these men to be comfortable with each other without having to expend emotional energy in building their account of trust with each other.

Scanning this brief, watered-down version of Greif's typology can inform us of some of the things men most need from their relationships: dependability, variety in closeness, trust, and a certain level of unconditional availability at unexpected, or even unreasonable, times. As noted earlier, all of these relationships are highly instrumental, but as we evaluate how much to work within the current structure of male relations, it is important to remember that this structure provides men with exactly what they need out of their relationships. If we can affect this typology and the fraternity-based hierarchies that they exist in, using preexisting channels of male relationships to provide their relational needs, while also improving their behavior towards themselves and others, then we ought to do so. Our aim, after all, is to build healthier male communities.

We can connect the challenges we are trying to remedy here to the rising "boy crisis," not just because universities have been forced to mete out more punishments, and not just because the Hollywood's fraternity fantasies are getting more intense, but unfortunately from the experiences of a few fraternity members themselves, especially those who found themselves in communities of self-serving, self-centered, and self-preserving men. While many recent graduates and current students report fraternities as having monopolies on connection, fun, and status, a 1988 graduate from the

---

30. Greif, *Buddy System*, 1–304.

University of Delaware tells a different story. He reports having a meaning-ful, productive interview-based pledging process. Although interviews have recently been abused to the point of deserving suspension, they can also be used, as the graduate pointed out, to plant the seeds for fraternity within fraternities, cultivating a knowledge of and among the brothers, in direct opposition to the fear- and power-based relations that harm the bodies and psyches of today's pledges.[31] In the 1980s, this absence of senseless hard-ship—or even sadism, which some of today's most troublesome fraternities appear to relish—kept the pledge process relatively sane: "I never felt like [pledging] wasn't hard enough, or that we had to go through more things to become closer. I don't need planned things to bring me close to people."[32] A generation ago, beyond the hardship, there was also a sense that even the planned nature of fraternities could not offer men what they needed. Connection comes through organic time spent together, investment in the currency of trust—not party-planning and alcohol. This is not to say that alcohol use and the many other vices that give fraternities a bad name now were nonexistent then. It means simply that fraternities could not exercise the same power on campus they can now. Many of the fraternity presidents in the ACC and SEC I discovered while researching for this book do not drink alcohol at all, as we'll see in the Part 2 of this book.

Materialism and Nepotism

One of the best ways to choose the fraternity that is right for you is to look at its alumni. Evaluate its finished products and ask, "Is this who I want to be?" This is the way many people select their college, profession, friend groups, and various other life choices. This is the right way to make decisions. Con-sider the options, evaluate the consequences, and make a decision based on those evaluations. It is logical, it is straightforward, and it keeps your priorities at the front of your mind. Unfortunately, nefarious forces by some have worked to warp those priorities. The version of manhood sold to our boys by some of the worst fraternities, film, and society's silent signals is based on violence and dominance—and materialism, which for better and worse, rules our era.

In 2013, Max Abelson and Zeke Faux published an article in Bloom-berg online that exposed some of the nefarious activities of high-tier frats in the post-grad world: "'Every Sigma Chi gets a business card,' Hails recalled. 'We're trying to create Sigma Chi on Wall Street, a little fraternity on Wall

---

31. Graduate, University of Delaware interview.
32. Graduate, University of Delaware interview.

Street."[33] Many college men join frats to attain lives similar to those of the business and finance majors that come out on the other side. Now, of course there are many fraternities that center on a variety of other majors, including those not related to Wall Street. However, it is important to acknowledge that the top-tier fraternities are the ones attracting the most rushes and pledges who are aiming for status and influence. Traditional views of manhood stressed the pursuit of humble, virtuous leadership. Nowadays, the quest for power and money is largely unconcerned with where the money is made or over whom power is held. This is why Hollywood's stereotypical fraternity boy has a poster of Leonardo DiCaprio as Jordan Belfort from *The Wolf of Wall Street* (2013) on his wall: They dream of becoming the next Belfort, but not getting caught. They want the freedom to act, as they will. The notion of being free to obey or serve is shunned. Without a moral guide for the powerful networking capacity of national fraternities, they devolve into self-interested boys' clubs that look after their own to their exclusive benefit, while preaching that other fraternity brothers should do the same.

A major reason men prefer hierarchical groups as relational mechanisms is that it often proves beneficial to show respect for a tiered system and loyalty to an individual ranked above them. When those to whom a man is loyal rise, so does an instrumental quid pro quo arrangement: The man rises to the now vacant position. A rising tide lifts all Sigma Alpha Epsilon, Kappa Sigma, or Pi Kappa Alpha boats, and the boats at the bottom are making as many waves as they can to follow their superiors up the food chain, both on campus and at the firm when applied in self-serving, self-centered, and self-preserving ways. This is by no means meant to be an argument for why fraternities ought not extend assistance to members who seek a job. That is the essence of a network. It is my intention, however, to highlight that the practices of the more nefarious networks, "whose Wall Street alumni guide resumes to the tops of stacks, reveal interview questions with recommended answers, offer applicants secret mottoes and support chapters facing crackdowns."[34] The point of the networks is not simply to create opportunity through affiliation but that those affiliations should assume a certain level of competence and character a student should have after spending three or four years immersed in a culture of heroic masculinity. A heroic man is networked to support the quality control environment on campus. He has already been assessed by virtue of how the fraternity formed his character. A heroic man is being networked because a new

33. Abelson and Faux, "Secret Handshakes."
34. Abelson and Faux, "Secret Handshakes."

context needs him to add value there in ways beyond the value he added as a college student to his brothers and to his campus.

Penn's Alpha Epsilon Pi, which gave up its charter in 2012 to escape sanctions for hazing, got a member into Morgan Stanley for the fourth year in a row in 2013.[35] That same year, Dartmouth College's Alpha Delta, an inspiration for the 1978 comedy *Animal House* sent someone to the New York-based firm from the fifth consecutive class days after a New Hampshire court reprimanded the chapter for providing alcohol to someone underage.[36]

When fraternities engage in self-serving, self-centered, and self-preserving behavior, they are not just undermining the ability of those outside of their network to get a job, they also subvert the whole fraternity's purpose of creating better men. Every fraternity states that as its goal in some form and many achieve it. However, when self-serving, self-centered, and self-preserving men take the lead they sabotage the competence and character of their members when enhancing their job prospects, they reward without reason and promote low expectations and can often set men up to be coddled and purposeless. Fraternity leadership and alumni should find the conviction to subject their members to the scrutiny that men in community together ought to be applying to each other, as they seek to become heroic together, again, as every fraternity posits as a main objective. When fraternity networks fail to do this, it becomes clear that their fraternity failed to promote a moral standard in their membership, and this failure perpetuates itself as they avoid the heroic masculinity so needed in the world today.

A heroic network recognizes the requirement that brothers favor each other and seek to serve their younger counterparts, by mentoring and aiding them as they search for a place to carry out their identity as value-adding men. Although many fraternities do this, the high-tier fraternities are working their way into the high-tier fields on Wall Street, where forty-seven of the nation's fifty biggest companies are headed by fraternity men, and in Washington D.C., where 44 percent of all Presidents, 76 percent of current Congressmen, and all but seven of all forty-seven Supreme Court Justices since 1910 came from the fraternity system.[37] We need not reduce the influence of fraternities, we simply—though with difficulty—need to help structure fraternities so that their influence is channeled to positive and heroic ends. We want fraternities to pipeline heroic men into every area of society. Colleges campuses and the world needs the heroic men that fraternities provide.

35. Abelson and Faux, "Secret Handshakes."

36. Abelson and Faux, "Secret Handshakes."

37. UWgreek.com, "Fraternity Facts."

3

The Early Days of Fraternities

"I think it starts off as devotion to the rituals and the traditions and then, by extension, it becomes devotion to each other. Those two things happen concurrently, because when you're pledging you're learning traditions, but you also become committed to the other people, and you're becoming committed to helping the other people learn the traditions."

—NICK FISCHER, UNIVERSITY OF VIRGINIA

A meeting between five members of Union College in New York on November 25, 1825 changed the landscape of college life and masculinity in America.[1] These five men were recently unemployed after an organized military company had been dissolved. Ever since the company's dissolution, they felt what one described as an "aching void," and so they gathered together to form a society for literary and social purposes. The very next day, they gathered again in order to conduct a formal initiation before naming their organization Kappa Alpha Society. This was the beginning of fraternities and Greek life in America.

Fueled by the game-changing use of steam power, as historians note, the Industrial Revolution began in Britain and spread to the rest of the world, including the United States, by 1830–40 and changed the nature of

1. Syrett, *Company He Keeps*, 13. This entire chapter is a summary of Syrett's book and citiations will only be used for exceptional or major quotations.

27

social formation and connection.[2] In a time of rapid social, educational, and professional change, fraternities provided American men with networks, ideas, friends, and allies in the face of a rapidly changing American landscape. For all these reasons, as Syrett explains, they spread rapidly in the second quarter of the nineteenth century. Soon, there were fraternities on every campus in the New England and the mid-Atlantic regions, as well as some scattered throughout the South and the Midwest. The fraternities had a dual purpose—education and camaraderie—and the pursuit of these values allayed many anxieties that men had in this era.

By making the pursuit of education a fundamental purpose of fraternities, they were taking on a role that universities of the day were not created to do. The role of the university was instead to train individuals for the ministry, and university life was filled with prayer, recitation, and related studies. The schedule was very strict, and the faculty were overbearing. One scholar of the period described the curriculum by saying:

> By no educational criteria derived from any time, place, or philosophy, can the early nineteenth-century American college curriculum as actually taught be made to look attractive. It consisted solely of a drill in Latin, Greek, and mathematics, with a cursory view of science and some moral philosophy and *belles lettres* as the capstone. The students disliked the curriculum and pursued their studies only grudgingly.[3]

Yet in the early 1800s, an increasing number of students went to university to enter a professional occupation. Fraternities allowed students to join together for meals, literary discussion, and academic pursuits outside the scope of tedious university activities. The constitution of Delta Kappa Epsilon details that "the objects of the organization are the cultivation of general literature, the advancement and encouragement of intellectual excellence." Many intellectual activities were mandated in fraternity constitutions. Alpha Delta Phi required each member to exhibit three essays per year, and Beta Theta Pi dictated that a member must deliver an essay at each meeting. Intellect and oratorical skill were key traits of a man in the antebellum period, and fraternities cultivated these skills.

Fraternities also existed to provide camaraderie and brotherhood. This camaraderie addressed underlying anxieties that many students had. Those who attended university were anxious to find companionship, as their matriculation required them to move away from home and their families. Fraternities met this need in a unique way by institutionalizing friendship

2. History.com, "Industrial Revolution."

3. Syrett, *Company He Keeps*, 16.

among like-minded peers, and requiring pledges to swear an oath of loyalty to their fraternity. In the case of Delta Kappa Epsilon, for example, a new member was required to pledge, "I will cultivate in myself and among my fellow members a spirit of kindness and good will."[4] Author and Professor Nicholas Syrett writes that "Fraternities provided a model for family that was comforting to fraternity men separated from their natal families. The familial model was also reassuring because, like one's real family, fraternal ties were presumed to last a lifetime."[5] The fraternity family provided a replacement for the biological family during the college years of a fraternity man. The fact that fraternity bonds were permanent and could not be broken on a whim made members willing to place their trust in each other.

University students were also anxious about competition with their peers and the uncertain job market that they would face after college. Many parents had paid for three or four years of college education for their child, and the fear of disappointing their parents overshadowed these young men as they entered the job market. Furthermore, these students were taking large steps downward, as they were moving from seniors in college to a freshman position in the workforce and the world at large. This created uncertainty in fraternity members about their place in society. Economic trends in the antebellum period only heightened these anxieties. Land ownership was decreasing, and so fewer fathers were able to pass down land to their sons. Competition in professional fields was increasing as a result, and the capitalist economy heavily valued the "self-made" man, one who could make it on his own. Fraternities responded to these anxieties by providing brotherhood, and pledging undying loyalty to each other. Syrett writes, "[G]roups encouraging young men to swear loyalty to each other in college and throughout their lives beyond graduation—fraternities—were many men's answer to this anxiety."[6] Elsewhere, he adds, "Loyalty to one's brothers was prized above all else because it was precisely the competition with other individuals that made men so anxious."[7] If a fraternity member was confident of his status among his peers, he was less likely to be anxious regarding his status in society.

The confidence that fraternities gave their membership was significant, and is evidenced by their good behavior. Historian Leon Jackson analyzed the Harvard riots of the late eighteenth and early nineteenth centuries. He discovered that members of fraternities, specifically Phi Beta Kappa, were

4. Syrett, *Company He Keeps*, 29.
5. Syrett, *Company He Keeps*, 30.
6. Syrett, *Company He Keeps*, 46.
7. Syrett, *Company He Keeps*, 38.

the least likely to have participated.[8] The students that rioted did so to gain recognition, but members of Phi Beta Kappa already recognized a manly dignity in each other, and so they did not feel the same need to rebel. Syrett summarizes the issue adroitly when he writes: "Their propensity to participate in the acts of revolution that swept across U.S. colleges between 1776 and 1860 may well have been tempered by the *feeling* of revolution inherent in belonging to a college fraternity, as well as by the dignity and manliness that fraternity men believed inhered in that membership."[9] When a man was unconditionally accepted by his fraternity brothers, he was a better student, and a more confident and peaceful man.

The dual purpose of fraternities not only alleviated the anxieties of many, it also helped prepare young men for the world beyond in two principal ways: They developed men for professional life, and they taught men how to be a gentleman. The second quarter of the nineteenth century oversaw the continuation of important economic trends. A shortage of land sparked a surge of industrialization and urbanization, which, in turn, led to an increasingly capitalist and mercantilist economy. This economy valued the individual. The self-made man was defined as one who had command over his destiny, and relied upon himself for success. He succeeded in business through hard work, skill, and ingenuity. All men were judged by what they made of themselves in the world.

Fraternities not only cultivated community, they also cultivated an independence and resilience in their men that prepared them for a changing world. They primarily accomplished this through rivalry with other fraternities that mirrored the competition that these individuals would face in the professional world. Simply belonging to a fraternity was not enough for members; these men wanted to be in the *best* fraternity. An excerpt from Alpha Delta Phi's constitution gives insight into these fraternity competitions:

> Qualifications for membership in this Society shall be a union of good general scholarship and ability: a laudable emulation and diligence in the pursuit of learning: those qualities of mind and heart which will endear one to his fellows throughout all the pursuits of life: and a moral character above suspicion and reproach. And none shall be eligible to this society solely on the ground of literary excellence, or of social feelings, nor shall private friendship or sectional prejudice be allowed any weight in making such selections.[10]

8. Syrett, *Company He Keeps*, 37.
9. Syrett, *Company He Keeps*, 37.
10. Syrett, *Company He Keeps* 62.

The ideal fraternity man was a complete man: intelligent and of strong moral character. Fraternity chapters corresponded with each other, boasting of these traits in their members. Brown University's valedictorian was graduated from a chapter of Delta Kappa Epsilon and "[our chapter] still occupies the front rank at Brown both in scholarship and popularity."[11] Middlebury's chapter wrote that they had five of the top students in the class, and Lafayette's chapter detailed that they had four out of the eight junior orators. Good scholarship, as Syrett tells the story, was lauded by fraternities, but they also valued extracurricular activities. Fraternity men sought elected offices in literary societies, skill in oration and debate, appointment to honor societies, and more. At Yale, a literary editorship was a mark of popularity and intelligence, and was particularly coveted by fraternities as a result.

While fraternities had a reputation for being filled with wealthy students, in reality, they often filled their ranks with men of less substantial means. This allowed men of lower and middle classes to display their talents, and work their way up in society through the pursuit of academic and literary excellence. This pursuit of excellence, fueled by competition with other fraternities, was critical in preparing young men for the professions after graduation.

Fraternities also emphasized character-building, which underscores an important point: Fraternities did not automatically make a man; rather, they helped young boys grow into gentlemanliness. An observer of a fraternity situation at the University of Wisconsin in 1911 wrote:

> Let the fraternity man realize that the fraternity has not placed the stamp of "man" upon him, just because he has been initiated, but that the fraternity has given him a chance to "make good" in the world.[12]

Members of fraternities developed into young men through the community of like-minded brothers. Fraternity men realized that to gain respect as a man, they had to live for people other than themselves. A fraternity man did not pursue success for himself in sports, extracurricular activities, or academics. One student wrote in his memoir of Yale, "To be musical and indulge in music privately was a sure sign of freakishness, as bad as private drinking."[13] This is because activities were pursued with and for other people, not for self-indulgence or self-recognition. Fraternity men were known to take music lessons as a way to show that he could lead men. The

---

11. Syrett, *Company He Keeps* 63.

12. Syrett, *Company He Keeps*, 128.

13. Syrett, *Company He Keeps*, 139.

Yale student continued in his memoir, "There were routes upward for men who could write what the college magazine wanted, or make the music that undergraduates liked; and a broad path, much trodden in my day, for the energetically pious who could organize religion, and sell God to the right kind of undergraduate."[14] Just about any activity, from athletics to art to religious pursuit, was valuable as long as it was pursued with and for other people in the college. Syrett sums up the section by writing, "The activity had to be communal: The collegian without respect was the one who did all for himself and nothing for his college."[15] The concept of living for others is critical to a proper understanding of masculinity. Fraternities lived out this concept in their daily lives, with young men also seeking to be refined gentlemen, a pursuit that prepared them for secular society after graduation. A gentleman possessed a certain dignity through his appearance and conduct. In contrast, fraternities rejected men that did not assert themselves and were under the thumb of others. They rejected people who blindly followed orders without thinking for themselves. Such weakness of character opposed the values that fraternities actively pursued.

Fraternity men believed that physical appearance was a reliable indicator of an individual's character. A virtuous man presented himself well in both dress and stature. A gentleman was also sociable and had good manners. William Hammond of Amherst described a fellow student that he admired, saying "He is the most finished gentleman in every good sense of the word, I ever saw: most thoroughly conversant with society, without an atom of frippery or a shade of the *petit-maitre*."[16] A gentleman did not keep to himself. He was a man of status that interacted with society without showing off. Noah Webster's adviced fraternity men to choose their friends wisely. "You can always select, for your intimate associates, men of good principles and unimpeachable character. Never maintain a familiar intercourse with the profane, the lewd, the intemperate, the gamester, or the scoffer at religion."[17] Fraternity men realized that they were judged by the company that they kept, and during the antebellum period, they strove to be gentlemen of good character who kept each other accountable. Through these endeavors, fraternity men prepared each other for the secular world at large, shaping it in ways that others could not.

The social and professional benefits that fraternities provided spurred their national expansion in the nineteenth century. Fraternity chapters

14. Syrett, *Company He Keeps*, 139.

15. Syrett, *Company He Keeps*, 139.

16. Syrett, *Company He Keeps*, 65.

17. Syrett, *Company He Keeps*, 67.

blossomed into national organizations, which only enhanced the advantages that fraternities already provided. The spread of fraternities across the nation increased during the 1840s and 1850s. While the spread was temporarily halted in the 1860s due to the Civil War, it began again in the 1870s. From the beginning, fraternities were interested in establishing "sister chapters," which connected fraternity chapters at other colleges across the nation, and grew them into national brotherhoods. This alignment with chapters at other schools differentiated fraternities from other organizations on campus, such as literary and debate societies. It also contributed to the distinct identity that fraternities were developing for themselves. These attributes of fraternities in the nineteenth century increased their professional and social value to students.

Chapters at different schools frequently corresponded with each other. Each chapter would elect a secretary for the purpose of corresponding with other chapters in the fraternity. The secretary of Delta Kappa Epsilon at the New York Free Academy sent a letter to his counterpart at Michigan University, stating:

> Our late convention has inspired each man with new energy and a stronger determination (if possible) to strive increasingly to the object of our glorious Fraternity—we are gratified to hear of your continued and increasing prosperity—tidings of this kind add an additional lustre to the name of ΔKE and find an echo in our own hearts always respondent to the individual and combined interest of our widespread brotherhood.[18]

Such language demonstrates that the national camaraderie of fraternities was powerful, and it caused individual men to strive for excellence together.

Syrett's research shows that fraternity hired administrators, who were often alumni, to coordinate the uniformity of chapters across the country. In order to maintain membership in the national organization, a chapter had to uphold the fraternity's values and preserve its good reputation. The reputation of a fraternity was important to its members due to the close relationships that these men had with each other. Therefore, they greatly cared about the people that they affiliated themselves with. Nathan Corbin, a fraternity member in the Michigan chapter of Delta Upsilon, described the ideal fraternity man when he wrote, "I sincerely hope that the fraternity will never expose itself to the danger of being compelled to recognize other than true gentlemen and careful scholars as its members. We are judged as a whole as we are known through individuals."[19] This emphasis on reputation

18. Syrett, *Company He Keeps*, 79.
19. Syrett, *Company He Keeps*, 79.

and excellence sparked a key development in the community of fraternities. A fraternity brother was bound to defend the honor of his fellow brothers, and he was also required to confront his brothers, and correct their misbehavior in an effort to improve their character. These expectations were set forth in the founding constitution of many fraternities. Specifically, Alpha Delta Phi's constitution states:

> Furthermore, it shall be the duty of each member of the Society, openly and faithfully to defend the intellectual and moral character of every brother member whenever it may be unwarrantally attacked: and to correct and silence if possible, all false and malicious reports calculated to injure the reputation and prospects of any member of this society. And further every member shall consider himself morally and religiously bound, as far as he is able, under all circumstances, to consult the interests of every brother member. He shall also by all expedient means endeavor to correct the faults he may observe in the conduct and opinions of every brother, which may have a tendency to injure him, in the estimation of his friends, or bring reproach on the Society.[20]

Fraternity membership and community sparked positive character development as brothers defended each other and held each other accountable. Such actions formed young men into scholars and gentlemen who were prepared for the professional world at large.

For these men, this community and social benefit extended after graduation. As Syrett describes it in his book, "Fraternity alumni associations, reunions, and clubs also allowed men to prolong intimate friendships, based partially on nostalgia, throughout their adult lives."[21] Previously, intimate male friendships ended when a man got married, unlike friendships between women, which frequently lasted for life. Postgraduate fraternity functions allowed men to continue these friendships on a communal basis.

The tangible benefits of national fraternity membership were significant as well. Most of these benefits were directly due to the efforts of alumni. Fraternities held annual alumni conventions and established regional alumni associations that purchased halls in major cities for the use of dues-paying alumni. These halls were outfitted with restaurants and overnight guest rooms to provide a fraternal sanctuary in the middle of these cities. They printed various materials for the fraternity, such as newsletters and catalogues of alumni and current members. These catalogues were expensive, with steel engraving and a coat of arms for each chapter of the fraternity.

20. Syrett, *Company He Keeps*, 91–92.
21. Syrett, *Company He Keeps*, 81.

Members became avid catalogue collectors so as to be able to identify their brothers at other chapters. Fraternity badges, or pins, also became a way for members to identify each other when they were not personally acquainted. The catalogues, pins, and other memorabilia and collectibles were funded by alumni eager to promote fraternities across the country. Such privileges of fraternity membership allayed many students' anxieties about their future and their place in the world, which was a critical boost of confidence for young men as they stepped into manhood.

Universities have an enormous opportunity to recover the more heroic aspect of fraternity history. Perhaps Greek Week should be more than games, sports, and skits. Perhaps non-exclusive awards should not be used to manage bad behavior. What fraternities were also given awards for a fraternity debate competition or an essay competition. What fraternities also have a to produce their own high-quality shorts films related to a theme chosen that each year by the president of the college. What even fraternities had to compete by writing original music and producing theater connected to some annual theme. What if fraternities were competing for year-round for the annual "Fraternity Cup" or the "IFC Cup," which included multiple events and activities year-round that spanned the range of student academic disciplines from business to education to STEM with a huge cash prize. For example, first place may win $20,000 and last place $2,000 and everything in between. In other words, if universities invest in heroic fraternities that is exactly what they will get in the form of pro-social outcomes.

4

The Evolution and Impact of
the "Frat Film" Genre

"You know what, we're not a bunch of drunk, rambunctious men who
do nothing but take advantage of girls. . . . We are better men and we
have created a culture in our fraternity that puts that on display."

—STEVE EGNACZYK, OHIO STATE UNIVERSITY

The Eternal Party

Larry "Pinto" Kroger (Tom Hulce) and Kent "Flounder" Dorfman
(Stephen Furst) hesitantly walk to the front of Delta house. They are
there to try their luck with Flounder's brother's fraternity when Pinto tells
him he heard it's the worst house on campus. Just then, a mannequin crashes
through a window to their feet. As they near the front door, they pass by a
drunk John "Bluto" Blutarsky (Jim Belushi) holding a goblet of cheap beer,
and watering the front lawn with his first few drinks. Bluto graces Pinto and
Flounder's shoes with the same stream, and invites them in, where scores of
drunken and drinking partiers are dancing, making out, and breaking stuff
ad nauseam. This is how we are introduced to Delta House's lovable antihero
losers and a future preoccupation of fraternity life.

Every artistic creation is an artifact, capturing the present culture,
and influencing the future of that same culture. On paper, *Animal House*

36

reenacts screenwriter Chris Miller's own fraternity hijinks, but as much as the film encapsulates some element of the past, its significance, and the significance of other films like it, lies in the genre's influence on young men who yearn for the college life they see on-screen: brimming with destructive partying, hazing, girl-chasing, and racial homogeneity.

Movies like *Old School* (2003) set up college students to expect that the college experience is the pinnacle of the human experience. When Mitch (Luke Wilson) moves into a house beside a nearby state college, recently married Frank (Will Ferrell) and young father Beanie (Vince Vaughn) all see it as an opportunity to relive their college days. The film repeatedly derides adult life, emphasizing that even a feeble-looking navy veteran would—and does—die trying to recapture "good times" at the fraternity. Beanie agrees with him, arguing that the ability to party is more important than family. "I have a wife and kids. Do I seem like a happy guy to you, Frank?"[1] Later, he doubles down, ironically asking Mitch, "You think I like avoiding my wife and kids to hang out with nineteen-year-old girls everyday?"[2] The film ends with the guys moving on from the fraternity, but leaving the audience with the implicit message that nothing is more fun—at any stage of life—than the parties and sexual antics of fraternity life. The takeaway is that the highest good available for pursuit is *fun*.

Animal House has done much to establish the expectations newly arrived freshman have about campus life. They know they are expected to drink heavily, as is very clearly spelled out in a scene where Katy (Karen Allen) and Boon (Peter Riegart) argue about Delta's toga party, which Boon wants to attend, against his girlfriend's wishes. "You're twenty-one-years old," she says. "In six months, you're going to graduate, and tomorrow night you're going to wrap yourself in a bed sheet, and pour grain alcohol all over your head. It's cute, but I think I'll pass this time."[3] Boon insists on going because, "It's a fraternity party, I'm in the fraternity. How can I miss it?"[4] The fraternity not only attracts, it compels. The expectation that young men have when they enter college is that drinking with your fraternity is your highest priority, a message that is reinforced by Delta's continual disinterest in academics throughout the film.

During a party at Delta house, Katy keeps arguing: "Is this really what you're gonna do for the rest of your life? . . . I mean hanging around with

---

1. Phillips and Gurland, *Old School*.
2. Phillips and Gurland, *Old School*.
3. Landis, *Animal House*.
4. Landis, *Animal House*.

a bunch of animals getting drunk every weekend."[5] And Boon says, "No! After I graduate, I'm gonna get drunk every night."[6] The film is instructing its viewers, and the films that follow, that the true fraternity experience doubles as a staging ground for incipient alcoholism, but functions as a faux grown-up fantasy of never actually growing up. That messaging accounts for why the overuse of alcohol and other substances have become such a staple of the stunted manhood some fraternities promote. Although they may also consider alcohol "cool" or "sick," given its benefits as a social lubricant, college students don't consume alcohol in such immense quantities for the "cool factor," or for its ability to function as a social lubricant. Many likely overconsume to self-medicate. Young men today are struggling with a deep sense of purposelessness, and that carries with it enormous anxiety, which *The Place Beyond the Pines* (2012) lays it out on film. The movie follows the lives of an outlaw, an ambitious police officer, and each of their only sons. One son suffers from a fatherless home by way of a bank robbery-turned-shootout and the other by divorce. What it shows is that each son ends up with similar—though redeemable—problems of substance abuse and violence from their respective experiences of fatherlessness. The two boys use alcohol, marijuana, oxycodone, and ecstasy to numb their sense of being "lost" and their sense of fatherly loss. They each turn violent, lashing out in an attempt to express their emotional turmoil.[7] The film concludes with both boys on a mission to find their fathers, however paradoxical this is, given that one lives with his father, and the other's is dead. These two seventeen year-olds are dramatized versions of the ones that are flooding into the arms of the fraternity system. The challenge this poses for the Greek organizations is how they are going to step up to the plate, and provide a healthy model for manhood and purposeful lives that fatherless or father-weak homes cannot. Unfortunately, many fraternities have failed to rise to the challenge to date, and have become havens for substance abuse and other misconduct instead.

Van Wilder (2002) is another good example of the expectations that are set for students coming into college, particularly when it comes to young men and their encounters with the opposite sex. If you scroll through IMDb's list of the titular character's most memorable lines, you are treated to pages of hilarious but woman-objectifying, oversexualized, and nudity-related quotes that all indicate that the best man at the college is the one who can go farthest with the girl of his choice, without regard for emotional

5. Landis, *Animal House.*

6. Landis, *Animal House.*

7. CianFrance, *Place Beyond the Pines.*

commitment to his any of his hookup partners or other moral consider-
ations.[8] Though the film is humorous, and may actually intend to take a
critical stance towards the partying and pursuit of girls that are now staples
of many fraternities, it is important to uncover what kind of good life this
genre of film is pushing.

In *Old School*, we can see how this vision is meant to be internalized.
Nudity and overt sexuality are applauded for dodging the seemingly un-
avoidable potholes of adult and married life. By rejecting any responsible
standards, the pursuit of a monogamous relationship, and even conceptions
of the age of consent, *Old School* communicates that random sex with beautiful women is an exciting goal that ought to be pursued at all stages of life.
At the end, the film takes a mild stab at redemption when its young male
protagonist Mitch moves out of the fraternity house to focus on a career, a
meaningful relationship with love interest Nicole, and genuine adulthood.
But a last-minute change of heart after the fraternity and its partying are
saved from disbandment does little to undo the message that is pounded into
our heads for the vast majority of the film: When considering whom to have
sex with and when, consent, commitment, and the dignity of either party
play no role. In this way, *Old School* echoes *Animal House* in its praise of pro-
miscuity. *Animal House* is a far less sexualizing film, but several of its stories
stand out for their promotion of reckless and inconsiderate male sexuality.

During a road trip to Dickinson College, an all-girls school, in Flounder's brother's car, the film promotes a mainstream conception of hookups as
acceptable—and even impressive when pulled off successfully. Otter, already
established as a lady's man, is the brains behind the Dickinson scheme. His
goal is to hook up with an attractive Dickinson girl, and maybe set up his
friends too. Outside a bar, Otter and the Dickinson girl make out in the car,
removing some clothes in the process. They are suddenly interrupted when
the rest of the boys flee the bar. The girl screams, almost falling out of the
car with no shirt on, as Otter scrambles to catch up with his pals. The scene
is played for laughs, but the obvious disrespect and carelessness with which
Otter treats the Dickinson girl is a model of immoral manhood: Hook up
and run! Don't look back! The notion that it is acceptable for men to deceive
women into sexual encounters, of whatever kind, is a dangerous one that,
when we see it play out on college campuses, can all too often lead to young
men taking too many liberties with their female counterparts. A similar message is conveyed later in the movie when, at the fraternity's toga party, the
dean's wife shows up and is brought upstairs by Otter where they presumably

8. IMDb.com, "Ryan Reynolds: *Van Wilder*."

have sex. For young male viewers, the scene's meta-message is that sleeping with a married woman is not only funny but desirable and respectable.

In fact, both *Animal House* and *Old School* brush off the problematic nature of adults having sex with minors. In *Animal House*, Larry, a freshman, makes out with, and later has sex with, a girl he meets, only to later discover she is only sixteen. In *Old School*, similar events occur: Mitch, who seems to be in his late twenties, has sex with a girl at the party Beanie throws at Mitch's new house. Assuming the girl is in college, Mitch fails to investigate, only to discover that she is the sixteen-year-old daughter of his boss. This distresses him, but the movie routinely scoffs at any moral hesitation. Both of Mitch's friends, Frank and Beanie, agree he did nothing wrong. Not surprisingly, this is the message that the movie ultimately imparts, with Mitch effectively shrugging off any questions about the capability of a minor to consent.

Although in the real world, both Larry and Mitch are guilty of statutory rape, in the film, their ignorance of their conquest's real age, and the fact that they got laid, excuse any moral ambiguity in the eyes of the film's characters. In the real world, this fantasy communicates imaginary legal and moral loopholes to young male audiences. This carelessness on matters of statutory rape and moral constraints is concerning. Far more pernicious is what it teaches young men about consent. If our societal standard is that consent to sex cannot exist between a minor and an adult, and yet popular films about fraternity life ignore that standard, it is an easily transferrable attitude that can all too quickly gloss over the many other ways that consent is not and cannot be given. By degrading the importance of consent across an age gap, films like these degrade the importance of consent entirely. This is what makes so many impressionable fraternity men educated by "fraternity films" dangerous: Consent is no punch line. Yet its devaluation occurs in movies as recent as *Frat Star* (2017). The film follows the efforts of Nick Cooper (Connor Lawrence) to join the Phi Delta fraternity on his campus. During the pledge process, he is assigned a scavenger hunt that involves sneaking into a sorority house and awakening a young woman with a sexual act.[9] Now, this is softened by Nick's discomfort with the task, which leads him to obtain consent from the woman he wakes up. (Though is this really enough to satisfy our moral qualms?) The fact remains that Nick was apparently willing to complete his pledge activity before he even knew whether he *could* gain consent. Once again, young male viewers are shown how little value they should place on *consent*.

9. Johnson and Serbu, *Frat Star*.

Given that these films are being sold as comedies, it is worth saying that just because it is important to value and respect something like consent does not mean it cannot or should not be used in an attempt at comedy. Rather, jokes about sensitive topics should be depicted in ways that account for the strong tendency of impressionable young viewers to mimic off-screen the humorously distasteful and immoral behaviors they see on-screen. Consider the impact fraternity films have had on hazing. The forceful and humiliating initiation of freshmen on screen is a staple of fraternity movies, as *Animal House*, *Old School,* and *Frat Star* all demonstrate. In *Frat Star*, for example, during the Phi Delta fraternity's pledging process, the pledges are required to prove their worth to the fraternity in a hazing process that involves forced drinking, paddling, and mandatory sexual acts with women. In this film and others, hazing is, like consent, the butt of many jokes.

In *Old School*, an ancient-looking veteran, covered in lubricant, wrestles topless college girls and dies. Pledges are tied to cinder blocks and then thrown off the roof.[10] In *Frat Star*, pledges go on the aforementioned illicit scavenger hunt, they drink half-naked and to the point of sickness, and they are required to sacrifice schoolwork in service to the fraternity.[11] In *Animal House*, Flounder accidentally kills a horse, there is forced binge-drinking, and students are awakened with fire extinguishers.[12] In *American Pie: Beta House*, a selection of five pledges are brought in front of the Beta brothers, and are presented with a board of fifty tasks to complete by the end of the semester, ranging from the mildly perverted, to the dangerous, illegal, and lewd, The tasks include getting their "ass signed by a stripper," having sex with a professor, stealing an ostrich and placing it in another house, and stealing from a rival fraternity.[13] Another hazing practice, instituted by a different fraternity, required students to have sex with a sheep, which one student does, and finds traumatizing but, again, this is made the butt of a joke.

Young men are not more likely to haze or be hazed because they are seeing violent and humiliating forms of hazing on-screen. They are more likely to haze or be hazed because they see these practices depicted as *funny*. Images of young men being forced to drink to the point of sickness while being physically abused occur, in films like these, with a smile and the message that the trauma, humiliation, and violence are worth the price of fraternity admission. As a result, the vehicle and tone that carry these pictures promote and condone, rather than warn and proscribe.

10. Phillips and Gurland, *Old School.*
11. Johnson and Serbu, *Frat Star.*
12. Landis, *Animal House.*
13. Waller, *American Pie Presents: Beta House.*

The Brother from Another Planet

Films that endorse racist attitudes in fraternities are few and far between, even in an implicit sense. However, many fraternity movies do adopt a stance of tacit approval toward racist fraternity practices. Although virtually all predominantly white fraternities accept brothers of color, films often portray a false tokenism that inadvertently reifies their ignorance and racialization of college life by filmmakers. It seems that it is hard for filmmakers to accept the fact America has made significant progress on race and the many white men have non-white friends because they love their non-white as brothers (with no agenda). From the start of the fraternity film genre in 1978, no film has explicitly excused or promoted racist fraternities. This is likely due to the progressive nature of Hollywood and racism's taboo status in mainstream American culture. But that does not prevent movies from reinforcing racist habits in fraternities.

Tokenism is a buzzword that is nearly ubiquitous in fraternity movies and conversations on race relations. In the context of race, a standard issue Americans need to answer for is the presence of the "token black guy," regardless of whether they are discussing a student body, a politician's staff, a friend group, or a fraternity film. There are pieces from popular outlets such as *Salon* and the University of Miami's student publication the *Tab* that describe the experience of being black in a white fraternity, which demonstrate the tokenism, patience, and tolerance of racism required to exist in that space, but fraternity movies routinely gloss over this.[14] In *Frat Star*, the scene where we are first introduced to all of the pledges and are given their nicknames, one black student joins his white brothers-to-be, and is given the nickname "Token."[15] The purpose for his presence is thus reduced to meeting an unspoken quota, presumably so that the fraternity can avoid any accusations of racism, but he is allowed no agency of his own. Token's reason for joining a fraternity has, of course, nothing to do with him belonging there. Given the yearnings for community and acceptance that lead most freshmen to join a fraternity, they are shortchanging the character of fulfillment, by making him a false symbol of their nonexistent acceptance of students of color. Lest it appear I am reading too far into a nickname, this throwaway "joke" is playing on an earlier scene between upperclassmen. One expresses concerns about diversity in the fraternity, which his brothers dismiss with ignorant or sarcastic comments. All fraternities—real or imagined—see themselves as service-oriented organizations that look to

14. Kasai, "Black Guy"; Bass, Jr., "Only Black Guy."

15. Johnson and Serbu, *Frat Star*.

support both their members and the needy outside of the fraternity. It is fundamentally anti-fraternity when these films reinforce the practice of accepting black students for the benefit of perceived diversity and tolerance.

Some films, like *Animal House* and *Old School,* do not really take up the issue of race. Either they do not have any black pledges—or even black characters—or they utterly disregard race in their treatment of characters. Others, however, instruct racism, in a broader sense, that can be internalized, both by future fraternity members and the culture, at large. *Van Wilder* and its sequel *Van Wilder 2: The Rise of Taj* play into these kinds of racial stereotypes, most noticeably with students of Indian descent, but also with Jewish and black stereotypes, reducing each of these characters to their culturally assumed qualities. The film's failure to portray these characters in three dimensions has little to do with actually making people believe that students of Indian, Jewish, and African descent meet the criteria for their respective stereotypes. The consequence of these portals is that they maintain and reify the racialization of human relationships in ways that do not exist in more fraternities today.

"Frat" Films that Criticize

Not all fraternity movies glorify fraternity life. Some raise questions about the darker side of it, and still others are full-on critiques. It is not necessarily incumbent on all fraternity movies to cast a critical eye on fraternities, and for those that do, it by no means ensures that the result will be a better-quality film. A little criticism, however, does beget greater diversity of thought and consideration among those who consume the fraternity genre, and that, of course, includes fraternity and would-be fraternity boys.

Director Todd Phillips, who has already featured prominently in this chapter, is not only a prophet of fraternity misbehavior, but also a former critic. The genesis of his career was in documentary filmmaking, which include his 1998 documentary, *Frat House,* which was commissioned by HBO but never aired. HBO decided not to release the film because Phillips and his co-director, Andrew Garland, were accused of unethically abusing waivers, alcohol, and paid reenactments of rumored hazing practices to make the final product, resulting in some combination of fact and fiction, as Phillips and Garland set out to reveal—and critique—the facts of "real" fraternity life.

At the start of the film, one brother is convincing a freshman at rush week to "commit to me right now," with promises of reliving high school, partying, protection, women, brotherhood, and popularity.[16] Alcohol is key here: It provides brothers with an intoxicating platform to proffer social bribes to potential pledges who willingly accept them. Alcohol is at the center of every function, tradition, and lifestyle for the fraternities depicted in the documentary. Members drink beer and liquor while pledges drink to their limit. Thus, they prove their worth, accept their assigned punishment, and earn their reward. Mixers and parties are themed after, and operate around, alcohol. They facilitate fraternity among brothers, and fraternization with "sisters." A cheap elixir, alcohol is also used to medicate the stunted emotional states of the many college students in Warren Farrell's *Boy Crisis*, but alcohol ultimately deepens their crisis, culminating in numerous suspensions.

Though *Frat Star* is dangerous in many ways, given its twisted vision of women, hazing, and alcohol, the film does have an inkling of a conscience. Films like *Animal House* and *Van Wilder* see the trade-off between alcoholism and grades, maturity, and the general ability to make good decisions as a no-brainer: Drink until you cannot! Nick, the film's main character, is not so sure. He wrestles with those trade-offs throughout the film. The fraternity promises an escape from lovesickness, responsibility, and boredom—but at what cost? Is the alcohol and accompanying misconduct-laden "–ism," worth it? During the hazing process, Nick appears to be the only one among the pledges who is unconvinced of the legitimacy of going through these rituals of submission both for their content and intent. He pushes through until he is kicked out for lying about his family's wealth because of the pressure exerted on him by his roommate, father, and his own suffering in the wake of an embarrassing breakup. This lukewarm disapproval of hazing for the more sensitive or moral among us is an acceptable contribution to the discussion of some fraternities' shortcomings. In the same way it softly criticizes alcoholic behavior, *Frat Star* tries to signal to its viewers that, at least for some people, the fraternity system is not worth the cost of hazing. By the end of film, Nick's internal struggle has come to a head. He yells at himself, angry that he has been rejected from the fraternity, even while he finally, reluctantly, commits to what he seemed to have known all along: Alcohol does not remedy problems; it only inflames them.

Hookups and Sweethearts

The fraternity film genre has a notably muted approach to relationships, but it is worth exploring what they criticize, and what else they perhaps ought to

16. Phillips, *Frat House*.

criticize. *Frat Star* may actually have the most robust criticism of the mainstream fraternity view of women. The sports and pop culture blog *Barstool Sports* recently released a humorously intended interview with fraternity members about the role of "doorman" at fraternity functions. When asked about who to let in, the doorman responds that they must be a brother, friends with one, or, finally, female.[17] In *Frat Star*, women are seen as sexual space-fillers in physical, romantic, and emotional capacities. Nick is introduced to numerous women at fraternity parties, persuaded by his would-be brothers that a hookup is a fraternity man's calling and the only way to get past his heartbreak. He refuses at first, partly because he develops an attachment to a special sorority sister, but he caves and appears to pay some consequences. A party montage shows the couple making out with strangers of the other's gender to make each other jealous in a strange, roundabout way of getting to know each other that both seems to work for, and against, them. *Frat Star* knows that this is the method that the most twisted fraternities sponsor for the men they are developing and demonstrates to its audience that, if you want a meaningful relationship with a woman—and you just might—then this hedonistic fraternity-sorority hookup culture is not for you.

Goat (2016) is a dramatization of real events that is almost entirely silent on hookup culture, save a couple of throwaway lines when both members and pledges acknowledge the immediate satisfactions of hookup culture. The most noticeable of these lines is when Will (Daniel Flaherty), by all measures a loser, is told by Brad (Ben Schnetzer) he should consider dropping from the pledge class. Will is incensed at the idea and lists off all the benefits of being even a pledge to the fraternity, including: "I'm having sex for the first time in my life."[18] Brad disregards the comment, taking no issue with it, but the audience is given a sense that this is a flimsy reason in the eyes of the filmmakers. The idea that fraternities are worth the torture inflicted on him for the "in" they provide with women and various other perks is condemned by *Goat*. The only similar subtext occurs because Brad's having a girlfriend apparently making him less of a fit for the fraternity life, though it does not really ever make a problem for him getting in.

The absence of anything resembling sexual assault in *Goat* is striking, but *Frat House* documents it as it appears to happen in the context of the fraternity party scene. The opening scenes of the documentary are among the most shocking, especially as Phillips and Garland choose to plunge the audience straight into the raucous partying of rush week at SUNY Oneonta

17. Barstool Sports, "Science Behind a Frat Party."
18. Neel, *Goat*.

where mobs of college students are flooding bars, getting drunk, and later filtering out back to their houses and apartments. On the way out, the crew catches a brother and the closest thing to a date you can find at a function like this. They follow the two to the young man's home, commenting on how they do not know each other, and that the young woman now seems to regret having agreed to have gone with him. The young couple light a bong that they smoke together and the rest of the evening is left to the audience's imagination. This is the life everyone knows that the highest tier fraternities offer their members, but *Frat House* lets the audience feel the danger that it poses, and the sense of entitlement that exists within it. Most startling, perhaps, is the lack of inhibition, or self-awareness, about this dark side of fraternities that the men (and some college women) have in them. The fictional accounts in *Frat Star* and *Goat* have characters that transcend the toxic mindset that is being force-fed to them, regretting and resisting its pull. *Frat House* has no such characters, indicating that the dominant fraternities of 1998 have no such characters either. One has good reason to believe that progress made by women's movements and American culture's development of a recognition that women are their own agents means the vision of women in *Frat House* is increasingly rare, but the idea that these worldviews are extinct given how much these attitudes still dominate many films would be naïve.

Alcohol

Goat (2016) both covers and critiques the overuse of alcohol by fraternities. Early in the film, producer James Franco appears in a minor role as an alumnus and potential role model for the brothers at the fraternity house. They all get drunk together, and we last see Franco's character passed out on a couch covered in vomit, likely blacked out and possibly even an alcoholic. This underscores the multitude of problems fraternities have with alcohol: Not only do they get to exist without authority, and in possession of vast amounts of liquor and beer, but that they actually can have negative long-term consequences, as illustrated by the drunken alum.[19] Films, as we have seen, are providing some not-so-subtle messaging to teens that this is what is expected of them and what they should expect in college, which is only reinforced by those upperclassmen and alumni who are responsible for mentoring each incoming class. It is ultimately an abuse of power that, in the case of *Goat*, appears to stem from the culturally well-known desire of graduated fraternity brothers to relive "the best four years of their lives."

19. Neel, *Goat*.

Goat points out the fruitlessness of chasing after this juvenile experience, during college and beyond, is not only unfulfilling, but also embarrassing.

The film's more potent focus is on hazing, which it portrays as a life-and-death-like power over pledges by drunken upperclassmen. In the film's climax, the main character's roommate, Will, suffers a heart attack, apparently brought on by the stress of pledging a fraternity. The tragic scene is difficult to watch because Will and his fellow pledges appear to have made it through the worst of the torture: They are *this close*. Will had, by then, been made to drink a full keg with his class, under threat of sex with the titular goat. He was nearly suffocated with duct tape. His upperclassman masters subjected him to forced labor. As an audience, we think he has already paid the price of admission, and merits the reward he sought. When he dies instead—and pays the ultimate asking price—we are instead left wondering whether it was worth it. That, after all, is *Goat's* point: Real-life fraternities engage in similarly immoral and dangerous hazing rituals—why aren't we asking them that question?

Given *Frat House's* central concern, the biggest hurdle for co-directors Todd Phillips and Andrew Garland was acquiring real-life hazing footage. To get it, the young men from the titular fraternity house demanded that they undergo the hazing process, too. The speed with which the real-life role of the co-directors disappear into their assigned roles is remarkable. Almost from the start, they are treated no differently from all the other skinny nerds looking to pledge a fraternity.[20] Moreover, the brothers pull no punches, subjecting the two directors to grueling physical tasks, abusive lineups, and serious psychological strain.

The requirements were so intense that Garland was hospitalized and could not continue the initiation, leaving Phillips to finish it alone, all while the cameras stayed on. This experience takes up most of the film and occurs at Muhlenburg College in Pennsylvania, but the first portion of the film focuses on another fraternity at SUNY Oneonta, where the crew is driven off the campus by threats to their lives from protective fraternity brothers. Although the members had initially agreed to have their traditions filmed by Phillips and his crew, they reneged on the agreement after beginning to feel the secrecy of their activities was threatened, and perhaps knew to be shameful.

20. Note that the making of *Frat House* is reminiscent of the 1971 Stanford Prison Experiment in which real-life Stanford University Professor Philip Zimbardo hired male students for "a psychological study of prison life," and then randomly assigned participants, after a "stability test," to take on the "real life" role of guard or prisoner, only for the entire experiment to be halted six days in due to the disturbing brutality of the guards.

The little we are able to see of the SUNY men's practices reveals the usual: Freshmen stripped of their individuality, and their ability to sleep a minimally healthy amount—as far as freshmen are ever capable of this. For long stretches, they also remove any sense of safety. Shortly after they start pledging, the brothers instruct the pledges to avoid the documentarians, and threaten the crew, seeking to hide the processes by which they refine fresh meat into fresh men.

Frat Film Perspectives

Frat Star takes a "not for everyone" critical overview, which seems to suggest we should simply dissociate from those who live the fraternity life. However, in order to build a redemptive narrative for American fraternities, we need to give our criticism both teeth and heart, while debunking the appeal of a fundamentally destructive lifestyle, in the case of some fraternities. We also need to seek a way to redirect the desires of potential pledges into a heroic kind of fraternity. *Goat* and *Frat House* are the beginning of this, but we must go even further to advocate for the advance fraternities are institutions that add value to other students on campus.

At first blush, *Frat Star* seems to be a cheap grab for adolescent attention, which it essentially is. On a deeper level, however, it also carries a self-aware satirical edge that cracks fraternity jokes, but also cracks jokes about its fraternity jokes, and that approach is sufficiently successful it is worth pondering whether we also ought to be joking about the shortcomings of depraved fraternities. Amid all the jokes, the audience becomes aware that the real joke is on the real fraternity brothers who are being mocked for their proliferation of alcoholic, sexual, racial, and pledge-directed abuse. The middling amount of no-harm-done wrongs in fraternity movies, as a whole, is likely an accurate depiction of many fraternity chapters, though many are either more harmful or less harmful than they are depicted on film.

When fraternity films praise and criticize, however, they are really either making a call to action for real-life men to emulate misconduct, or taking critical aim at the more pernicious and dangerous behavior in which fraternities engage. When a student pledge educator sees the scene in *Animal House* where Flounder shoots a blank at a horse, the same thought occurs to that brother, and perhaps stimulates his imagination to consider making a pledge shoot a horse for real. Conversely, when a fraternity president sees *Goat*'s lineups, we can only hope that it does not persuade him to make his freshmen endure similar psychological torture, but instead reminds him of even more pernicious hazing practices that put pledges in even more serious harm's way and is—again, we hope—turned off to that even darker prospect.

Watching fraternity misconduct on-screen triggers images of far worse and more disgusting conduct for those knowledgeable about fraternities. This, in fact, seems to be at the root of the fraternity film genre's biggest errors. *Goat* seems to pull the least punches in this regard, but, even as an R-rated film, it fails to convey the scope of the misconduct in fraternities that lead to pledge deaths and long-term trauma, from "kicking pledges with steel-toed boots, beating them with a metal pipe, and urinating on them, among other horrific offenses."[21] Again, *Goat* tries to replicate that as best it can with the threat of goat sodomy, the forced overconsumption of alcohol, and physical abuse during lineups, but it is obvious that no film, including the *Frat House* documentary can ever fully depict what is happening to the country's young men when they are sent off to college.

Like *Animal House, Frat House* is a product of its time. *Frat House* was completed in 1998, only fourteen years after *Animal House* all but single-handedly revived American culture's interest in fraternity life. At that point, fraternity movies were not nearly as popular as they were to become over the next two decades, so the imagination for abusive behavior within a fraternity was not as developed as it is now. This is not to say that fraternities were not ever harmful between the mid-1980s and the year 2000, but it is worth recognizing why the largely harmless fun of *Animal House* and the not-quite extreme behavior of *Frat House* are no longer capable of speaking to the current state of the fraternities today that often find themselves suspended or expelled. We know from fraternity leaks at Swarthmore College, for example, and the many investigations, suspensions, and news stories that fraternity corruption runs deeper than films like *Animal House, Van Wilder*, and *Old School* ever imagined.[22] In the real world, none of the misconduct is ever funny, and the most dangerous fraternities are sadistic, twisted, and degrading. We also know, however, that the image of fraternity life portrayed in popular films perpetuates a stereotype of fraternity life that does not exist on most college campuses. They exaggerat the negative and ignore the existence of the predominant positives.

21. Hopkins, "Shocking Hazing Incidents."
22. NBC News, "'Rape Attic.'"

5

Those Who Harm and the Harm They Do

"If you know someone in a fraternity who is a terrible person,
he was a terrible person before joining the fraternity, and
the fraternity didn't make him that way. However, there are
fraternities that harbor and allow that kind of behavior."

—CHAD FRICK, CLEMSON UNIVERSITY

The Young Bull Mob

There exist groups of young males whose misconduct rivals that of the worst fraternity. They are just as self-serving, self-centered, and self-preserving. It is widely agreed that they are intelligent, and can function socially, yet they have been repeatedly referred to as delinquents, mobsters, hoodlums, and hell-raisers.[1] When they congregate together in their late teens, a band of brothers, free of family, females, and father figures, they have been known to enter into a "state of heightened testosterone and aggression," a disruption that can cause deviancy.[2] No one member overwhelmingly dominates another, and there is no one more experienced to guide them because they are all about the same age. That only makes things worse. Their bodies are raging with hormones, so they suffer from bouts

1. CBS News, "Delinquents;" Daley, "Troublemakers."
2. PRX, "Living on Earth."

of aggression, which they inflict on others. Although these groups of individuals are sometimes known as "young bulls," these characteristics actually describe adolescent male elephants. Much like young adult men who suffer from dad-deprivation, the brutality of their unchecked aggression did not receive widespread attention until they began to kill.[3]

In the late 1970s, Krugar Park, South Africa's largest conservation area, found itself with more elephants than space.[4] The logical solution was to relocate some of the adult elephants to another park. But no vehicle then existed that was sturdy enough to transport adult elephants. So researchers decided the only thing to be done was to kill the adults, and save the children who were still small enough to be moved.[5] The government veterinarian who approved the plan knew that problems might develop, but the results were far worse than anticipated. The elephants, who ended up at South Africa's Pilanesberg Park, grew into troubled teenagers. As the Park's field ecologist Gus van Dyk explained: "I think everyone needs a role model, and these elephants that left the herd had no role model, and no idea of what appropriate elephant behavior was."[6]

Game rangers first realized there was a problem when large numbers of white rhinos started turning up dead. The rangers photographed the crime scenes, and began looking for clues: Had any elephants been in the vicinity of the deceased?[7] By the time the park understood the scope of the problem, nearly three dozen white rhinos, or about 10 percent of the park's entire rhino population, had been killed.[8] Those murders, along with rising incidence of elephants charging tourist vehicles, led the rangers to take the drastic step of killing five of them.[9] When that solved nothing, Jock McMillan, a local elephant caretaker, began following elephants around to determine precisely what was happening. He watched an elephant hose down a target rhino, then stalk a small group for hours at a time. Finally, he saw an elephant push a rhino to the ground, kneel on its chest, only to rise again, and kick it.[10] At last, the rangers decided to bring in role models for the elephants. "Typically, older male elephants travel with two *askaris*."[11]

3. Murphy, "Young Elephants."
4. Murphy, "Young Elephants."
5. CBS News, "Delinquents."
6. CBS News, "Delinquents."
7. Daley, "Troublemakers."
8. CBS News, "Delinquents."
9. CBS News, "Delinquents."
10. CBS News, "Delinquents."
11. Daley, "Troublemakers."

The Swahili term describes "young male warriors in training," and the hope was that the incoming elephants would "have a paternal effect."[12]

Unusually sturdy trucks were designed to transport the adult elephants, and thus an old herd came to congregate with a young one. A new hierarchy was soon established, with the old bulls "sparring with the younger elephants" to keep them in line. This had the welcome side effect of lowering the testosterone of their youthful counterparts.[13] The murders stopped, and so did all the harassment.

The Challenges of the Pledge Process

The story of the young bull mafia is a useful allegory for the misconduct that routinely occurs during of the pledge process, and the assault, harassment, hazing, and heartbreaking death that can result when old bulls are missing. Fraternity men across the country would benefit from asking older alumni to serve as the "old bulls" for their fraternity. The pledge period, in particular, provides fraternity men with an important opportunity to get older alumni involved—and reconnected—to their chapters. Consider asking alumni to present at your pledge events—not so that they can relive the glory days of their college experience—but to keep the pledge experience from becoming too raucous. Be direct about what you need: "If you think we're going too far, stop us!" It's a mark of maturity to be humble enough to ask for guidance and accountability.

As a rule of thumb, fraternities should not plan pledge events they would not feel comfortable engaging in when their chapter's older alumni, the president of their national headquarters, or maybe even a pledge's father, is present. If you don't think older alumni would approve, it may be a sign you are going too far, which is all the more reason it is so important to involve older local alumni during pledge activities, team-building events, and parties. In fact, the older the alumni, the better, as mature adults will be that much better versed in risk analysis. They will help keep fraternity members, new pledges, women guests—and the brotherhood itself—safe.

The most disordered fraternities are the ones most lacking mature male guidance. The ones lacking mature male guidance are the ones most populated by self-serving, self-centered, and self-preserving college men instead of heroic men. This is what so often triggers a bad pledge experience for everyone, including those that descend into crime and tragedy. Fraternity men gain nothing from suspensions at the end of a pledge term. Heroic

12. Daley, "Troublemakers."
13. CBS News, "Delinquents."

fraternities, on other hand, welcome someone with greater insight in to help guide the choices they make before the pledge process begins. I know of one fraternity in the South that has already used this heroic model successfully, and other fraternities should consider adapting it to their needs. Not only does the presence of older alumni help your fraternity avoid activities that will lead to a suspension, alumni will have the presence of mind to ensure that the pledge experience benefits pledges and brothers alike.

Fraternity chapters should consider planning a long meeting every semester, several weeks in advance of pledge season, to discuss how to plan for a truly heroic pledge experience that provides reasonable boundaries for the initiation process that remain consistent with your fraternity's mission and values.

The task is easier if you ask yourselves: "What do we need to do to make our pledge process successfully initiate men so that they find our strengths, and in what ways can our older alumni help us achieve this goal?"

For those that refuse to request help, be aware of the pitfalls of your decision. A lot of young men have told themselves, "It's no big deal. Nothing bad will happen. Everyone does it." But the Abolish Greek Life movement didn't spring from nowhere. Every year, self-serving, self-centered, and self-preserving fraternity men rationalize the vast quantities of booze they buy, the many girls they "host," the torments of their pledges—and the calls to abolish fraternities only get louder.

From Alcohol to Alcoholism

Many of the worst tragedies and cases of fraternity self-serving, self-centered, and self-preserving misconduct involve consuming copious amounts of alcohol in the absence of heroic men. Young fraternity men are attracted to the immense volumes of the very substances that will make them vulnerable to maiming, death, and a proclivity to sexually assault their female peers. Now central to the standard college experience, high school students invariably anticipate partaking of—or at least being surrounded by—vast quantities of alcohol on college campuses, regardless of their past experience "partying" or their future desires "to party." The Mayo Clinic associates alcoholism with "problems controlling your drinking, being preoccupied with alcohol, continuing to use alcohol even when it causes problems, having to drink more to get the same effect," and with other patterns.[14] Although this cut-and-dried medical description of alcohol abuse is reminiscent of much college humor (and bragging rights), it accurately describes the 20 percent of college

14. Mayo Clinic, "Alcohol Use Disorder."

students who qualify as alcoholics, and the approximate third of respondents who binge drank at least once in the past month.[15] Imagine the candor if students had not been answering questions from the National Institute on Alcohol Abuse and Alcoholism, but were recounting their "wild" evenings with close friends who valued and accepted that behavior.

These habits and expectations are formed as early as rush week, or even the very first few weekends of school. During rush, fraternities put their wares on display for freshmen, and older potentially interested candidates, in an effort to lure them to their houses with alcohol, women, and activities. A college senior compared it to a "market," explaining that fraternities "want to look as good as possible, have the funnest possible events, the funnest possible parties . . . trying to sell themselves and get the best possible kids. They want to get the most applicants."[16] During rush, fraternities compete with each other for attendees and prospective pledges with "sake-bombing, casinos," and other alcohol-soaked markers of "maturity." Freshmen flock to the bounty of fun and alcohol regardless of their interest in any of the fraternities.[17] Alexandra Robbins uncovers what this looks like in her journalistic exposition of a year in the life of various fraternity boys, which included a freshman's description of his rush week experience at Town College: His first night at a Delta Rho party put him face to face and "elbow to elbow" with huge masses of students, dangerously heavy, and house-made, alcoholic drinks, weed, blaring music, and, of course, girls, girls, girls.[18] As chaotic as that sounds, and probably felt, leaked minutes of fraternity meetings at Swarthmore College reveal that booze-soaked and weed-infused parties are a highly organized and well-funded operation throughout the academic year.[19] They help ensure that freshmen are "dead set on rushing, lured by the hookup to parties, drinks, and girls."[20]

Substance abuse is the second most common reason colleges suspend Greek activity from their campuses. Between 2017 and early 2019, my research team tracked nearly 225 individual suspensions, a number that includes 100 more suspensions than the previous two years combined, with substance abuse was the precipitating incident in nearly half of them. If you color these numbers with the fact that universities have an interest in downplaying the amount of binge-drinking and drug abuse on campus

15. NIAAA, "College Drinking."
16. Senior, Cornell interview.
17. Senior, Cornell interview.
18. Robbins, *Fraternity*, 5–6.
19. NBC News, "'Rape Attic.'"
20. Robbins, *Fraternity*, 5–6.

to assuage parental concern and ward off legal trouble, that some amount of partying and underage substance abuse is sanctioned by a number of schools, and that college investigations tend to uncover relatively little of what goes on in fraternities, then we can begin to paint a picture in our minds of the prolific role alcohol plays in fraternity misconduct. But we also know it culturally, even if its omnipresence renders us oblivious sometimes: It's in every movie, it's in most former college students' memories, it's in music, and it's exactly what the average American eighteen-year-old expects from his college experience. The other challenge with substance abuse is that more and more drugs are laced with fentanyl and more fraternity men are falling victims to early deaths.

Without knowing the particulars of each suspension, you might assume that colleges are taking opportunities to suspend fraternities and students whenever a violation is made known to them. This is not so. When Dan Niersbach, president of the Indiana Student Association and Indiana University, commented on the Interfraternity Council's (IFC) decision to indefinitely halt all social and recruiting events by Greek organizations in 2017, he described it as an escape hatch: "I see this as a way out of a situation," he said, noting that it was helping ensure the fraternity didn't "cause more harm down the road."[21] Earlier that year, the College of Charleston suspended their Pi Kappa Phi chapter for two years pursuant to alcohol violations that led to hazing and the "revenge-lynching" of a brother in his room after a drunken episode in which, unprovoked, he punched another brother. The mass assault of the twenty-one-year-old was preceded by a menacing Facebook message: "We will get 80 bros behind us to bury you, you [expletive] queer."[22] The 2019 suspension of all fraternities at the University of Vermont was precipitated by the death of freshman Connor Gage from "hypothermia, which was worsened by being severely intoxicated." Found dead in a snow bank after apparently trying, and failing, to climb a fence, his blood alcohol level "was measured at 0.2 percent, more than twice the Vermont legal limit of 0.08 percent"[23]

In 2017, Cornell University's chapters of Kappa Alpha Psi and Pi Kappa Alpha were each put on interim suspension and a year-long probation "as a result of incidents determined to include hazing and alcohol consumption."[24] Beyond simple suspension and probation, Cornell is requiring students to complete anti-hazing education, and undergo a member

21. Van Wyk et al., "IU Fraternities Suspend Social."
22. Yee, "Five Fraternities Shut Down."
23. Loftus, "Student's Final Hours."
24. Musto, "Two Fraternities."

overview before they are allowed back on campus, a newly popular practice among many colleges. The same year, Creighton University suspended Phi Kappa Psi until 2025, a nine-year ban, when "Christopher Wheeler, a Creighton student at the time, was accused of attacking another Creighton student with a pocketknife at Gallagher Residence Hall."[25] The stabbing kicked off an investigation into the fraternity's activities, which uncovered a disturbing pattern of hazing, drug use, and supplying minors with alcohol. A similar outcome occurred when the University of Nebraska at Lincoln suspended Phi Gamma Delta for three years. The fraternity was found guilty of rampant alcohol use, hazing, and "inappropriate sexually based behavior, including a pattern of sexually harassing conduct," involving inappropriate comments outside their house during a women's march two months prior to their suspension.[26] They too will only be allowed back on campus after being better educated on alcohol, drugs, sexual misconduct, hazing, and women's issues.

There are also a number of cases where fraternities are suspended for alcohol and drug-related offenses alone. In 2017, Penn State University suspended Delta Tau Delta when a student was found drunk and passed out on the street after one of their parties. Crowds of people passed by him, assuming something was wrong but also that someone else would take care of the student.[27] Soon after, Penn State suspended Delta Upsilon until the following fall after the fraternity organized two parties in three weeks that involved underage drinking.[28] Their third suspension of the month came down on Pi Lambda Phi, who "violated University expectations by making alcohol available to guests on three separate occasions. . . . [which] violated the capacity of the fraternity house and the expectations for dry social functions."[29] This all came in the midst of the school cracking down on fraternities following a student's death earlier that year, and it is all happening because fraternities are not simply allowing and enabling the consumption of alcohol these days, they are also encouraging it, especially among underage students.

In 2019, the University of Vermont got rid of all Greek life following Connor Gage's death and the University of North Georgia suspended Sigma Alpha Epsilon (SAE) when an underage student was hospitalized for excessive alcohol consumption after a party where brothers were drinking

25. Szalewski, "Drinking, Drug Distribution and Hazing."

26. Szalewski, "Drinking, Drug Distribution and Hazing."

27. Ratchford and Krize, "Student Found Drunk."

28. PennState, "Fraternities Lose Recognition."

29. PennState, "Fraternities Lose Recognition."

even while they were on probation."[30] Wichita State University suspended Beta Theta Pi following a "Thirsty Thursday" event involving "MD 20/20, 30 packs, bottles of vodka and whiskey, alleged kegs, and bags of wine specifically to get women drunk."[31] The specific target of getting women drunk off of cheap bags of wine is particularly worrying. To what degree, if any, is the gross overconsumption of alcohol at the fraternity house intended to make it easier to break down consent and inhibitions of the opposite sex?

The pattern here is simple: College students are drinking in the numbers and volume we expect them to be (maybe more), administrations wait until someone is really hurt or, worse, dies, and then the suspensions roll in. Nearly every suspension involving alcohol or drugs that provides any details on the investigation mentions some injury, assault, or death that triggered punitive action. The problem of substance abuse seems to be compounded by the fact that colleges and universities only take action after someone has been seriously hurt. Improvements should certainly be made to the way we respond to fraternity missteps, but stopping there provides only temporary and reactionary satisfaction to these problems. In order for fraternities to play a healthy and positive role in society, we need to influence them much earlier in the process such that the irresponsible drinking and drug use that led to so much harm are mitigated in the first place. But, in order to do that, we need to acknowledge and explore the trend in fraternity suspensions and think about why they do not make men more virtuous or heroic.

The Crisis of Out-of-Control Hazing

Hazing has to be one of the most confusing concepts at play in fraternity activity to the average outsider. The idea that nearly one hundred thousand young men would choose to be initiated into North American Interfraternity Conference-affiliated fraternities knowing that hazing was a distinct possibility or, in some cases, guaranteed might shock most non-Greeks or those who did not attend a traditional four-year college.[32] Perhaps is not surprising, as I discuss later, that perhaps what guys want is initiation and that often devolves into bad kinds of hazing. The worst of it is typically confined to a few top-tier fraternities comprised of self-serving, self-centered, and self-preserving men in the absence of heroic men, and are most intensely experienced on the biggest, most sports-obsessed campuses, as with all of the other issues with fraternities. In their case, we must ask why are

30. Capelouto, "Student Taken to Hospital."

31. Linnabary, "Beta Theta Pi Suspension."

32. NIC, "Fraternity Stats."

they willing to risk so much of their well-being to join a semi-secret society? We also need to ask, what is hazing attempting to accomplish and can we achieve those same goals in a way that is heroic.

In the winter of 2019, a sorority was accused of "forced drinking . . . toe-licking [and] the dunking of students in ice water."[33] Then two unnamed fraternities were suspended for three years, in one case, for forcing members to,

> eat expired food, perform 'acts of servitude' and get dunked in a large trash can filled with icy water for giving wrong answers during a biweekly lineup," the other for making new members clean the house and do members' laundry. They also taped new members to poles or walls and threw food and other items at them. And they required new members to write and create "stall stories," described as "a pseudo pornographic newsletter" with pornographic images that were posted around the fraternity house.[34]

In many cases, universities don't provide many details for many hazing suspensions. One such suspension occurred in February 2018 at the University of Miami when the school suspended all fraternities. President Gregory Crawford said, "we must act for the betterment of individuals and the whole" in his statement about the suspension.[35] Advance measures were taken by the University of North Georgia, when the school suspended SAE, Phi Mu (sorority), and Kappa Delta (sorority), prior to completing an investigation, and without releasing many details, though one SAE brother claims they are alcohol-related and another acknowledges the role of hazing allegations in the suspension.[36] At Southern Methodist University, all we know is that "members were forced to consume onions, hot sauce, eggs and milk, and were required, or encouraged, to drink alcohol."[37] That almost seems benign compared to the unspeakable cruelty of fraternity brothers at Louisiana State University who were accused of "kicking pledges with steel-toed boots, beating them with a metal pipe and urinating on them, among other horrific offenses." One student alleged that he had hidden in an ice machine, naked, for up to forty-five minutes to avoid being beaten. He was later forced to lay on broken glass, next to another pledge, while

33. Associated Press, "Forced to Lick Members' Toes."

34. Leonard, "Fourth Fraternity Disciplined;" Associated Press, "Forced to Lick Members' Toes."

35. Baker, "Suspends All Frat Activity."

36. Wade, "Hazing Reports."

37. Cardona, "Hazing Investigation."

being urinated on and milk crates were thrown at them.[38] At Florida State University, in 2018, a warrant was put out for the arrest of Oliver Walker, a non-student member of Alpha Epsilon Pi, who had been charged with battery after he was given approval to hit another twenty-year-old member "as hard as he could" after the student was named "scumbag of the week."[39] His victim was left unconscious, and would later end up hospitalized for a skull fracture and hemorrhaging after the brothers lied, claiming he had slipped. Only weeks later, at the University of Florida, Delta Chi was suspended for four years when a pledge nearly died of alcohol poisoning. After a "big brother night" where the pledge drank sweet tea vodka and was forced to foot race other pledges, he was taken to a hospital with a blood alcohol content of .324, all while the brothers refused to call 911. Doctors claimed that the pledge had come within five minutes of losing his life.[40]

At Texas A&M, Phi Gamma Delta was suspended until 2022 for their role in the death of recently pledged freshman Joseph Little. The preliminary autopsy results stated that his death was caused by an "unnatural" seizure that occurred at an off-campus housing complex, likely caused by the alcohol, drug, and hazing violations that led to the fraternity's suspension.[41] In 2017, Kappa Sigma's chapter at Georgia Southern University didn't kill anybody, but a student was beaten and knocked unconscious while blindfolded during "gate night," which involved twelve gates, with the last granting admission to the fraternity—but only after the student was "slammed onto the ground" at Gate 7.[42] Once the student recovered enough to disclose his gate night beating, he began receiving death threats from other fraternity members.[43]

A 2018 incident at Texas State University led the school to suspend all Greek life, following the "alcohol-related" death of one of its students, Matthew Ellis.[44] A month prior, Southern Methodist University had also suspended Kappa Alpha when a school investigation from the spring "found evidence of things like paddling, new members [being] forced to consume alcohol and jalapenos until they vomited, and forcing them to wear soiled clothing."[45] Either fraternities are becoming more violent and irresponsible with their pledges, or the high-profile student deaths of 2017

38. Hopkins, "Fraternity Members Arrested."
39. Tallahassee News, "Battery Incident."
40. Rosa, "Pledge Nearly Died."
41. Okolie, "Houston Teen's Death."
42. Enfinger, "Hazing, Assault and Threats."
43. Enfinger, "Hazing, Assault and Threats."
44. KXAN, "Pledge's Death."
45. ABC13 Houston, "Suspended for Hazing."

and 2018 are forcing universities to perform more diligent investigations of hazing on their campuses.

An unnamed fraternity from Lehigh University was removed from campus for five years in 2019 after allegations of "coerced consumption of alcohol, lineups, servitude, sleep restrictions, and other degrading actions regarding new members," which are all supported by a notebook police found.[46] Sonoma State University suspended Tau Kappa Epsilon for hazing "in the form of paddling and intimidation," at an "informal chapter event."[47] The write-up in the *San Francisco Chronicle* notes that the Greek life at Sonoma State did not have established on-campus living arrangements, possibly limiting the university's ability to oversee fraternities, leading to their ability to haze more harshly.

An unnamed fraternity at Temple University dissolved in 2019 after they were reported for hazing with "knuckle pushups on bricks or cement, planking, squats, carrying bricks, and jumping into a river."[48] Also in 2019, Southern Mississippi University suspended Sigma Chi. Although they already had a bad reputation with drinking and drug violations, the suspension was punishing the fraternity for having pledges hold seats for brothers at football games and making them wear coats and ties. This seems harmless, but further investigation by campus police uncovered weapons and evidence of alcohol, drugs, and physical violence on two separate occasions. Cases like SMU's are interesting because they were triggered by seemingly minor offenses that ended up revealing far more destructive practices. If we accept that minor violations can be our technical pretext for attempting to curb the more pernicious misconduct involving fraternities, perhaps this trend towards a heavy right hand of punishment is a healthy one. In a world where Navy SEALS, male athletes, and fraternity men haze and sometimes want to be hazed and exclusive groups rely on, well, exclusivity, we need to think carefully about what hardships we allow and force our young men to be subjected to as they pursue status and acceptance in their social groups.

Sexual Assault and Harassment

Nearly a quarter of all women in college are sexually assaulted, a rate that is three times higher than that of women who experience sexual violence, in general.[49] This problem can be further isolated to the self-serving,

46. Associated Press, "Forced to Lick Members' Toes."
47. Hernandez, "Bans Fraternity Chapter."
48. Associated Press, "Forced to Lick Members' Toes."
49. U.S. Department of Justice, "Rape and Sexual Victimization."

self-centered, and self-preserving men fraternity house, where fraternity men are three times as likely to rape a woman, and 87 percent of the sexual assaults that involved alcohol in these spaces were committed by serial perpetrators.[50] Disordered masculinity thrives in the absence of heroic men. Again, this is the epitome of being self-serving, self-centered, and self-preserving. Instead of concluding simply with a "#NotAllMen" standpoint, let us instead survey the circumstances of, and responses to, sexual abuse cases from the past few years so that we can then answer, "#WhyTheseMen." In these stories, we see a pattern. These are not heroic men but self-serving, self-centered, and self-preserving men. In fact, at times sexual violators are not brothers in the fraternity but non-Greeks who are attend fraternity events looking for opportunities to take advantage of being in the presence of a selective group of women.

One of the most important things to recognize when discussing sexual assault in any setting is that for any number of reasons sexual assaults are rarely reported. That is why we rely on survey numbers from the U.S. Department of Justice (DOJ) to cut through the fog created by stigmas and shame that repress victims. Since 2017, fraternity suspensions for sexual assault have seen a noticeable increase, starting out at five that year, rising to fifteen in 2018, with three in just the first months of 2019.

As we explore 2017 first, it is important to notice that all five suspensions that year also cited alcohol and drug abuse as factors in the university's decision to remove the fraternity (or fraternities) from campus. This should signal what we should probably already have some knowledge of, which is that the sexual assault problem, as the DOJ numbers point out, is very much intertwined with the problem of substance abuse. That February, SAE (Sigma Alpha Epsilon) was suspended by Northwestern University. A party where alcohol was being served to minors happened at the fraternity's house, which SAE was only investigated after some sexual assault allegations were made that four women were given a common date rape drug and "two [were] possibly sexually assaulted."[51] The University of Central Florida took action against Lambda Theta Phi that June, suspending them following "a slew of complaints."[52] There were issues of underage drinking and hazing at one of the fraternity's house parties, but it came to a head when a brother had sex with a girl who was "severely mentally, physically incapacitated" who could not give consent. Photos of the victim were passed around the

50. Foubert, et al., "Campus Rape."

51. Bookwalter, "Sexual Assault Allegations."

52. Wolf, "Sexual Assault and Hazing."

fraternity.[53] The IFC banned all fraternities at the University of Michigan in November of that year after multiple students were put in "near death situations," and it was found out that there were "claims of sexual misconduct involving fraternity brothers" and other violations.[54]

In an interesting case in May 2017, Drexel University suspended Tau Kappa Epsilon for alcohol violations, but had already been on an interim suspension for a sexual assault investigation into the house and had three separate instances of sexual assault allegations prior to being suspended, though the official explanation from Drexel does not include sexual assault as a reason for suspension.[55] This case highlights a qualitative difference between sexual assault violations and most others that may explain why we see comparatively few suspensions for them as opposed to alcohol violations even though the numbers demonstrate that there are more sexually assaulted women on college campuses than there are alcoholics. This fact is consistent with our knowledge that women underreport, but in cases where there are reports and universities still fail to take full, proper action against perpetrating parties, as in the Drexel case, there needs to be reform.

Thankfully, 2018 showed that the need for such reform did not go unnoticed. That year, the patterns we saw in 2017 started to crack. There were three times as many suspensions for sexual assault and, out of all, only three of them involved related alcohol violations. This suggests that 2018 was a year of universities trying to take sexual assault violations more seriously in their own right. The first suspension of the year kicked off with Clemson University removing all fraternities on an interim suspension after an off-campus Delta Chi event where a sexual assault case was reported.[56] This scale of punishment for just one reported assault is a step in a completely new direction. The only thing that remains to be seen is if it will have the impact of properly communicating to fraternity members and college men broadly that sexual assault will not be tolerated will have an impact on case rates.

Just a month later, Cornell University's Zeta Beta Tau chapter was suspended and put on probation after finding out about the fraternity's practices of a "pig roast," which is a contest that awarded points to new members who slept with the heaviest woman. The school is going to require the members to "undertake training programs on sexual violence, participate in events during the university's Sexual Assault Awareness Week and hire a live-in adviser," and the fraternity will take it upon itself to perform an internal review

53. Wolf, "Sexual Assault and Hazing."

54. Harmon, "Hazing, Assault Allegations."

55. Snyder, "Drexel Suspends Frat."

56. Associated Press. "Clemson Suspends Fraternity."

and release members as necessary.[57] Here is another progressive move in response to the objectification of women, not just their assault, which is a good sign, especially since the fraternity has responded cooperatively. Temple University's suspension of Alpha Epsilon Pi is one of the few that also involved alcohol violations. AEPi's suspension is indefinite following issues of underage drinking, and three sexual assault allegations: "[A] female student said she attended a party and was given several drinks. She blacked out and later awoke in bed with one of the fraternity members."[58] Two of the accusations came from nineteen-year-olds.

The University of Central Florida's suspension of Lambda Theta Phi from the year before seems to be ineffective as they had to suspend another fraternity for more sexual assault allegations. Alpha Tau Omega was suspended after two students, twenty-six-year-old Jack Smith and twenty-year-old David Kirk, who were not members, raped a girl at an ATO party. She claims she "blacked out" around midnight and regained consciousness while being raped and hearing them say things like, "my turn, my turn." She blacked out again and woke up partially dressed on the bathroom floor, at which point she began contacting friends about what had happened.[59] This is another interesting case as the two perpetrators were not members of the fraternity, but ATO was held responsible because it happened at their party, which will disturb apologists who take the "one bad apple" approach in assessing the guilt of fraternities for the sins of their members. UCF had yet another sexual assault suspension that year as a woman from Arizona is suing Delta Sigma Phi for making "revenge porn."[60] The lawsuit alleges that a brother taped a sexual encounter with the woman and sent it to other members in the fraternity, that somewhere around two hundred people saw it, and that "the fraternity [maintained] a secret Facebook page called the Dog Pound, where members posted nude videos and images of their "conquests" without the women's consent."[61] At Central Michigan University, Phi Sigma Phi was permanently expelled from campus with no option for appeal: "A trail of repeated similar accusations against Phi Sigma Phi over the past several years shows a significant threat to the safety of our students."[62] The dangers Phi Sigma Phi posed were related to hazing and a recent student death, but also sexual assault allegations, the concerns about

57. Porter, "Cornell Frat Suspended."
58. Lattanzio, "Temple Suspends AEPi."
59. Cutway, "UCF Suspends Frat."
60. Sundby, "'Revenge Porn' Lawsuit."
61. Sundby, "'Revenge Porn' Lawsuit."
62. Jordan, "Student's Death, Sex Assault."

which "have been affirmed multiple times by [CMU's] inability to find witnesses willing to discuss allegations."[63] This rationalization for reaffirming fears based on an inability to find witnesses is also a big step for universities, and another that we will have to evaluate in the coming months and years as to its effectiveness.

Later in 2018, the University of Northern Colorado suspended Sigma Chi as they investigate twenty-one claims over the past three years of "sexual harassment, sexual misconduct, and possession of controlled substances," eighteen of which came in 2018, and only three of which do not include some complaint of sexual abuse or misconduct.[64] University of Nebraska-Lincoln had another problem with sexual assault when the SAE chapter was sued for sexual assault by a woman who attended an off-campus, SAE-sponsored party in October of 2018. She claims that the brothers served her alcohol "until she became incapacitated" and woke up at the fraternity's house on campus "to find she had been sexually assaulted by an unknown assailant."[65] The lawsuit focuses on her charge that the fraternity does not have proper policy, procedures, or staff members to prevent sexual assault at their parties, particularly the one she attended.

The last three suspensions of 2018 occurred in December. At the University of Central Arkansas, Kappa Sigma was suspended for alcohol, hazing, and sexual assault violations. There was an allegation of sexual assault because the woman involved was unable to give consent.[66] If there were a vanilla flavor of fraternities' problems, it is wrapped up in this suspension: alcohol, hazing, and violating principles of consent. The University of Tennessee placed an unnamed fraternity on interim suspension while they investigated rape allegations against the fraternity: "Two female students reported being drugged and sexually assaulted at a fraternity house on Nov. 29."[67] The year's last sexual assault suspension was handed to Tau Kappa Epsilon at the University of Nevada, Reno for a "songbook" that has songs that encourage heavy drinking and sexual misconduct towards women on top of promoting violence towards other fraternities on campus.[68] The school is now navigating the difficult task of trying to identify if the fraternity was in direct violation of their code on sexual conduct by simply having a songbook that condones and promotes the behavior that, if performed, would

63. Jordan, "Student's Death, Sex Assault."
64. Silvy, "21 Complaints in 3 Years."
65. Dunker, "Alleged Sex Assault."
66. Associated Press, "UCA Suspends Kappa Sigma."
67. Kast, "2 Students Drugged, Raped."
68. McAndrew, "Frat's Songbook Promotes Sexual Violence."

have certain been violating, given the preference for white female students by brothers in charge of admitting guests to a party.[69] A more recent suspension we found for sexual assault was at the University of Nebraska-Kearny, and it was handed out to just one brother from Sigma Lambda Beta, Miguel Guzman, and it was given by "the Executive Office of the International Fraternity."[70] He is being charged with first degree sexual assault and faces up to fifty years in prison for the alleged rape at an off-campus house.

Although fraternities frequently rebut criticism by saying their members should be treated on an individual basis: One bad apple does and should not spoil the whole bunch. But there is a difference between the corporate standards that fraternities have always held themselves to, and writing off entire types of organizations based on the actions of a few of those organizations and only a few of those organizations' members. As Nicholas Syrett points out in his compelling history of fraternities, *The Company He Keeps*, the willingness to be accountable for the mistakes of your members of lesser ability and character is essential to the function of a healthy, traditional fraternity.[71]

Racial Abuse and Exclusion

Many fraternities have broken with their racially exclusive histories. Nowadays, diversity extends to accepting members with varying ideas of masculinity, and an LGBTQ+ orientation. It also involves the proliferation of fraternities created specifically for minority communities, including fraternities that are Black Greek Letter Organizations (BGLOs) and part of the National Association of Latino Fraternal Organizations (NALFO). This evolution on the part of the members of the North American Interfraternity Conference (NIC) and Interfraternity Council (IFC) is admirable, but, a lot of the time, incomplete. Fraternities routinely do a poor job of including minorities. It doesn't help that mandatory dues can be wrongly interpreted as proxies for race, almost automatically disqualifying both poor black and white students. In fairness, there are some fraternities that want to remain white-homogenous and, in those cases, there is still much work to do. It is also the case on many campuses that racial minorities simply do not want to join predominantly white fraternities because they prefer to join predominantly ethnic fraternities and that should be encouraged. It is unfair to assume that if a fraternity is all white it is because they do want non-white

69. Cills, "Women Sue for Gross Fraternities."

70. KSNB Local 4, "Arrested for Sexual Assault."

71. Syrett, *Company He Keeps*, 51–78.

members. Ethnic minorities have options and sometimes they choose, on purpose, to join ethnic Greek organizations. For example, I could have pledged a predominantly white fraternity at Clemson but I chose instead to pledge a historically black fraternity. I can only think of a few fraternities at Clemson that would have rejected me at the time because of my race. The fact remains that the lack of racial diversity is not always a sign of discrimination, and I reject the notion that a predominantly white fraternity has to prove that it is not racist by pledging an ethnic minority and them making him the "diversity and inclusion" chair whose job it is to recruit minorities. If fraternities are seeking, first and foremost, men who want to be heroic diversity will follow. Great men want to be around great men regardless of race. Heroic men want their fraternities populated by other heroic men because heroic masculinity has no race.

Even as there are many pushes for greater racial inclusion and opportunity, there is still a significant resistance to such change from some self-serving, self-centered, and self-preserving fraternities. In an anecdote from the beginning of Alexandra Robbins' book on the inner workings of fraternities, Jake's Pakistani friend, Arjun, tells a girl at the Delta Rho party that he is "def" interested in pledging that fraternity and others in the top tier, and Jake internally reflects, "he'd heard that top-tiers at [Town College] rarely gave bids to minorities."[72]

Fraternity suspensions for racism are even more rare than they are for sexual assault on campus, likely because of how blurry the line can be about actionable racism, as most of these instances involve racist chants, statements, and posturing. In 2017, there were only two cases of fraternities being suspended for racism, six in 2018, and, interestingly, two in the first months of 2019 alone. In 2017, Baylor University suspended Kappa Sigma for racism, and the fraternity is no longer welcome on campus or as a part of the national chapter after a "Mexican themed party," which two hundred students came to protest, leading to the suspension.[73] Several social media posts documenting the incident show students at the party in sombreros, ponchos, construction worker outfits, and even "brown face."[74] In fairness, it is questionable if the mere having of a culturally themed party constitutes actual racism. Taco Tuesday where everyone wears Mexican attire could be considered by some as, in fact, celebrating the beauty of Mexican culture. Other cases, however, may be clearer. For example, The University of Louisiana-Monroe also suspended their Kappa Sigma chapter in 2017 when some

72. Robbins, *Fraternity*, 7.

73. Adams et al., "Racist Mexican-themed Party."

74. Adams et al., "Racist Mexican-themed Party."

screenshots of the fraternity's group message were released that included racist comments. The conversation started with one student asking for recommendations on topics for an argumentative paper, and the responses got more and more racist, mounting to "'The difference between the n-word [sic] and black people.' And, 'why black lives don't matter.'"[75]

In April, the University of Arkansas-Little Rock suspended Chi Omega, a sorority, and Pi Kappa Alpha, both for racism. There was a "racially insensitive" video released from a co-hosted Greek function on a bus where members of both organizations can be heard singing a song by Lil' Wayne, using the N-word as excessively as the song does.[76] In the same month, California Polytechnic State University suspended all Greek life indefinitely after photos were released of multiple members in two fraternities wearing racially disparaging outfits. Members of Lambda Chi Alpha and Sigma Nu dressed as gang members, and some Lambda Chi members were also pictured wearing blackface.[77] The university also stated that they have found instances of "racial profiling and cultural appropriation" within Sigma Nu.[78] Even though all sororities were suspended as well, University spokesman Matt Lazier said the decision "included racially charged and insensitive events, sexual assaults, hazing and alcohol-related deaths," etc, which are all problems that have primarily been driven by fraternities, not sororities.[79] Again, the line is not always clear if these were instances of racism (as malice) or simple ignorance, which should be used as a learning opportunity.

In 2019, Syracuse University suspended fifteen Theta Tau brothers after a video surfaced of the suspended students "using racial and anti-Semitic slurs, mocking gay sex, and simulating the assault of disabled people."[80] The students have been suspended for two years, but do have the option to appeal while students and other organizations like The Foundation for Individual Rights in Education oppose the suspensions on the principle of the First Amendment.[81] As the second suspension went so far as to make light of the sexual abuse of disabled persons, something appears to be wanting in our understanding of fraternities such that we seem unable to explain such a monstrous fixation on that particular subject.

75. Ducre, "ULM Suspends Kappa Sigma."

76. KARK, "UA-Little Rock Suspends Sorority, Fraternity."

77. Associated Press, "California Suspends fraternities."

78. Associated Press, "California Suspends fraternities."

79. Associated Press, "California Suspends fraternities."

80. Whitford, "Suspended for Racist, Homophobic Video."

81. Whitford, "Suspended for Racist, Homophobic Video."

Out of the ten suspensions in the past three years for racism, it is important to note that in only two of them did the suspending organization include any reason other than racism to justify their punishments. The fact that racism stands alone, however, with none of its related suspensions having to do with alcohol, signals that universities are considering racism more broadly as a stand-alone issue when it occurs without any other violations. It also shows that the faults in our Greek system go deeper than removing hard liquor, or even all alcohol, from the fraternity house. Even if fraternities stop drinking, and it decreases the hazing and sexual assaults that happen on campus, we will still be left with a full spectrum self-serving, self-centered, and self-preserving men who may be racist.

6

What the Best Fraternities Do

"We're looking for guys who give a damn. What I mean by that is everyone thinks it's cool to not care. We want guys who care, and we want guys who give a damn about themselves, about us, about the school, about the community, about the country, about the world, and we want people who are going to make the world better."

—CHAD FRICK, CLEMSON UNIVERSITY

Aiming Higher

What most universities ask of college fraternities is that they be less bad than the worst stereotypes seen in the news and depicted in movies. Universities want more accountability and more punitive measures to make men less bad. But being less bad is not virtuous. Telling men not to haze or to merely *avoid* sexual assault is not inviting men to excellence. It's not character forming. It's inviting them to the mediocrity of the lowest common denominator. What does it require of a man to not cause harm? How is *not* causing harming aspirational? How is "don't be dangerous" directional? It's formation by negation. It's not enough. Men in fraternities deserve something more motivational, challenging, and inspirational. Not being bad is too easy. This is why the future of college fraternities must be a call to heroic masculinity—*men using their power, presence, strengths, and creativity for the benefit of their brothers and those around them.* It's a call to live lives of excellence, honor, and virtue. It's an invitation to put themselves in the position to always add value to their campuses. Heroic masculinity is an invitation to set up men for holistic success so that if anyone were to say anything negative about their chapter, they would sound foolish. This would relieve fraternities from justifying themselves on the basis of philanthropies they support, or the alumni donations they raise, to the positive impact of their characters on campus life. Instead of saying in response to calls to abolish fraternities, "but look at how much money we raise for cancer?" The response would be, "but look at how much better off our college is because the men in our chapter make the lives of everyone around them better by refusing to haze pledges, and by insisting on treating everyone with respect, regardless of gender, ethnicity, or race." Whose lives are better? The brothers in the chapter, all of the women on campus, their peers on campus who are not in Greek life, faculty and staff, and all other stakeholders involved in campus life.

I am not arguing that philanthropic work is not admirable or worthy, but I am pointing out that philanthropy says nothing about a man's character. During the 1920s and 1930s, the mafia would murder people on Friday, host a fundraiser on Saturday, and sit in church on Sunday. For heroic fraternities, philanthropy is to be expected. What distinguishes average fraternities from the greatest fraternities is that the latter strive to be men of exceedingly extraordinary character and add value to entire campus community.

Earlier, we examined how young men are arriving on campus with real challenges and struggles. Many arrive full of self-doubt. Others are just one day away from giving up. Others are struggling with narcissism and addictions. Still others are plagued with anxiety and depression. America is desperate for a generation of men whose lives can be characterized by their benefit to others, and there's no better institution on a college campus to form such men than college fraternities. Fraternities are not just fun. They are vital for producing outstanding men who live above reproach. Fraternities do not exist merely so that men can have fun while being "less bad" than in other chapters. They exist because they provide an exceptional opportunity for young men to find acceptance, a band of brothers, initiation into adulthood, an epic amount of fun, personal and professional development, an aspiration for excellence, and the formation of honor and virtue.

Abolishing Greek Life is a False Solution

At present, there is a call to remove Greek life from college campuses altogether. Through a network of Instagram accounts where students post their negative experiences and grievances against fraternities and sororities, there is a growing rallying cry to "Abolish Greek Life" (AGL) on all campuses because Greek like is seen as perpetuating classism, racism, sexual assault, hazing, and so on. Writing in the *Washington Post*, Kate Cohen believes that fraternities are irredeemable and that colleges should just "abolish the problem."[1] I believe Cohen is dead wrong. Abolishing fraternities will not put an end to hazing, sexual assault, or drug and alcohol abuse. Men will form secret societies in other ways on or off campus, and continue creating the community they want and need. Ivan Petropoulos, writing for Duke University student newspaper argues that the abolition of fraternities will not abolish vice on campus. He continues:

> Perhaps this is most clear with rates of sexual assault. Harvard, for example, leveraged extreme sanctions on fraternities and sororities and greatly disincentivized membership within these organizations. Despite this, the university found that rates of sexual assault remained "largely unchanged" from 2015, when the policy had not yet been announced, and 2019, a full two years after it took effect. Similar results can be observed at Princeton. An internal survey from 2008 details that 28 percent of female undergraduate students at Princeton identified themselves as victims of sexual assault. Beginning in 2012, the university took action against Greek organizations and banned them from recruiting freshmen. Furthermore, when this policy was announced in 2011, the university stated that it "[did] not recognize fraternities and sororities." However, four years after the university officially stopped recognizing Greek organizations, and three years after they severely restricted the presence of these entities on campus, a 2015 survey found that 27 percent of Princeton's undergraduate women experienced some form of sexual assault while on campus. This represents an insignificant change in the level of sexual violence women at Princeton suffered during the time before and during the time after the university formally abolished Greek life.[2]

Petropoulos knows that critics might respond that Harvard and Princeton did not go far enough. But the fact remains that even if fraternities

---

1. Cohen, "Abolish Fraternities."
2. Petropoulus, "Problem with Abolishing Greek Life."

are abolished students are going to form social organizations. Petropoulos observes that "thirty years after officially abolishing Greek life, Amherst College announced, somehow, in 2014 that 'students caught as members of underground fraternities, or in 'fraternity-like organizations,' could be suspended or expelled." Even though Amherst College rid itself of fraternities three decades ago, "the college still found that 29 percent of their female undergraduate population would suffer from sexual violence while enrolled."

So why is it, then, that fraternity men are reportedly three times as likely to commit rape? Petropoulous argues:

> This phenomenon is a direct result of individuals predisposed to committing these offenses self-selecting into Greek organizations. In the absence of these organizations, these men do not simply disappear from campus. Rather, they form exclusive and unregulated clubs or friend groups to continue their abhorrent behavior. For example, Harvard recently found that 47 percent of female seniors who associate with Final Clubs—non-Greek, all-male organizations of Harvard undergrads—have experienced "nonconsensual sexual contact since entering college." This is the highest rate of sexual assault experienced amongst all student groups Harvard surveyed.[3]

AGL will not prevent men with terrible characters from enrolling in college. While men need to be held accountable for sexual assault to the fullest extent of the law, men also need to be invited by universities to heroic expressions of their humanity with their female peers in all aspects of campus life. Character matters and if universities only rely on punishment for character formation schools will never form the men they need and want. Colleges should raise the expectations of the kinds of character virtues they expect their students to display, and recruit students accordingly. A high-performing student with a reckless moral character makes the college campus worse off. Are universities willing to raise their standard so that evidence of good character is also a part of the recruiting and admissions process, even if it means recruiting less competitive students in some cases? Petropolous concludes by noting, "The ugly truth about Greek life is that it is not what plagues Duke's campus. We are. Greek life does not make sex-offenders out of good people, nor does it make us any more exclusive than we naturally are as humans . . . Conversations on campus should thus not focus on how to regulate organizations, but individuals within them." AGL will not abolish the presence of students with low moral values. Sadly, the spirit of AGL advanced on the campus of Duke University. Seven fraternities

3. Petropoulus, "Problem with Abolishing Greek Life."

decided to disaffiliate from the university in 2021: Alpha Delta Phi, Alpha Tau Omega, Delta Tau Delta, Kappa Alpha Order, Pi Kappa Phi, Sigma Chi and Sigma Nu.[4]

Writing for student newspaper at the University of Richmond, William Bartnett, the 2021 President of the Interfraternity Council at the university, rightly observes, "Greek life organizations are only as good as the people in them. Becoming better will only be a result of changes in individual behavior, and that onus is not lost on Greek life leaders. But like any community of people and organizations, it is directly shaped by policies, resources, and its environment."[5] It is character that matters in Greek life—just like anywhere else. And since students are impacted by the incentive structures around them, this question matters greatly: "What are individual chapters and universities doing to incentivize excellent character?" How are they investing in fraternities so that they add value to the entire campus? If fraternities need good people, what universities and fraternities doing to recruit good people to campus and encourage them to be heroic during their years in college and beyond? Any negative externalities of Greek life will not be resolved by abolishing Greek life but by using fraternities to infuse the campus with heroic masculinity. In this scenario, everyone at the university wins.

Using punitive reforms to make fraternities less bad will also not create or cultivate excellence of character. It is important to remember that fraternity men want to be great men, and we should put them in positions where they can attain excellence. Two significant ways universities punish fraternities is by temporarily or permanently suspending them. Suspensions and threat of suspensions, however, fail to make fraternities better, and they do not invite men to practice pro-social virtues.

In 2017, we found about thirty-four fraternity suspension cases across the entire country reported in the news. In 2018, that number had spiked to one hundred and one, demonstrating at least an increase in the popularity of this method of discipline with many fraternities who had experienced no punishment the year before receiving suspensions. As we approached the COVID-19 pandemic, fraternity suspensions grew at an alarming rate. We found thirty suspensions reported in the news in the first two months of 2019 alone, almost matching the suspensions in all twelve months of 2017. That this spike clearly did not serve as a deterrent indicates that the threat of suspension of both the temporary and permanent varieties are not effective at discouraging reckless and harmful behavior. Instead, it all but functions as a dare, encouraging men to go as close to the line as possible

4. Sheridan, "Seven fraternities disaffiliate."
5. Bartnett, "Fraternities aren't going away."

without getting caught. Nicholas Syrett's *The Company He Keeps,* which traces the history of white fraternities makes it clear that fraternities have always been counter-cultural, feeding off the idea of resisting the demands of authority as a means of asserting their independence, and confirming their adulthood. Given America's history of individualism, it's not surprising that some young men and some fraternities end up cultivating a culture of disordered self-focused masculinity instead. It is only natural that there would be staunch opposition to the presence of such men, and rightly so. While the emphasis on safety and accountability are both worthwhile up to a point, especially if they are primarily punitive in orientation, fraternity men deserve to be held to the higher standards of the missions and values of their own fraternity charters.

The pattern we see in the reeducation programs and mandatory training prescribed by colleges to reform reckless fraternities do not inspire a self-motivated desire to practice the habits of self-improvement and become increasingly heroic. Providing sexual consent, anti-hazing measures, substance abuse, and the like, are a good starting point, but they fail to ask the deeper psycho-emotional questions: What self-perception and personal values make men vulnerable to reckless behavior, and what can the university do to help fraternities impactfully address this? What are some of the struggles and root causes that fraternities are uniquely positioned to address to sabotage disordered masculinity and inspire heroic masculinity? These are the types of questions that "risk management," is not equipped to ask. To prevent abuse of all kinds and create lasting change, we must invite men to use their use their presence, power, strengths, and creativity to benefit their brothers and the larger community. What follows are six ways fraternities can cultivate heroic masculinity, while accounting for the issues that young men face, as well as their good motivations for wanting to join fraternities in the first place. Many of them are unarticulated, yet true.[6]

Acceptance and True Friendship

The first way fraternities cultivate heroic masculinity is by creating an atmosphere of acceptance and true friendship. Most American men are desperately lonely.[7] A whopping 58 percent of men on college campuses report feeling lonely, and with Generation Z (born between 1997–2009) and Generation Alpha (born between 2010–2024), in particular, we are seeing

6. Note that Patrick Hagerty has a similar list. I am building his helpful framing. See Hagerty, "Why Guys Join Fraternities."

7. Braucher, "Pandemic of Male Loneliness."

astronomical instances of loneliness and social isolation.[8] Although many fraternity pledges are arriving on campus with high school networks of close friendships where they were accepted, deeply known, and loved "as is," some are not. High school guys are fully aware that college is a time to make new life-long friendships. Most spend their entire lives watching their fathers live friendless local lives, and they do not want that future. They also know that they need friends. They need to be accepted and loved by men who consider them brothers. Men need other men to help them grow and develop into better men, and guys pledge fraternities because they know that on the other side of their initiation ceremony lies a path to permanently obliterate isolation, and create some of the best friends he'll ever have. What they seek is brotherly love, something that they are prepared to say to those who accept them. As Jeff Hemmer writes:

> A man needs a brother or two—friends whose bonds run deeper than watching football or drinking beers together. He needs intimacy that exposes him and makes him vulnerable. He needs a fellow man to challenge him, to correct him, to challenge him . . . There's a delicate balance though in forging such a friendship. It must be intentional, not accidental. But it cannot be forced. The best places a man can look for a friend like this are the place he already inhabits. . . . Where there is a common goal, a unified direction for two men to fix their faces there can be this sort of friendship.[9]

Outside of sports teams, there is no better organization on college campuses for men to forge these types of friendships than in a fraternity. This is why fraternities exist, and the vulnerability of relationships, which allow men to be truly known by other men and accepted for their true selves is not what is depicted in the movies about Greek life. Modern culture has all but erased the possibility of deep platonic intimacy between men as brothers by too often eroticizing the healthy affection that men can have for each other. For some, this has blocked openness to deep friendship but fraternities provide a safe space for men to be fully vulnerable, seen, and known, without fear of rejection.

There is an African proverb that says, "If you want to go fast, go alone. If you want to far, go together."[10] The acceptance that fraternities provide improves the mental health and self-esteem of the men who join them. In fact, "being rejected by a group, lowers our self-esteem. It also makes us

8. Lewis, "Loneliness Among Teens Has Increased;" Iberdrola, "Generation Alpha."

9. Hemmer, *Man Up*, 35.

10. Cacioppo and Patrick, *Loneliness and Social Connection*, xv.

far more aware of social cues, forms of social information about group dynamics that might help us better navigate social environments. . . . Rejected individuals also have heightened tendency to conform to the opinions of others."[11] Living as an independent person without a network of close friends handicaps a man. This is one of the reasons why receiving a bid invitation to pledge a fraternity can be such a powerful moment in a man's life. Our bodies and brains were made for connection. We were not designed to live in isolation.[12] As Cacioppo and Patrick observe, "the attempt to function in denial of our need for others, whether that need is great or small in any given individual, violates our design specifications."[13] When people are lonely and isolated they are more likely to lack self-confidence, to "adopt the consensus opinion," not think for themselves, and be coerced even to the point of betraying their true selves.[14] Fraternities can provide a massively important source for human connection. When brothers are kind and generous with each other it "leads to social acceptance and the healthy feeling of connection."[15] When guys are isolated, independent, and alone, loneliness can threaten their sense of purpose, which is fundamental to a sense of well-being and thriving.[16] This is one of the reasons that alienation, isolation, and loneliness are risk factors for suicide. Suicide is the second leading cause of death for males ages fifteen to twenty-four. Loneliness and isolation can lead to "declines in executive control and self-regulation that lead to impulsive and selfish behavior. The ability to respond actively and purposefully also declines, replaced by passivity, negativity, and sometimes even clinical depression."[17] Social acceptance helps college men with their social regulation skills and, when they are in a fraternity that practices heroic masculinity, rather than disordered masculinity, they are better able to regulate their impulses, be less selfish, and respond actively and purposefully to the challenges of life. When people feel rejected and excluded "they tend to become more aggressive, more self-defeating or self-destructive, less cooperative and helpful, and less prone simply to do the hard work of thinking clearly.[18]

11. Cacioppo and Patrick, *Loneliness and Social Connection*, 119.

12. Cacioppo and Patrick, *Loneliness and Social Connection*, 126–27.

13. Cacioppo and Patrick, *Loneliness and Social Connection*, 126–27.

14. Cacioppo and Patrick, *Loneliness and Social Connection*, 183.

15. Cacioppo and Patrick, *Loneliness and Social Connection*, 215–17.

16. Cacioppo and Patrick, *Loneliness and Social Connection*, 215–17.

17. Cacioppo and Patrick, *Loneliness and Social Connection*, 215–17.

18. Cacioppo and Patrick, *Loneliness and Social Connection*, 215–17.

Another important reason that men need close friends is that every man has an Achilles' Heel and an unethical vulnerability. Every man has a major weakness or two "which threatens to bring him down and destroy everything he has accomplished."[19] Patrick Arnold writes, "His particular weakness isn't necessarily pedestrian in nature, but may originate in the heart, the seat of values; in the stomach, center of emotion; or in the genitals, source of passion. Whatever their locus, all males—especially the most successful ones—have major weaknesses. A man who doesn't know this is a fool."[20] Every man needs a friend or two who knows these weaknesses and can help him fight against them. He needs friends who can hold him accountable, and help him take responsibility for these weaknesses so that they do not consume his life and eventually ruin him. When fraternity brothers are letting each other be fully known and seen, it become difficult to hide some of those dark tendencies and weaknesses. Fraternities are great places for providing men with the friendships they need to better exercise self-mastery and self-control. Fraternities are places where men can find friends to help them break their addictions. Since we all are addicted to something, there is no shame in fraternity brothers helping each other fight addictions to food, drugs, alcohol, sex, pornography, sugar, social media, cell phones, nicotine, adrenaline, working out, and so on.[21] If a man believes that he can go it alone without having a couple of brothers he trusts to fight for him, and with him, against his inner demons, he is naïve, and will likely pay a steep price for it. I would argue that a man who does not seek help with those things is also a fool.

Fraternities fill a need for social acceptance and connection and, when practiced in a heroic way, can even restore mental health and contribute to significant thriving. Cacioppo and Patrick recommend four simple steps to achieve social connection (E.A.S.E.) that helps people thrive.[22] These four steps are the basis of accepting others and being accepted that fraternities have expertise in facilitating. First, a person needs to extend themselves to pursue positive social interactions. Second, a person needs to make an action plan for social connection. It needs to be intentional and purposeful, but one where being exploited is not the price paid for connection. Feeling lonely makes us fall victim to being people pleasers but healthy connections are dignity affirming. Third, a person needs to be selective. Human connection and acceptance needs to be meaningful and satisfying for everyone and

---

19. Arnold, *Wildmen, Warriors, and Kings*.
20. Arnold, *Wildmen, Warriors, and Kings*.
21. Lembke, *Dopamine Nation*.
22. Cacioppo and Patrick, *Loneliness and Social Connection*, 237.

"not according to some external measure."[23] And, finally, a person needs to expect the best. People need to be optimistic about the potential for real connection and patiently wait for it to develop within the complexity of human relationships. Fraternities provide the best that acceptance provides: dependability, variety in closeness, trust, and a certain level of unconditional availability at unexpected, or even unreasonable, times. What is so extraordinary about fraternities is the entire pledge process, from the informational meetings through initiation, fulfills steps in building the connection needed for acceptance and friendship. No wonder so many men in college are drawn to them.

Brotherhood

The second way fraternities cultivate heroic masculinity is by fostering brotherhood. Finding acceptance and connection with a few men during the pledge process is a great experience but it gets even better when a pledge is brought into the larger brotherhood of his entire fraternity. All men need the sense of belonging a tribe provides. Fraternity brotherhoods provide the connection and camaraderie that lead men to thrive despite life's challenges. Jeff Hemmer says it well:

> Men need a tribe. Boys need a band of men to initiate them into manhood. Men need a band of brothers where they can belong. Alone is not good. It takes other men to cultivate [heroic] masculinity in others. A tribe gives a man a place where he can share his identity with others on a similar quest, working toward a common goal.[24]

In other words, a fraternity gives a young man a place to share his identity with others on a similar quest, as they work toward a common goal. Fraternity is derived from the Latin word, *fraternitas*, which refers to "brotherhood," and there is nothing more honorable and praiseworthy in a young man's life than to accept the challenge of heroic fraternity, with a loyal brother at his side. It's not just that brotherhoods are good, men actually *need* them. Brotherhoods are vital to a man's survival and fraternities, by design, provide one of the best environments in which to nurture deep acceptance, encouragement, and personal development with a band of brothers in a young man's campus chapter. Sebastian Junger observes that "adversity often leads people to depend more on one another, and that

---

23. Cacioppo and Patrick, *Loneliness and Social Connection*, 240.

24. Hemmer, *Man Up*, 41–42.

closeness can produce a kind of nostalgia for the hard times . . ."[25] This is one of the reasons older men will look back on their college years, and say that they were among the best years of their lives. They had a close band of brothers to walk through adversity with them. According to Junger, a "lack of connectedness allows people to act in trivial incredibly selfish ways." A fraternity that challenges men to heroism is a fraternity of men who are willing to make generous sacrifices for the good of their brothers.

It takes a community of men to help each overcome fears, insecurities, and self-doubts. It takes a brother's hope to inspire hope when disappointment and discouragement are at the door. A heroic fraternal brotherhood can build a man's self-confidence, and help him become the outstanding man he yearns to be. A brotherhood can help a man find his true self, so that he can truly be the person he actually is, instead of the one that everyone wants him to be or thinks he should be. One of the realities about being a college-bound high school student is that there is so much pressure on so many students to define their worth according to external measures, including athletic performance, academic performance, the expectations of parents, religious communities, material goods, and financial success that many guys have never been free to be themselves. Many men arrive on campus with a lot of uncertainties and insecurities about their identities, wondering whether they have what is takes to succeed in all those arenas with performance measures. Karen Horney refers to this as "basic anxiety."

> A wide range of adverse factors in the environment can produce this insecurity in a child: Direct or indirect domination, indifference, erratic behavior, lack of respect for the child's individual needs, lack of real guidance, disparaging attitudes, too much admiration or the absence of it, lack of reliable warmth, having to take sides in parental disagreements, too much or too little responsibility, over-protection, isolation from other children, injustice, discrimination, unkept promises, hostile atmosphere, and so on and so on.

What this means is that every man arrives on campus with some questions and doubts, about his ability to live up to his own expectations, and those of society, generally. For many college students, the love that they received from their parents may have been conditional, based on meeting parental expectations for success. For example, a student may have experienced greater love and celebration when he received good grades, or when he scored a goal, than for being the person that he is, regardless of his ability to perform.

25. Junger, *Tribe*, 92.

It is actually quite normal to be confident about one's ability to perform in one arena, while lacking confidence in another. Knowing that distinction is the basis for humility. For example, a young man could excel at sports, but be plagued with social anxiety when it comes to meeting a group of strangers. There is often a disparity between who a college man actually is, and the one that he believes he ought to be. There could also be a tension between who a man is, and what he believes other people require him to be in order to respect and love him. Facing doubts and insecurities are all part of the transition into adulthood, but when they are handled in a disordered way, they can destroy a man and his relationships. These insecurities and uncertainties can be the birthplace of real anxiety. Psychiatrist Karen Horney (pronounced OR-NAY) describes three ways that people tend to mishandle their doubts and insecurities: (1) moving against others, or the self-expansive solution, (2) moving toward others, or the self-effacing solution, and (3) moving away from others, or the resignation solution.

The Self-Expansive Solution

The self-expansive way of handling anxiety, uncertainty, and insecurity seeks mastery of the life's challenges through dominating both circumstances and other people. A self-expansive man is determined to overcome any obstacle that comes his way, even if it means stepping on people to accomplish his idealized goals. Horney observes that the self-expansive man believes that he "should be able to master the adversities of fate, the difficulties of a situation, the intricacies of intellectual problems, the resistances of other people, [and] conflicts within himself."[26] David Kelly explains that the self-expansive person craves domination over others for its own sake, which is inherently disrespectful of others, their individuality, their dignity, their feelings, the only concern being their subordination of others.[27] The self-expansive man has an indiscriminate adoration of strength and contempt for weakness.[28] He avoids uncontrollable situations, and never likes to put himself in positions where he might feel helplessness.[29] A self-expansive man exploits and manipulates others. He craves social prestige and recognition. He loves to be admired by others, is driven to be the best at everything, is obsessed with ambition, and is narcissistic and vindictive. This is the man who evaluates others primarily according to whether or not they can be exploited,

26. Horney, *Neurosis and Human Growth*, 192.

27. Kelly, "Expansive Solution."

28. Kelly, "Expansive Solution."

29. Kelly, "Expansive Solution."

and takes pride in his ability to manipulate others. At parties, he believes women's bodies exist for his sexual pleasure and will do whatever it takes to make sure she meets his needs either by force, emotional manipulation, making sure she gets intoxicated, or even putting sedatives in her drink. His masculinity is defined by successful sexual conquests and hook-ups at parties, spring break, etc. He tends to be vain and materialistic, "all things— inanimate objects, money, persons, one's own qualities, activities, and feelings—evaluated only according to their prestige value."[30] He evaluates himself according to the way he hope others see and accept him. No amount of achievements are enough for him. He always needs more. A man like this is deathly afraid of having limitations, being seen as incompetent, losing his social status, not being adored, and being humiliated.[31] This disordered attempt to alleviate doubts and insecurities through mastery is problematic because American society can reward such behavior in a convoluted way. A man like this can end up becoming MVP of his sports team or the president of a fraternity chapter. This kind of man is often misconstrued as someone who is "Type A," driven, an alpha male, but his character could very well have roots in an emotionally unstable place.

The Self-Effacing Solution

The self-effacing way of handling anxiety, uncertainty, and insecurity is by becoming a "nice guy" at the expense of your own identity. David Kelly summarizes the self-effacing person by highlighting his desperate need for affection and approval, an indiscriminate need to please others and to be liked and approved of by others, reflexive concern about living up to the expectations of others, and his focus on the lives of others rather than his own. For this kind of man, other people's wishes and opinions as the only ones that count, but though he appears to be humble, he is full of inordinate pride about how much he does for others.[32]

When it comes to relationships, the self-effacing man looks for a friend or a romantic partner who will take over his life, and will fulfill all of his major life expectations, as well as be responsible whatever good and evil occurs. This man overvalues love because he believes that love will solve all problems, alleviating his fears, doubts, and insecurities. He often believes that he does not deserve boundaries, and should be undemanding and contented with little, including ambition or any materialist desires. This man

---

30. Kelly, "Expansive Solution."
31. Kelly, "Expansive Solution."
32. Kelly, "Self-Effacing Solution."

believes he should seek to remain inconspicuous, and take second place. He is first to belittle himself. He believes everyone should always be modest, and is deathly afraid of people abandoning him. He is afraid of being alone. If he breaks up with a girl, the self-effacing man will immediately try to get into another relationship as soon as possible. The fear of being alone is so strong that he is willing to let his friends abuse him, or let women emasculate and emotionally manipulate him, rather than be unattached and disconnected. The thought of not being in a relationship or having friends immediately around is unbearable for this man. He would rather be abused than be alone.

He is afraid of making demands on people because he does not believe that he is worthy of such demands. He fears being a burden and liability to others. He is constantly sublimating his thoughts, wishes, and desires to those of others. He is willing to meet the needs of others in perpetuity, even if it means the regular neglect of his owns needs. He does not want to risk rejection by standing up for himself, which is why he dreads "having or asserting expansive wishes." He can't tell his girlfriend "no," so his friends never see him. If he's asked if he'll participate in an activity he does not like, he'll always agree to it because he fears risking rejection. Unsurprisingly, self-expansive people and self-effacing people often end up dating each other or becoming fast friends. The self-expansive person is looking for someone to control and the self-effacing person, who is entirely other-directed, is looking to be controlled. It is match made in dysfunction.

The Self-Resigned Solution

The self-resigned man's way of handling anxiety, uncertainty, and insecurity is by checking out and not caring. He just wants to be left alone to do what he wants to do as long as he doesn't hurt anyone. He has resigned from caring. As Karen Horney observes, "The very essence of this solution is withdrawing from active living, from active wishing, striving, planning, from efforts and doing." He does not want to be bothered. He's content playing videos, smoking weed, and hooking up with a girl or two.[33] Here's how the self-resigned man develops, according to Karen Horney: He goes through childhood like any promising young man. He is full of energy, rambunctious, silly, curious, possibly ambitious in school or in sports. He may show remarkable energy or gifts. He may be creative and resourceful. He may appear to have long-term interests. Then a period of distress occurs: He experiences some sort

33. Horney, *Neurosis and Human Growth*, 259–90. Note I will be summarizing her main points in the rest of this section.

of deprivation, anxiety, depression, trauma, or despair about a failure or some unfortunate situation. This is when he begins to lose his zest for life. His wings have been clipped through a series of major or minor disasters or deprivations. Anxiety, depression, and addiction can settle in. Unsure about who he is or where he stands, he will become alienated from himself and, in our current culture, he may lose himself on the internet where he becomes the person he is not in real life. To relieve his inner tension and discomfort, he detaches and becomes a spectator to his own life. The absence of any serious striving for achievement and the aversion of effort emerges. He will procrastinate over simple things like completing an application, doing his homework, washing his car, cleaning his room, or even bathing. Or he may do them despite inner resistance, slowly, lethargically. This will be confused with laziness, but it is not. It's resignation. There will be an absence of goal-direction and planning. What does he want to do with this life? He will not know. The arrogant driven narcissist wants success. The doormat wants love. The resigned young man, however, has no idea, and gets annoyed when people ask. He just wants to be left alone. He just wants to chill, and he is irritated when you interrupt his resignation, and ask him to do something. He restricts his own wishes by ceasing to wish for things for himself. He becomes detached, and keeps his emotional distance from others. This is a common narrative in cases of college male suicide: He cared so much for others, he was so warm and helpful, so friendly, a friend to everyone. He had good grades, or he was a star athlete, or he took care of his mom. Regardless, no one knew he was struggling. He was detached, and no one knew.

The self-resigned man is hypertensive to outside influence, pressure, coercion, long-term commitments, and rules. This is often confused with rebellion. He'll have an aversion to change. He'd rather stay "as is" than work on self-development; he just wants to get by. He's abandoned the drive for actual mastery. He no longer wants to be really, really good at something, or he's just given up trying. "What's the point," he asks. He withdraws, so no one knows his joys, his pains, his sorrows, his fears. He lacks self-confidence but knows how to perform for adults: So he may get good grades, perform well on the football fields, or get a great summer job. Why? Because he knows that as long as he performs for adults, people will leave him alone. He may then simply resign himself to shallow and vain living to distract himself with pleasure, the vain pursuit of the prestige and honor he wishes he had in real life, and he adopts the vanity of mirroring himself to others as a distraction. He feels, thinks, does, believes in whatever is expected or considered right in his environment—his family, his church, his school. All the while no one knows he is dead inside.

The self-resigned man is deathly afraid of needing others, of ties, of closeness, of love. He's afraid of being too attached to anyone for too long. He will sabotage and end a great relationship, if necessary. He won't take risks or move out of his comfort zone because he is afraid of finding flaws within himself or of making mistakes. He avoids situations that might lead to criticism or rebukes. When asked to run for a leadership position, he will say, "no" because the best way to never be criticized is to never put oneself in that position in the first place. Even though the self-resigned person appears not to care, he does, and his pride is reflected in the fact he believes in his of self-sufficiency, independence, and stoic strength to provide direction for his life.

Most people find themselves experiencing some combination of one or two of these behaviors, if not all three, from time to time, depending on the circumstances. The truth is most of us mishandle anxiety, uncertainty, and insecurity, and it hurts us in the long run. We know that we need other people to help us see our blind spots, and so the way that we mishandle our wounds does not take over our lives. For a college man, there are few places better suited to help him identify and dismantle disordered approaches to handling the vicissitudes of life than a college fraternity. A new family of relationships helps each new brother find his heart and thrive. Heroic fraternities create an environment, through friendship and brotherhood, where men are honest about the imperfections they see in each other. They are committed to doing whatever it takes to not leave a brother self-expansive, self-effacing, or self-resigned. Heroic fraternities create a culture when brothers will call out these tendencies, and do whatever is necessary to help their brothers purge them because they truly want what is best for each other. Formation happens in a fraternity where friendship, acceptance, and brotherhood meet. Heroic fraternities use friendships built on trust, love, and respect to help their brothers find their strengths, and push each other forward in the journey of self-improvement for the benefit of those around them. When acceptance, friendship, and brotherhood work in harmony, they act as a repellant to a culture of self-serving, self-centered, and self-preserving men, and can help free men from the tyranny of being self-expansive, self-effacing, and self-resigning. The self-improvement journey begins when fraternities use the pledge process to help new brothers find their strengths.

Pledging and Initiation: Helping a Man Find His Strengths

The third way fraternities cultivate heroic masculinity is by helping each man in the fraternity discover more of his strengths through the pledge process and the remaining years as an active brother. Pledging a fraternity should be both extraordinarily fun and powerfully formative. Many men arrive on college campus unclear about the full range of ways they can add value to the lives of those around them. For too many men, their high school years were so dedicated to building a resume that they don't know why they matter outside of academics, sports, and other extra-curricular activities. To become an adult, men need to be initiated into adulthood and develop a framework in which to understand what it means to use their lives for the benefit of others. They need direction. A path. They need guidance in what heroism looks like in daily life. One of the misconceptions about the pledge process is that older brothers need to break pledges down so that they can build them back up. This concept is adopted from the military and other institutions that believe that men function best as a unit if stripped of their individuality. Why? For the military, unity is a matter of survival, and individuality can lead to death. Thus military needs to build men up to help them reimagine themselves as an integral part of the team because that is what active military duty depends on. Fraternity life is not a matter of life and death, and adopting a military framework for pledging is often a net negative. The misguided notion that a fraternity needs to "break men down" like soldiers is irrelevant to fraternity life, which is why it so readily feeds into the types of disordered masculinity that result in suspensions. "Breaking people down" just to mess with them undermines the purpose of a brotherhood dedicated to the betterment of all of its brothers. Fraternity man, former college IFC president, and Air Force Veteran Pat Hagerty, who deployed twice to Iraq and survived over one hundred and fifty mortar attacks, has this to say about both his fraternity and military experience and notion of "Break Them Down, Then Build Them Up:"

> This is, by far and away, the most foolish comment made by brothers during a fraternity's new member program to justify hazing. It seems like pledge marshals believe that they are now drill instructors, and that is what is expected in a new member program.
>
> I want to let you in on a little secret—there is no such thing as breaking them down to build them up in the military!
>
> I served five years in the military, deploying twice to the Middle East. I have been to boot camp and numerous training schools, and the concept of stripping a man of all his dignity to only rebuild him isn't part of the military mindset.
>
> Instead, the military focuses on finding people who already have the foundation and potential to contribute to the team.

From there, the training programs are focused on building on that foundation in order for recruits to meet their potential.[34]

What if fraternities adopted the military's formation model using the pledge process to focus on building on the strengths men already have, rather than a fraternity film-influenced model that messes with guys, based on a misapplied theory. Given that young men are arriving on campus riddled with shame, anxiety, depression, and addictions, what they need most is a pledge process that introduces challenges and obstacles that builds their self-confidence. Navy veteran Steve Swan described the purpose of basic training as something designed to "Break down individualism. Push you beyond what you thought you could do. Teach you precision at following directions."[35] This was training for combat, but fraternities are not training for combat readiness. One of the goals of pledging is to strip away any self-serving, self-centered, and self-preserving reflexes to reform the pledges into men who are made for others and are willing to sacrifice their own preferences for the good of the fraternity.

Being initiated into fraternity life helps men experience these essential truths:

1. Life is hard.

2. You are not that important.

3. Your life is not about you, and

4. You are not in control.[36]

When brothers listen to each other's stories and walk with each other through the trials and tribulations of transitioning into adulthood on a college campus, the pains, sufferings, anxieties, and mental health issues that recent high school graduates often endure are often ignored on the basis of misplaced ideas of privilege that don't recognize what the data really indicates: these young men are struggling.[37] Committing their lives to being a benefit to others is, however, one the most powerful ways to persevere through stress, trauma, and adversity. When the pledge process is performed properly, it actually functions as training in altruism, or the "unselfish concern for the good the good of others; we wish to give another a leg

34. Hagerty, "Break them Down."

35. Swan, Twitter message to author.

36. Rohr, *Adam's Return*, 32–35.

37. Farrell and Gray, *Boy Crisis,* 15–39.

up . . . without concern for our own gain."[38] Research shows that an altruistic disposition in college was among five predictors of medical, psychological, social, and occupational success decades later.[39] When the pledging process is designed to impart meaning, purpose, and intentionality, it sets men up for success for years to come. Along the way, pledges begin to discover new strengths, as they are given opportunities to lead and serve in ways that they once would have considered impossible. Pledging is the first step in a college man initiation into adulthood—and it is very much needed.

For thousands of years, ancient and tribal cultures around the world developed sacred rituals to mark the transition from boyhood to adulthood. There was a formal process where a boy would be welcomed into the community of men and elders. As Patrick Arnold explains, "males need a holy space at a distance from the feminine world, and they require rituals there to reenact and reinforce their masculinity, which needs constantly to be re-experienced and won anew."[40] Unfortunately, modern American life lacks any male initiation rites of passage into adulthood so, as Arnold notes, modern males "are left to initiate themselves—usually and unconvincingly—in gang rites, drinking bouts, punk mutilations, and the like, without any supervision or adult help."[41] In many American communities, that makeshift substitution is defined by physical domination (athletic performance or an aesthetic physique), sexual conquest, and the consumption of drugs and alcohol. In the ancient world, however, initiation into adulthood occurred in three stages:

1. Separation/Departure: A man needed to leave his familiar environment to embark on a journey that would test him, and earn him a new virtuous future. To learn that he could not remain a child for the rest of his life, he had to leave the comfort and safety of home.

2. Order/Initiation: A man needed to encounter a range of obstacles and challenges to overcome as he grows beyond the passivity of boyhood to find hidden strength with the help of older guides and friends to find and achieve his purpose. He needs to be pushed beyond what he previously believed he could do so he can gain the self-confidence of self-reliance and the ability to learn. Men need self-confidence to act in their own best interest, and that of others. Self-confidence embues men with the courage to do what is right,

38. Schiraldi, *Resilience Workbook*, 133.
39. Schiraldi, *Resilience Workbook*, 133.
40. Arnold, *Wildmen, Warriors, and Kings*.
41. Arnold, *Wildmen, Warriors, and Kings*.

no matter the consequence. Self-confidence is the birthplace of prudence, which helps men enact justice on behalf of others, gain fortitude, and learn self-control.

3. Return and Reintegration: After confirming that he can fend for himself, and have impactful agency, the world needs a man to contribute to bettering others and the world around him. To accomplish this, he must integrate himself back into the ordinary world while retaining a deep sense of purpose and meaning. The most dramatic marker of this reintegration is when a man graduates, leaves campus, and enters the next stage of his journey in a new location.

For fraternity men, the rite of passage into adulthood is an integral part of the college experience itself. A teenager leaves his home (stage one), pledges a fraternity (stage two), and receives his initiation rite, (stage three). He is then welcomed as a brother, and sent off into the world. He knows that from his initiation forward, his is no longer an independent man. He is a man who has a trustworthy band of brothers. He spends the remainder of his college years building up his brothers so that they can excel.

But it all starts with the pledge process. Because it is so formative, it cannot be reckless. There's too much at stake. The world doesn't need any more selfish men. Pledging is intended to help a man discover his strengths, which is why *every pledge activity should have a distinct purpose, and be philosophically defensible in light of the fraternity's mission and values.* Those leading the pledge process should think deeply about ways to challenge new pledges to bring out their best qualities. At the end of the pledge process, a new brother should be more confident about his heroic identity, having learned new things about himself, which readies him to give himself to his brothers because he loves them deeply and wants what is best for them. Pledges are not entertainment.

Fun and Happiness

The fourth way fraternities cultivate heroic masculinity is by helping brothers experience fun and happiness. The one thing people should notice when they see fraternity brothers together is immense laughter, regardless of the time of day or the location. Fraternities should compete to be the most fun communities and produce the most laughter on campus. If a fraternity chapter is not fun, it is seriously doing something wrong. Fraternities should commit a significant amount of its annual budget brainstorming in the creative production of fun, both for themselves and the entire campus.

The production of fun is important not simply because "college students are supposed to have fun" but because fun is also formative, holistically beneficial, and increases the quality of life, and everyone's mental health.

At root, fun is the production of positive emotions, and positive emotions are key to happiness and thriving. Martin Seligman describes positive emotion as feelings of "pleasure, rapture, ecstasy, warmth, comfort, and the like."[42] Positive emotion also includes "hope, interest, joy, love, compassion, pride, amusement, and gratitude."[43] When viewed this way, we see that fun casting a net far beyond parties and intramural sports competitions. The potential for fraternities to create the conditions for people to experience enjoyment, pleasure, hope, laughter, compassion, pride, and gratitude are almost endless. Fraternities need to draw on their imaginations to conceive of a broad range of ways they can produce positive emotions for their brothers and those around them, including their peers outside of Greek life. What makes a fraternity fun is not the number and size of their parties but their ability to create positive emotions whenever brothers are together, day after day. Too many fraternities restrict the way fun is imagined. There are many variations of fun on many campuses that have yet to be explored. Positive emotions are experienced through things like spending time with people you care about, doing activities that you enjoy (hobbies), listening to uplifting or inspirational music, and reflecting on things you are grateful for, including those things that are going well in your life.[44] Parties have their place, but an expanded notion of fun should include things that make the fraternity brotherhood even stronger. The more positive emotions men in fraternities experience, the stronger they are mentally, and the better able they are to persevere through stress, adversity, and trauma. Fraternities should intentionally focus on increasing happiness among their brothers and their campuses. In the discipline of psychology, "happiness" comprises two things:

1. Feeling genuine heartfelt, positive emotions on a fairly regular basis, such as contentment, gratitude, joy, inner peace, satisfaction, inspiration, enthusiasm, hope, awe, amusement, curiosity, and love.

2. Feeling overall satisfaction with one's life and self, and believing that they are meaningful and worthwhile.[45]

---

42. Seligman, *Flourish*, 11.

43. Madeson, "Seligman's Theory."

44. Madeson, "Seligman's Theory."

45. Schiraldi, *Resilience Workbook*, 95.

Fun, happiness, and positive emotions are associated with "psychological thriving:" higher self-esteem, emotional stability, greater self-confidence, less anxiety and depression, better coping skills through adversity, occupational thriving. Outcomes that involve psychological thriving include enjoying work and school, being more engaged at work, being more productive and creative, earning a higher salary, and so on. "Social thriving" involves greater satisfaction with family, friends, dating relationships and marriages, a greater ability to cooperate with others. and medical thriving. Outcomes include living longer, a stronger immune system, more energy, faster healing from wounds.[46] Research shows that while 50 percent of our experience of happiness is genetic, 40 percent is derived from intentional happiness-enhancing activities, and the remaining 10 percent depend on our circumstances.[47] This means that fraternities have the opportunity to contribute to 60 percent of the ways most people experience happiness. This leaves fraternity leadership teams with a vital budgetary and programming question: What happiness-enhancing values and circumstances are we creating for our brothers that are consistent with our mission and values?

An additional contribution of happiness is engagement. Engagement happens when you are enjoying something so much that you may lose track of time. Some psychologists call this "flow." Flow refers to immersion that occurs when the perfect combination of challenge and skill or strength is found, such that time flies right by.[48] Fraternities can increase engagement by: creating activities that brothers really love; helping guys live in the moment, appreciating good things regardless of daily activities or mundane tasks; spending time in nature, watching, listening, and observing what happens around them; and helping brothers identify and learn about their character strengths, giving them things to do where fraternity brothers excel.[49]

Hollywood screenwriters lack the knowledge to imagine what real fraternity leaders across America's college campuses do day-to-day, which is why their plots focus on reckless behavior and parties at the expense of everything else. Heroic fraternity chapters, however, have the skills, expertise, and creative resources to conceive of multiple opportunities throughout the week for increasing the experience of happiness amongst their brothers, ranging from laughter-filled meals together, to playing video games, to providing opportunities for men to share some of their struggles with each other. When fun is expanded to show its true potential, it becomes clear

---

46. Schiraldi, *Resilience Workbook.*
47. Schiraldi, *Resilience Workbook.*
48. Madeson, "Seligman's Theory."
49. Madeson, "Seligman's Theory."

how and why fraternities have the dynamic capacity to make the men who join them significantly better off than the general university population.

Personal and Professional Development

The fifth way that fraternities cultivate heroic masculinity is by providing opportunities for personal and professional development. Young men can gain leadership experience by serving in a leadership role in their chapters, hosting résumé workshops, using alumni networks for internships and job placement after graduation, and so on. These are all ways that men have access to developing skills with professional value. Fraternities provide young men with the infrastructure to experience accomplishment, achievement, mastery, or competence for its own sake, which is vital to flourishing, happiness, good mental health, and self-confidence, regardless of any deeper meaning, or ability to positively impact relationships.[50] Licensed professional counselor Melissa Madeson explains that accomplishment is the result of working toward and reaching goals, mastering an endeavor, and having the self-motivation to finish what one sets out to do.[51] This contributes to well-being because it provides opportunities for individuals to look at their lives with a sense of pride, knowing that their efforts made a positive difference. Accomplishment includes relying on internal motivation to strive toward things or working toward something just for the sake of the pursuit and improvement.[52] Fraternities can create opportunities for accomplishment amongst its members, by helping others in their personal lives, or the chapter as a whole; by setting SMART goals (specific, measurable, achievable, realistic, and time-bound); by creating occasions to reflect on the past successes of individual brothers or the chapter as a whole; and by pursuing creative ways to celebrate everyone's achievements.[53]

Fraternities provide an ideal environment for members to find realistic opportunities to experience accomplishment and achievement within the fraternity itself. Likewise, they provide multiple opportunities for fraternity men to participate in leading different organizations across campus. Celebrating participation, accomplishment, and achievement at award dinners, on social media, with recognition through the national offices, and beyond, are all ways that fraternities benefit young men, and put them in a position to succeed and excel. Heroic fraternities are the ones that are intentional about

50. Seligman, *Flourish*, 19; Madeson, "Seligman's Theory."
51. Madeson, "Seligman's Theory."
52. Madeson, "Seligman's Theory."
53. Madeson, "Seligman's Theory."

springboarding their membership into achieving academic success, job place-
ments after college, and everything in between and beyond. Alumni can play
a crucial role in expanding these opportunities if they are willing to focus on
the personal and professional development of their younger brothers.

Heroic Character Formation

The sixth way fraternities cultivate heroic masculinity is by helping the men
in their chapters develop character. Heroic fraternities strive to transform
good men into great men. A man joins a fraternity because he believes his
brothers will better him. Former Colts NFL defensive tackle Joe Ehrmann
explains that masculinity is built on a two-part framework. First, heroic masculinity is defined by the quality of the relationships it cultivates.[54] "It ought
to be taught in terms of the capacity to love and to be loved. If you look over
your life at the end of it . . . life wouldn't be measured in terms of success
based on what you've acquired or achieved or what you own. The only thing
that's really going to matter is the relationships that you had."[55] What kind
of friend are you? What kind of fraternity brother are you? How do you treat
women? What kind of father and husband will you be? What kind of son or
sibling are you? What kind of student are you? How do you relate to your
professors? For Joe Ehrmann, "success comes in terms of relationships."[56]
Relationships provide us with ways to reciprocate feeling supported, loved,
and valued by others by offering the same to those around us.[57] Humans are
not inherently designed to survive in isolation. We are necessarily interde-
pendent for survival. Research shows that sharing good news or celebrating
success fosters strong bonds and better relationships.[58] We also know that
"responding enthusiastically to others, particularly in close or intimate relationships, increases intimacy, wellbeing, and satisfaction."[59]

Successful relationships are key to perseverance, which is crucial for
recovering from stress, adversity, and trauma. Good relationships increase
our social intelligence—skills that help us relate well to others.[60] Socially
intelligent fraternities produce men who are "likable, respectful, believable,
genuine, positive, approachable, interested, and enthused. They [will] tend

54. Marx, Jeffrey, *Season of Life*, 36.
55. Marx, Jeffrey, *Season of Life*, 36.
56. Marx, Jeffrey, *Season of Life*, 36.
57. Madeson, "Seligman's Theory."
58. Madeson, "Seligman's Theory."
59. Madeson, "Seligman's Theory."
60. Schiraldi, *Resilience Workbook*, 161.

to listen more than they speak and are really attuned to other people's feelings.[61] They both prepare us and give us the capacity to benefit those around us. Most young fraternity men pledged their fraternity, in part, because they wanted to increase their social intelligence, and gain relational skills to help them relate better to others, believe it or not. Most young men will likely not say this publicly, or perhaps even articulate it to themselves, but fraternities give men in the brotherhood an opportunity to love and to be loved in ways that provide certainty that other men in their fraternity will support and, if need be, defend them. Although research shows that the absence of love can lead to poor medical health, outside of sports, society provides young men with few ways to experience brotherly love. Love contributes to resilience because it "positively impacts performance of the giver and receiver by increasing happiness."[62] Fraternities provide ways to practice and offer love that wants what is best for one's brother—be it in class or past midnight at a party. To love your fraternity brothers is both a choice and a commitment, especially when it's difficult: In the midst of strong disagreements, or when we don't feel like it.[63] The experience of deep fraternal love can also lead to positivity resonance—"fleeting moments of warm, mutual connection with others, in which we feel safe and good."[64] These are often those late-night "heart-to-heart" talks where men talk about their relationship troubles, processing a parental divorce, the disappointment of a graduate school rejection, and the like. Positivity resonance can also happen on a road trip, in a tent, on a day hike with a few brothers, even at dinner and the movies. The point is that social intelligence makes fraternal brotherhood stronger, and more helpful. Given what the research shows, I believe that one of the absolute best ways that a college man can find relationships and build his character is to join a fraternity.

Joe Ehrmann's second criterion for healthy masculinity is that all men "ought to have some kind of cause, some kind of purpose in our lives that's bigger than our own individual hopes, dreams, wants, and desires. At the end of our life, we ought to be able to look back over it from our deathbed and know that somehow the world was a better place because we lived, we loved, we were other-centered, other-focused."[65] This is completely consistent with heroic masculinity. Men need a cause outside of themselves that draws them away from being self-serving, self-centered, and

61. Schiraldi, *Resilience Workbook*, 161.

62. Schiraldi, *Resilience Workbook*, 164.

63. Schiraldi, *Resilience Workbook*, 164.

64. Schiraldi, *Resilience Workbook*, 164.

65. Marx, Jeffrey, *Season of Life*, 36.

self-preserving. Men need meaning and purpose that do not allow them to be self-expansive, self-effacing, or self-resigning. Having a cause allows us to belong to, and serve, something beyond the self, and it deeply captivates how we direct our lives.[66] Men who live with meaning, purpose, and a cause are generally happier and more resilient. These inner strengths of mind and character enable them to respond well to adversity, stress, depression, and anxiety.[67] Research shows that looking forward to a meaningful future stimulates one to set satisfying goals, make plans, and work hard to succeed and be healthy.[68] When we commit ourselves to challenging causes that matter, meaning and purpose increase.[69] When a man has a purpose in life that provides him with meaning, he is far less willing to engage in reckless behavior that might sabotage his hopes, dreams, wants, desires, and inspirations. Because heroic masculinity orients men toward living in a way that benefits others, the natural consequence of a life well-lived is one that provides recognizable and tangible evidence that the world was made a better place by his presence.

Having good relationships, and a cause that transcends individualism, naturally forms the character of a man toward that which is heroic. Because a heroic man wants to be a great man, he will take responsibility for his mistakes, and use them as opportunities to learn. Fraternities provide a setting where men can fail and take responsibility for their failures, without the experience of shame. Shame does not emerge from making mistakes. Shame emerges from having your mistakes brand you as a worthless loser. When young men live in shame, they become posers, and posers live self-serving, self-centered, and self-preserving lives as a way to mask their insecurities, anxieties, and uncertainties. By contrast, men who experience resilience, and the happiness that follows, are men formed by outstanding relationships that demand the excellence needed to benefit others. Healthy relationships are the birthplace of sacrificially meeting the needs of others in ways that make communities thrive.

How to Refute Abolishment

The most effective way to silence the Abolish Greek Life movement, and put an end to media demands to remove fraternities from campus is to pursue heroic masculinity. What primarily makes a fraternity praiseworthy,

66. Silegman, *Flourish*, 19.

67. Schiraldi, *Resilience Workbook*, 2, 155.

68. Schiraldi, *Resilience Workbook*, 156.

69. Schiraldi, *Resilience Workbook*, 156.

on campus and in the community, is less about the philanthropic work a fraternity does, than the overall characters of the men who make up the membership of a fraternity. Arguing for the demonstrable heroism of the men in a fraternity is inevitably a much stronger argument than pointing to their philanthropy, which is but one facet of their impact on the community. Fraternity men who focus on acceptance, friendship, and brotherhood, who help their brothers find their strengths, create fun and happiness, provide personal and professional development, and orient men toward to the heroic will be men lacking sexual assault and hazing allegations for reckless behavior. They will never be suspended, and they will add nothing but value to the lives of their brothers and the campus community.

Heroic fraternities are open, vulnerable, and safe spaces for men to get help with insecurities, uncertainties, doubts, fears, pain, anxieties, and mental health struggles. Heroic fraternities are fraternities where men have the courage to ask for help if they are in distress rather than abuse drugs and alcohol to numb their pain and discomfort. If heroic fraternities threatened to leave the campus, they are the ones the faculty, administration, staff, and non-Greek peers, would plead with to stay. Heroic fraternities do need to attend regular seminars where they are taught to be less bad—or else! Heroic fraternities will be the safest places for women to be on the entire campus. Heroic fraternities only use their hands to build great men so they do not need to embrace the lowest common denominator position of "these hands don't haze." Telling others "we don't hurt you" is not the pursuit of excellence. It is the pursuit of mere decency. We already know what the hands of heroic fraternity members do: they help pledges discover the assets and strengths to use their presence, power, strengths, and creativity to benefit those around them.

Heroic fraternities accept imperfect men, forge deep friendships with them, and then release them on campus, and into the world, to make the world a much better place. Heroic fraternities are characterized by their contagious laughter, which makes them the most fun places to be on campus. Heroic fraternities are known for developing men personally, academically, and professionally. Heroic fraternities create men whose success is determined by the quality of their relationships, their commitment to something greater than themselves, and the help they provide to others. Every college campus needs more heroic fraternities, and it would make sense if every man wanted to join one.

7

The Heroic Fraternity Movement

I am calling for a national movement of fraternities who want to use their power, presence, strengths, and creativity to benefit their brothers and those around them.

Theta Chi at Clemson University offers a great model of heroic masculinity adding value to their campus. They understand what it means to use their presence for the benefit of their immediate community. For example, following Clemson's at home win over Wake Forest University one year, the men of the Eta Alpha chapter of Theta Chi sacrificed their time to make the Clemson community a better place by cleaning up the football stadium. This is exactly the kind of image of Greek life the entire campus needs to witness–that is, one defined by service to peers and others on campus. Community service and philanthropy should not be limited to off-campus activities. Your fraternity can make the world better first by making your campus better. Theta Chi's motto is "An Assisting Hand" and that is exactly what they are doing at Clemson: acting in a way that is consistent with their values and mission and making Clemson better in the process.

If you are a college administrator, we encourage you to use positive reinforcement to encourage the fraternities on your campus to aim for heroism. If you are a college student in a fraternity reading this book, I encourage your fraternity chapter to take a heroic pledge.

I am determined to ensure America's fraternities add comprehensive value to their brothers and their campus. Our goal is to make the notion of suspending them for misconduct—or criticizing them for misbehavior—unthinkable. I seek to eradicate fraternities as a risk management issue by reinventing them as a role model of beneficial excellence. I want fraternities that have them to eventually abolish the role of risk manager altogether. I believe the starting point for all fraternity events should begin with a social chair asking, "What is the best way for women and non-Greeks to have unbelievable fun, too?"

When your chapter needs defending, community service to adjacent neighborhoods near the college campus, and raising money for national charities, no matter how admirable is not the talking point. A fraternity's best attribute for justifying its existence must be the heroic character of the men that comprise it. Any group of college students can clean up a highway or raise money for research to cure diseases. What makes fraternities a fundamental good for college men, however, are the friendships it helps forge, the brotherly bonds it helps build, the initiation into adulthood it helps support, the professional development it helps provide, and the characters of the men formed by chapter who end up on a course to be outstanding leaders, co-workers, husbands, fathers, sports coaches, volunteers, and so on. Perhaps this is an opportunity for black Greek fraternities to lead in providing an alternative model of what fraternity life can be like for predominantly white fraternities since black fraternities are generally not the subject of complaints about men on campus. Black fraternities also provide a more active experience of extending the virtues of fraternity life after college. College campuses don't need fewer fraternities, they need *more* heroic fraternities, and *more* men who aspire to heroism. We don't need to abolish Greek life. We need to abolish the "Abolish Greek Life Movement" by silencing our critics with our heroism. Will your chapter join the movement?

This book does not have all of the answers to possibilities for change or potentialities for greatness on your campus but it is a modest proposal for what the future could look like. I trust fraternity men to figure it out. Every fraternity chapter culture is different and the way they express heroic masculinity will necessarily vary. That's the way it should be. If all of the fraternities on your campus are heroic, they will complement each other's strengths and make the campus better, by extension.

I've been in discussions with fraternity presidents across the ACC, the SEC, and the Big Ten. A revolution in Greek Life is currently underway, and I am asking you and your fraternity to join us. Have your fraternity read the book. Discuss it. Brainstorm. Debate it. Think about what it means to your brothers and your campus to privately and publicly express your fraternity's heroic capacities. Have the leaders of fraternity president councils on your campus read the book. Strategize a way to add value to the entire campus. Be creative. If your fraternity wants to join us, and is willing to publicly commit to heroism, please contact me directly. I am available on social media, by email, or through my website www.dranthonybradley.com. I want to hear your chapter's story.[1]

I am also willing to travel to any campus to speak about heroic masculinity to any fraternity, regardless of size. During the writing of this book, I had the privilege of addressing fraternities at the University of Virginia and the University of Mississippi. Those were some of the most memorable speaking events of my career. Heroic fraternities are the future, and if we are successful, college campuses and the entire country will benefit. Fraternities can save universities and America. Let's go!

1. Feel free to email me at abradley@heroicfraternities.com.

Part 2

In Their Own Words

8

Sigma Phi, the University of Virginia

Nick Fischer grew up in Howell, New Jersey. He served as President of Sigma Phi at the University of Virginia in 2021–2022. A major in political philosophy, policy, and law, he joined Sigma Phi because "It seemed like people really appreciated each other across differences," and because a lot of members "were just hilarious." He appreciates the rituals of Sigma Phi. "Not everything that Sigma Phi entails is available to the public," he says, "and that enhances what we do," noting that as "we learn Sigma Phi's history and traditions, we place ourselves within that tradition. The founders that we're learning about then become our ancestors, people who pass something down to us."

Q. What drew you to Virginia?

UVA was a popular place to apply to for people in my area who were interested in going to a rigorous academic school. It had the reputation of being a serious academic place, but also a fun and spirited atmosphere with fun sports teams. It came down to a handful of colleges for me, and I judged based on my visits that UVA was the best fit for the college life that I was trying to have, with that balance of school and fun.

Q. Why join a fraternity?

My vision of what college was going to be for me was a lot more academic than it turned out. Not in the sense that I'm skipping class or anything, but there's a lot more going on for me in college than what I imagined it was going to be like. I thought I was going to go there and be in the books and that it was about getting your degree and it was about being in class.

Plus, I didn't think fraternities had much substance. I thought it was about partying strictly. I didn't realize that they did anything else. I certainly did not foresee how important it could be to the people who were in it, so that wasn't part of my plans.

I realized here at UVA it was central to the social experience, at least for guys. When it came time to sign up for rush and everybody in the dorm building and in class was signing up for rush, I realized that if I didn't do this maybe I'd miss out on some kind of fundamental part of the UVA experience here, which in my opinion still is true. You can have a great time at UVA without being in a fraternity, no doubt, but it just opens up a whole other dimension of life here to be in one.

Q. How were your friendships different in high school from the ones you have at Sigma Phi?

I can notice a difference for sure. In our fraternity, there's a sense that we're not just friends, we're on a team together. There's a real sense of allegiance among all the guys and we take the title of "brother" pretty seriously. It means a lot to call somebody a brother.

When we have meetings to plan events or discuss whatever is going on, there's a very focused atmosphere. It's serious. We take seriously that we're all in this together and that we're doing a project in common. Our friendships are forged through these common experiences and being part of something rather than just living on the same street or being around each other in high school sports and what not.

We also spend a lot of time together. Our house is a really cool place to be at. In the case of the fifteen of us who live at the house right now, we are with each other all the time. It becomes a place of comfort. It becomes a place where you can go when you just need to relax, and that's the whole point. That's what makes this place valuable to people. We see each other's good days and bad days, which is not always true of the more selective and casual friendships you have.

A lot of times you're just with people when they're in a good mood, but we're around each other when we're in good moods and bad moods. That ties us together in a deeper way than the more casual sort of friendships do.

My dad was apprehensive. My mom was apprehensive. My mom is still apprehensive. They thought that it was going to be an *Animal House* type deal and that it wasn't going to be anything but a distraction. I understood that, and I still understand it, because there's a lot of places where that's how it is. We do our share of *Animal House* stuff, but it's so much more and it's worth it. I've conveyed that to them, and I think that they understand.

Q. Why are fraternities good for college men?

One important thing is that there's a lot of opportunities in a fraternity to lead and take responsibility. In a fraternity there's a ton of jobs. You need a president to be paying attention to the whole thing, you need a social chair to run the events, a treasurer to manage the money, house manager, secretary, and then on and on. In our fraternity a VP runs rush. There are so many jobs. There's probably over a dozen serious jobs that pop up over the course of the school year that involve actual leadership of other people and responsibility. They're usually elected positions, so you have to convince your brothers that you're the guy to do this. Then once you win, you now have to live up to the standard that you set and to the mandate that you were given.

These are prime opportunities for a college-aged guy to develop some leadership skills, because the brothers will hold you accountable. Guys call each other out all the time. It can be a rough and tumble atmosphere. When you screw up it gets noticed, and when you do things well it makes a visible difference in the lives of your friends. For a college-aged man, there aren't many opportunities to take on that kind of responsibility and be held seriously accountable.

Besides leadership opportunities, I think the best thing it offers guys is inspiration. If you join a good fraternity, with emphasis on the word "good" there, you're going to be around guys, especially above and within your pledge class, who inspire you to be a better person. You'll notice good qualities that your friends have that you can try to emulate. Ideally, you'll become closer to others who make you want to aim higher in life. But, of course, that's not guaranteed to happen. It's possible that by joining a frat you end up surrounding yourself with people who make you worse, and with all the time that you spend in your fraternity, that could do a lot of damage.

If you join a fraternity where you're going to be constantly around people who really are on a good track in life, that can turn you around. That can work wonders for you. For the most part, I honestly think the fraternity system is doing a service by putting them in close association with each other, and I've seen that firsthand.

Q. What is the rush process like?

Rush is once a year here, at the very beginning of the spring semester, and typically lasts for two weeks. There'll be an open house followed by three rounds of events. After open house, which is when guys go around touring all the different places, you'll ideally have between one hundred and fifty and two hundred rushees on your list. By the time the third round is over, the last round, you hope to have between twenty and thirty guys left from which to make your final cuts. That narrowing down will come from rushees leaving your process and from you cutting people out.

We aim for pledge classes of around twenty. There are just two weeks then from the informational meeting till bid day. Bid day is a huge celebration, where everybody is really happy that we're welcoming in new people. It's a really cool moment for the guys who are getting in. We throw them up in the air. It's awesome.

Between bid day and initiation is the season known as pledging, or "new member education," as you would say if you're in polite company. UVA has a rule that pledging has to be about a month and a half. They set a date for when initiation has to be taken place by. Suffice it to say that guys typically make the transition from pledge to brother well before the end of the spring semester, so they have a lot of time left in the spring to kind of enjoy being a member of a fraternity.

Q. Why Sigma Phi?

I looked at about five different places, and I was coming from New Jersey. I was an out-of-stater, so I had no idea what any of these houses were like. A lot of the people who were in-state have brothers and friends who go to UVA, and so they have their finger on the pulse of the fraternities out here. But I had no idea what anything was, so I was basically shooting in the dark. I was walking around, walking into whatever house I could walk into.

When I was rushing, the vibe in this house was different compared to the vibe in all the other places that I visited. The guys in here felt particularly authentic and relatable, and there is a ton of variety in here, which is what I noticed right off the bat. It seemed to be a fraternity that wasn't about wealth. It's not like we're all wealthy. It wasn't about appearance. It's not like we're all the best-looking people here. It wasn't intelligence. We have guys at all different levels with respect to those characteristics.

There are a lot of other houses where there's a really strong stereotype. You can tell immediately when you walk in that this is for these kinds of people, and that was not that way here. It seemed like people really appreciated each other across differences. And then many of the brothers I met were just hilarious. There was a lot of funny stuff happening in the house. That continues to be a characteristic of this place. We're constantly making each other laugh.

There was just a real sense of fun and authenticity here that I was eager to be a part of. It seemed like a very rich place, and the people spoke about it in this glowing way. And there still is that sense of an almost mythic status when it comes to Sigma Phi. The guys talked about it in an awesome way. They demonstrated what it meant to them, and when it came down to this house and one other house, I knew for sure that my gut was telling me to come here. My freshman roommate was from my high school. We ended up both coming here together.

Q. What makes Sigma Phi distinctive?

It's not dependent on one thing, but I can certainly feel the difference between Sigma Phi and other places. I think what it comes down to and what makes Sigma Phi unique in general is that the organization has a very particular character.

Number one, we are a secret society. We don't take that to the level of the Freemasons and such, but we do take seriously that Sigma Phi is for the brothers. Not everything that Sigma Phi entails is available to the public, and that enhances what we do. It makes it more special. It makes it more powerful for us to share those things amongst ourselves. That sense of privacy permeates the whole culture here, that sense of being in the world but kind of apart.

Another thing is that we're small. There's been fourteen total chapters ever, and only about half of those are still active, so nationally the community is very close. The alumni who run the national team are close to us. We know who they are. We know them personally, so that intimacy permeates the culture of the fraternity even within the chapter level. We're a very tight brotherhood.

Brotherhood matters a lot to us. It matters a lot more than it does to some of the other houses here, and that's not to knock them. It's just a question of what the organization is going to be about. Our organization is not about social opportunities or professional networks. It's about each other, and we have those other things as a byproduct. There's a strong identity here that has to do with our secrecy and our smallness, the main two things, and that creates a really special sense of brotherhood.

We're part of the Union Triad. We're one of the very first three ever founded. The fourth of March, 1827 is our founding date. Everything after us is a spinoff. We're the OG. Other fraternities were even founded in opposition to what we were doing. Delta Epsilon was founded to be a non-secret alternative to the secret societies that were being formed. Sigma Phi set the tone, and shaped how the rest of the process of fraternities starting was going to play out.

Q. Why is tradition important at Sigma Phi?

Our new member education, for instance, is in large part about absorbing our traditions, so it involves learning a lot of information. There are stories from our history and brothers in those stories that are very important to us. Knowing those stories and those names, those songs (because we have songs too) is how we form a collective.

Any group of guys can come together and become friends. But by learning Sigma Phi history and traditions we place ourselves within that tradition. The founders that we're learning about then become our ancestors, people who pass something down to us. Those traditions remain important even after new member education is over. I remember last spring I went on a hike. It was 2:00 in the morning, and a few of us decided that we were just going to leave the house and go on a hike. We found a place to hike for the sunrise, and while we were climbing up the hill at 4:00 in the morning we started singing one of our songs that we had all learned during new member education. It was a magical thing. The traditions are there to sustain that sense of magic, that sense of doing something special to us. Traditions are really powerful in that regard.

Pretty much everybody in here could rattle off a handful of key facts, even the guys who you would think are the least involved or care the least about history in general. Everybody is bound together by knowing some of these things, and feeling them.

In new member education when you study this stuff, you come across knowledge that not a lot of people have. Our books and stuff, they're only here at this house. It's really hard to get a hold of them. You're coming across stuff that's really special and unique, and you're one of the small handful of people in the grand scheme of things that gets to know these things.

You can even see that from the way things play out after guys graduate college. There's guys who are eighty years old who can come back here, and they start crying when they see what's going on at the house, when they see that what they did in college is still going on. The alumni have a life of their own. The conventions, the meetings they have, are just so awesome. This stuff really does stick.

Q. How does Sigma Phi cultivate a sense of devotion?

I think it starts off as devotion to the rituals and the traditions and then, by extension, it becomes devotion to each other. Those two things happen concurrently, because when you're pledging you're learning traditions, but you also become committed to the other people, and you're becoming committed to helping the other people learn the traditions. Learning the traditions becomes a collective process among the pledges. Devotion is an important word because it characterizes the way that guys approach being involved here.

For the guys who are in here, this is their bedrock involvement at the university. We do all kinds of stuff. We have club athletes. We have guys who run philanthropy organizations. We have people doing really serious research in class, but this fraternity is their foundation. It's their support network.

Another important thing is that all of us are at the house a lot. Guys are around each other all the time. Guys are constantly in this building, so you develop a sense of belonging to this place and it becomes part of your identity. It becomes inextricable from your identity.

There's nobody here who hasn't done anything to get involved. Everybody gets inspired to become involved in some capacity. The social chair, for instance, hears input from fifteen or so people who are interested in providing input on how to conduct our social events, and then a lot of them will help out in setting it up. The cleanups are a team effort. There's probably twenty brothers in here who have had a significant hand in the pledging process. Guys want to spend their free time doing stuff with the fraternity. There's been nights where our meetings, our elections and everything, didn't end until 4:00 in the morning because guys are willing to have those conversations until the conversation is over, no matter when it ends.

Between the pledging experience and the sorts of bonds and the sorts of traditions that you get involved in over the course of your brotherhood, guys end up pouring their entire heart and soul into this fraternity. It's cool to see. I never thought that people would care as much as they do about a fraternity, but they do, and it's real, and it makes it a lot of fun.

For the most part, we're each other's closest friends in life at this point. We see each other on good days and bad days, so I think everybody in this house has a story of a day when they were really going through it. For instance, our guy Kayvon, who is the president of the IFC, was dealing with a lot of crazy stuff earlier this semester. The university was putting pressure on him to restrict rush, and the chapters were putting counterpressure on him to not restrict rush. He was between a rock and a hard place, and things were getting kind of nasty. But our brotherhood banded behind Kayvon, and guys were here for him. We were talking to him constantly. We were offering him support, as one example. Even in the last few days, I think of people who have been dealing with difficult problems in their life. Guys are in their room, checking on them, "How are you doing?" Giving advice and stuff like that. We are really sensitive to each other's ups and downs, and we're really supportive in those situations.

There have been a lot of tears shed here. There's been a lot of arguments. There's been a lot of reconciliations. It is a master class in human relationships and going through it with people. There are relationships that have started here at the bottom, guys who didn't like each other, who now are quite good friends and who trust each other a lot. The richness of human relationships here is above average.

Q. Will pledges feel lonely at Sigma Phi?

That's the last thing that anybody in this chapter could possibly feel, and I know chapters where guys don't feel that tightly bonded to their brothers. I know chapters here where the word "brotherhood" doesn't mean squat. But here it's so opposite. If you're a member of this chapter you couldn't possibly feel alone. You're overwhelmed by attention and friendship all the time. It's real. It's not just a talking point. That is what we do on a daily basis here. That's the nature of our interactions with each other.

Q. What does excellence look like at Sigma Phi?

It goes back to the very beginning of our story. Our founders, when they were looking around Union College and the other colleges that started up chapters, were looking for people who would be men of strong character and high ideals. They didn't want to be associating and forming a club with a bunch of losers. They wanted to be around high quality men. The idea was that being around each other would have an iron sharpening iron effect. One of our greatest brothers was Elihu Root. He was a Secretary of State for the United States, among many other things. He emphasized this point: that by associating with each other we're actually improving ourselves. We're becoming better human beings by our association.

What that looks like today, in the twenty-first century, is brothers and pledges hopping in a car and going to the gym together and working out, strengthening body and mind in a side-by-side fashion. We have debates around the dinner table about politics, about the university, about Sigma Phi, so we're challenging each other intellectually. I think we have four guys who are on the IFC governing board, which is like half the IFC governing board. We host guest speakers now for the express purpose of coming in here and inspiring us to be better men. That is the point of these guest lectures.

When we introduce the history of Sigma Phi to our pledges, we emphasize the great things that Sigs have done in the past: winning wars, founding major organizations, getting involved in the world in a courageous way. College is the time when a boy turns into a man, and your fraternity is going to have a huge influence on how that goes for you, whether you want it to or not.

Our determination is for Sigma Phi to have a positive influence on that process, and by emphasizing excellence, and using all these resources that we have to promote excellence I think that we're doing that in a meaningful way.

Q. What is the community at Sigma Phi like?

It's really special. You can take it for granted. I know that I do. After spending enough time here you take for granted the nature of these relationships, but it really is weird how positive things are amongst each other.

One night we were at the Virginian Restaurant. When we walked in we had Kayvon with us and a bunch of other guys, and we announced that Kayvon just became the president of the IFC. Our whole section erupted in clapping and everything. That was an electric night.

Word gets around like that when something good happens to somebody. Whether they got accepted to a program here, or they won an election, birthdays, guys make a huge deal out of it. It's so much fun.

When you see somebody in the house, your first instinct is to start laughing, and to have a friendly and warm conversation. I'm going to miss living here. At the end of this semester I'm out. I'm going to live in an apartment with some people. That'll be fun too, but I'm going to miss being in this atmosphere where it's all love, all friendship, all fun, laughter all the time.

Q. Why do fraternities have a bad reputation?

The bad rap doesn't come from nowhere. There's a lot of fraternities where things like constantly being drunk and insulting women happens on a regular basis. There's a lot of organizations where the brothers are not looking for much more than an opportunity to do those things. There's a lot of places and a lot of guys who went to college and that's what they want out of their fraternity. Guys at those houses are going to do bad things to people, including each other. These are the people who overdose on drugs together. These are the people who send each other to the hospital hazing, and then it stains the reputation of everybody.

To a certain extent, fraternities are always going to be slightly transgressive because we're doing things like new member education, and that's always going to have a hazy public impression. But it does not have to be destructive. It's supposed to be positive, and it can be positive. What we try to do here is have a strong sense of purpose about what we do, about brotherhood, tradition, and excellence at life. You can take the procedures that we do as a fraternity and spin it in a destructive direction, but you can also spin it in a positive direction. That's the choice that an organization has to make.

It's also important to point out that a lot of fraternities get a bad rap as collateral damage for mistakes that other people are making. The mistreatment of female guests at a fraternity house, for instance, often takes place at the hands of a non-brother. It's a guy that got into a party and is not a member of the organization, and in those scenarios the house where it happened is going to suffer, and they hopefully learn a lesson. They need to be careful of who they let in.

Our fraternity, for instance, maintains a list of people who are not allowed in here, and during parties we maintain control of who enters the building. We have a bunch of sober brothers whose job it is to be vigilant about what's going on inside. In our bathrooms we have fliers telling people what they should do if they feel unsafe. There's a word you say to a certain person at a certain spot in the house, and that's your signal that you need some help.

Then we impart strongly on new members that there is zero tolerance for impropriety with anybody. You cannot try to extract from people what they don't want to give you. You cannot force yourself on anybody. You cannot approach social interactions with girls or guys in that manipulating kind of way. You have to build a culture where that is considered totally gross and antithetical to what you're about. If you build that culture strong enough you shouldn't have problems. Then you have to make sure that you guard the door well enough at parties. That's why people who don't have that kind of training are not coming in here.

Q. What kind of reputation should pledges expect?

That was something that I spoke to our pledges about on day one of them being here. At that point, even just as pledges, not even as brothers yet, everything that you do is now something that Sigma Phi is doing. You've taken on a brand now. You've taken on this larger identity. You now have a name attached to you that is like a magnet for people to attach attributes to.

People love to say this fraternity is this way, that fraternity is that way. Everything that these guys do is going to have an impact on our brand, and that can have enormous consequences. That determines in future years who's going to rush. You're going to have a bunch of guys who are going to hear this house is for these people and no longer rush there.

You have to be so careful about that. Reputation sticks. You make a mistake in 2005, you're going to feel the effects of that in 2022. It's truly hard to get rid of that stuff. To a certain extent, every chapter deals with reputation because we're all fraternities, and so people are going to throw the same accusations at everybody. But you have to be vigilant about that, and we do our very best. We make it a super serious message to the pledges that they cannot screw up with our name attached to them.

Messaging is so important with people. Pledging is all about the brothers putting on this big program. It's all about messaging, and communicating, and demonstrating this is what we're about, and having the pledges receive that, and respond to it. Crafting the messaging in that way is the name of the game.

Q. What should people think when they hear "Sigma Phi"?

What I want is for the Sigma Phis at UVA to be men who are an example of how to be. Guys who carry a presence. They walk into a room, and people think, "This is a serious person, this is a put-together person who is here with us now." Guys who speak well, who visibly care about others around them. Guys who are using their put-togetherness to lift up the people around them, guys who are dependable. Physical fitness is important too. It's a sign that you have discipline and that you work, and it's part of presence. Being somebody who looks capable of things is part of your presence, and that makes you a more powerful person socially.

The brand of the fraternity should be excellence as men in all these different capacities, and we should have a reputation for being that, and also for being really good brothers to each other. It should be obvious, it should be maybe even be annoying how clear it is that we have these deep friendships with each other, and that we care about each other. That's where a lot of the inspiration to improve comes from anyway. It comes from people caring about you. That's what I think our brand ought to be, and I think that people are internalizing that here, and I think that we're making positive steps in that direction.

Q. What's the pitch for Sigma Phi? What kind of guys are you looking for?

I wish that we were able to give a pitch like that at the informational meeting. We do things kind of weird here. We even talked in November about advertising and putting together social media stuff. For some reason, fraternities at UVA don't do that, so anybody who does that is then being weird and being out of bounds, so I wish we had that opportunity.

But I do deliver a pitch during the early rounds of rush, and I do give little commentaries about what we're about, what you can think of us as, when I meet guys for the first time.

What I would tell somebody who's rushing is if you're trying to join a fraternity at UVA you should join Sigma Phi if you're the type of guy who's in this for more than the superficial perks. If all you care about is being popular and having a fancy name, then there's other places that are going to do that better than we can. If you want a group that's just about hanging out, you just want to smoke and watch TV, other places are going to do that better.

This is the fraternity to join if you want to develop real lifelong brothers, and brothers meaning something real, not just some term, that will inspire you and help you as you grow into a man. Sigma Phi brothers care about each other in a way that is extraordinary, and it's going to be something really different that you'll experience for the first time in your life. If that's what you're here for, then this is the kind of place to go.

What we look for is guys who are interested in that, because it's easy to tell. It's easy to tell during rush if somebody is there for stupid reasons or if somebody is there because they're going to become actually an important part of your life.

We look for guys who have a positive attitude. We want to see guys who are smiling, who in conversation are interested in the brothers. It's a turnoff when guys come in there and think that they're a big deal, when they have just met you and they're a freshman and they're trying to sell themselves to you. Be interested in us. Be interested in what we have going on here. It's very easy to tell who has that kind of humble spirit.

Then, of course, we look for guys who are good candidates with what we're trying to do with excellence. We want guys who demonstrate that they're interested in becoming better men, guys who are interested in stuff in school, who have stuff to say about their classes, who have stuff to say about subjects they're interested in, history, science, whatever.

Guys who demonstrate an interest in physical fitness are great, too. We want to see that you're passionate about life, that you're passionate about getting better as a person, because then that means that you're going to really succeed in what we're trying to do here.

Rush is two weeks. We're trying hard to learn more about people than we can in that time period, but you can tell enough about somebody in order to make a judgment there. That's who I would invite to join Sigma Phi, and so far I think that's who joins. I love our pledges here. It's a good crop, and they are demonstrating that they care about this, and they want to be part of this.

Q. What will you remember after graduation?

The memories that are going to stick out to me the most are going to be the times when guys were really going through it, when guys were depending on us, and when I was depending on the guys to lift ourselves up—and when brothers came through and did that.

I can remember back in the fall when I had a big decision to make in my personal life in terms of career track, and I was torn up about what to do and making the decision was driving me nuts. The support and encouragement of a handful of brothers here was crucial in helping me get through that. Once I made that decision, it was crucial in helping me settle myself down and get back on track and focus on what I then had to do going forward.

Guys get dumped by long-time girlfriends and then they need a shoulder to cry on. They need somebody to listen up and say, "Hey, you're still worth it. You're still your own guy. You're still everything you were before." They fall short of their career goals and then they need somebody to remind them that you're not worthless because you didn't get the job or whatever. You still have opportunities.

You could make a mistake. You could do something wrong and then you need somebody to help you get back on track, and forgive yourself, and be forgiven. These are the human moments that I'm going to remember from this house, and I'm going to impart on my kids and on anybody else I talk to who wants to join a fraternity or is interested in joining a fraternity.

You're going to have these human moments that are going to give you friends that will continue to be there for you in that way long after you've graduated college. This experience doesn't end when you graduate. Like I was talking about with the alumni, people continue to be each other's best friends in life.

This experience has taught me how to be there for people and how to dedicate myself to others in a way that I know I would not have gotten without being here. I know that because of this experience I'm going to be a lot better at doing those things in the future, both with a family and with friends, and with the people at my job. I can't overstate what kind of difference this makes.

9

Alpha Sigma Phi, Clemson University

C had Frick grew up in Gaithersburg, Maryland. In 2021, he served as
president of Sigma Phi at Clemson University. A major in business management with a minor in history, he thinks "well-run fraternities promote
heroic masculinity," and that Alpha Sigma Phi already practices it. "A good,
strong fraternity will provide young men, particularly freshman and sophomores, with positive male role models who they can actually emulate, who
are close in age, and have similar lifestyles." Despite the many stereotypes, he
also doesn't think most Greeks are irresponsible. "In politics, they talk about
the silent majority," he says, "and the silent majority of Greek life are the
people looking for a social group that they can be a part of and grow themselves in." Under Chad's leadership his fraternity won awards at Clemson for
Alumni Development, Chapter Development, Fraternity and Sorority Life
Involvement, Philanthropic Service, and Scholastic Achievement.

Q. What drew you to Clemson?

When I was in high school, it was during the year that Hunter Renfrow
had that game-winner against Alabama, which put it on my radar. I love an
underdog story, I think we all do. I kind of wanted to be an underdog, and
I associated Clemson with underdogs. Senior year, I was thinking of where
I should go, where I should apply. I was driving home from school and a
Jimmy Buffet song came on. It's called "Boat Drinks." The song ends with

Jimmy Buffet saying, "I got to go where it's warm," and I thought, "Okay, you know what? Maybe I should do that. Maybe I should go south for school."

I wanted a school that was both academically challenging and social, a balance between having fun and being productive. I think Clemson offers that better than any other school in the country. I came and did a college visit with my best boy from high school, Jake Whitman. In the poem "Something in These Hills," Joe Sherman is saying that there's something in these hills that draws people here. There's a magnetic pull to Clemson, and we both felt that. I felt that. That's why I came to Clemson. It was the only school I officially visited. I thought, "All right, this is it. And I'm going to come here if I get in."

Q. Why join a fraternity?

I was 100 percent not going to join a fraternity. Never once considered it; it was an easy no. That's because I only heard the bad parts, those extreme outlier stories about ridiculous groups of kids who don't represent the whole group. The only reason I'd never heard or understood the benefits of a fraternity is because I'd never known anyone in one.

I think another reason I might have been reluctant is that I understood the stereotype surrounding people with the name "Chad." I was perhaps reluctant to fall into this trap, and I openly rebelled against the idea of fraternities because I didn't want to be a stereotypical Chad.

Jake Whitman was my roommate. He knew that he was going to join one. And I said, "No, there's no way." But he talked me into it and said, "You're doing yourself a disservice if you don't." There's another funny story: Behind the Esso Club, he said, "You're going to love it. You're going to regret not doing it." And he turned out to be right.

Q. How would you compare your friendships in high school to the ones you have here?

Fortunately for me, I had pretty strong friendships in high school. But I think the main difference was that in high school I had five best friends and then maybe twenty or twenty-five guys who I was close with outside of those core five. While at Alpha Sig the difference is just the scale. I have a hundred best friends here, and I feel this level of closeness with a hundred guys that I felt with my best friends in high school. I think the reason for that is when I was looking at it from the back end, as someone who served on the executive board with a bunch of my pledge brothers, we're all succeeding and currently progressing toward a common goal together, and that goal being improving the fraternity. I think that that's what binds us together: we're all on the same path. Whereas in high school, there are certain guys who are your friends, but they want to do certain things. But here, all working towards a common goal really unites us.

Q. Why are fraternities good for college men?

If you know someone in a fraternity who is a terrible person, then he was a terrible person before joining the fraternity and the fraternity didn't make him that way. However, there are fraternities that harbor and allow that kind of behavior. Those fraternities are the problem, because if that behavior is condoned, then it's allowed to grow. The fraternities you hear about on the news cause trouble with loud mouths, hedonism, and alcohol. And you only hear about them because they tend to be the most arrogant, the most obnoxious and the loudest. And I assure you that those fraternities are the outliers. In politics, they talk about the silent majority, and the silent majority of Greek life are the people looking for a social group that they can be a part of and grow themselves in.

I think well-run fraternities promote heroic masculinity. What I mean by that is that a good, strong fraternity will provide young men, particularly freshman and sophomores, with positive male role models who they can actually emulate, who are close in age and have similar lifestyles. For instance, if your role model was JFK or Ronald Reagan or The Rock, you might never be the president of the United States or a movie star. So what you learned from them or admire about them might not directly translate into your life as a college student. You might never be a movie star, but you will be a junior or senior in college one day, and it's helpful to have role models who are juniors and seniors in college.

The reason I say that is because when I was a freshman, there were older brothers in the fraternity that I looked up to. They're well respected, well spoken, carried themselves well, accomplished great feats in a short amount of time, guys with lofty goals, guys who want to save the world. Everyone loves them. That was who I wanted to become, and the fraternity allowed me to learn firsthand from them in a casual setting just by observing and interacting with them. That's one of the many reasons that I believe fraternities are good, because they promote heroic masculinity.

Q. What is the rush process like?

The rush process is pretty much the same for all IFC fraternities at Clemson. They'll register for rush, and then we'll have a large event called Smokers at Tiger Park, which is a relatively flat grassy area here in Clemson. At Smokers, fraternities will bring their large, open-sided pavilion style tents. Ours is 20 foot by 30 foot, which is the standard. Some are bigger and smaller. We'll all go set those up at Tiger Park, and then rushees, or potential new members, will come in. Freshman and sophomores meet the fraternities, walk around, and get to know a bunch of guys.

If our fraternity likes them, we will then vote later that day and decide if we want to send them to our first round. We usually do the first round at our fraternity house, but some do it at a bar. It gets more selective as you go on, and the group of potentials gets smaller. After the first round is the final round, and after the final round they get voted on. If they deserve and get a bid it's up to them to decide if they want to accept it or if they want to accept a different fraternity's bid. That's how rushing formally works for IFC fraternities.

What a lot of fraternities do here is have the pledges meet all the brothers. We schedule a time for them to meet with brothers through an interview setting. They'll sit down with them, they'll learn their name, hometown, and then there'll be a couple serious questions about their goals for after college, who their role model is, stuff like that. And guys can kind of pick and choose their serious questions. It serves two purposes. The first is that now a pledge or brother should never be nervous in a professional interview because they've done a hundred of them. Second, they get to know the brothers. It'd be easy for a brother to not come around for those eight weeks and never meet one of his future brothers. This serves the purpose of allowing everyone to meet all the brothers.

The pledge process cannot extend greater than eight weeks, so all fraternitieshere are done before eight weeks. And the pledge process isn't the way it looks in Animal House where you have to drink this handle or "I won't like you and respect you."

Q. How did you avoid drinking?

I don't drink alcohol at all, and I wasn't ever forced to. I live the lifestyle of a social college drinker, but I do everything except the actual consumption of alcohol. I'm the only person I know here at Clemson who doesn't drink alcohol. It's a choice that I made, and I'm strong and firm in my resolve and

I believe that the choice is right for me. I don't really have a problem. I get guys who will say, "Oh, you don't drink?" And I'll say, "Yeah." That's just part of it. Being confident in that decision is the way that I was able to get this far doing it. Like I said, I do everything except the actual drinking of the alcohol. And I think that's why I was able to get so far.

Q. Why Alpha Sigma Phi?

The football season started before my freshman year. I mentioned before that I hadn't known anyone in a fraternity. I had known someone in a fraternity, but I never knew he was in a fraternity, and I hadn't seen him since high school. When I came to Clemson he said, "Hey, come by my fraternity's tailgate." So I went to this tailgate, met a lot of people, shook a lot of hands, and it was kind of awkward at first. Everyone there was from two separate fraternities, so I was trying to figure out who was in Alpha Sig and who was not.

Then I ended up sitting next to this guy named Jake Edwards. He was a senior while I was a freshman. To paint the picture, our tent is up in the back-yard behind the Esso Club on Oak Street. He was smoking a cigarette towards the back of the tailgate. Somehow I ended up talking to him, and he started asking me about what I'm interested in, what I'm looking for in a fraternity. I realized, "You know what? I'm not really sure. Wasn't even thinking about rushing one." The way that Jake Edwards portrayed himself to me was that he's the luckiest man in the world that Alpha Sig chose him, that he doesn't belong there, but he's glad to be there. I thought that was interesting.

And then we started talking about politics. He told me that the previous summer he had worked for Senator Tim Scott in the Senate, and that he got that job through Alpha Sig. He said, "Now I want you to look at me." And I was looking at him the whole time. I said, "What do you mean?" He's said, "I'm a big, bumbly, clumsy guy, got bad facial hair, kind of balding. Look what Alpha Sig did for me. Imagine what it can do for you." And I said, "Wow, okay. I guess that's exactly what I needed." That was the catalyst. I realized, "Damn, I guess I have to rush Alpha Sig."

Q. What parts of Alpha Sig's mission are your favorites?

I would describe our guys as fun loving, but who still care about their future. They're not going to throw away their future or their potential or their opportunities for some four-year long bender, four-year long party, or whatever it might be. Our value proposition and competitive advantage, aside from the integrity and authenticity of our brothers, is our geographic diversity. Talk about campus and community involvement, leadership, and a culture of continuous self-improvement. What I've liked to say is that if you started in Massachusetts, drove all the way down the east coast of Georgia, and your car breaks down or you got a flat tire at any point, there will always be a brother within an hour that will pick you up. That means that they'd be close enough to do it, and that they'd be willing to do it because they're your brother. We also have guys in the Midwest, guys in Wyoming, Illinois, Michigan, Ohio. We talk about our geographic diversity a lot. The reason for that is because fraternities here at Clemson are strictly Northern, strictly Southern, strictly DMV, whatever it might be. But we like to have a bunch of different people so we can have diversity of thought and all that. That's what college is all about: meeting new people.

We also talk about campus and community involvement, particularly on campus. We're pretty involved in student government. Last year, we pulled off the Alpha Sig three-peat. The student body president, Jonathan Gundana, was an Alpha Sig. The year before, the student body vice president, Andrew Kwasny, was an Alpha Sig. And then the year before him the student body president, Mason Foley, was also in Alpha Sig. That was what we were looking to pull off. And we accomplished that.

Community involvement as well. We sponsored 12-mile Park, which is a public park here in Clemson. We clean it every Sunday just to keep it looking natural and beautiful. There was trash floating in the lake and on the lakeside. We pick it up and make sure that there's no evidence of people ever having been there. And then leadership. In every realm, being an Alpha Sig has been a masterclass in leadership. What I tell potential rushees is that if they want to become a leader and they think they're not there yet, or if they believe they are and they want to improve, joining Alpha Sig will really help them because they'll get to learn from some of the best leaders on campus.

The last thing I'd say is the culture of self-improvement. We always send in our group chat that graph emoji where it's trending upward. One story I'll tell is this: Payton Griffin, a brother in my pledge class, is an incredible speaker and a very impressive individual. He's just a guy I'm proud to call my friend and brother. He was asked by president Clements' son to travel around the United States, go to high schools and be a recruiter for the football team. He turned that down and he couldn't give me a good explanation, but that's how impressive he is. We were doing our final round of rush at the Sky Box, which is our fraternity house. We sent Payton out to give a speech, trying to give these guys the persuasive hard sell. We know that he is good at it because he is a great speaker. He said what I just told you about geographic diversity, what sets us apart from others, and gave the whole speech. Everyone loved it. We're all clapping. Rushees were all clapping. He turned away from the little stage we had set up, and then went back and said, "And we throw bangers." The reason I thought that was important is because that was an afterthought for us at Alpha Sig, and I think that is what distinguishes us. If you go through rush, obviously you want to party. Obviously, you want to meet girls, have a good time with your friends at college, and we do that. We definitely do that. Thursday, Friday, Saturday, and then the rest of the week is spent planning Thursday, Friday, Saturday. But that's not the most important thing to us, and I believe that's what makes us distinctive. Like I said, it's a balance between having a ton of fun and self-improvement.

Q. What does brotherhood mean for you all?

Since I mentioned Payton Griffin, I'm going to keep bragging about him and tell another story about him. Last year, I didn't have a car here at Clemson, and Payton Griffin did. There are a lot of places that you'd want to go at Clemson. I have a note of rides that I owe Payton because he drove me around so many times sophomore year. I'm at sixteen right now. That's just one example of what it means to be a brother. This guy picked me up sixteen different times to take me where I wanted to go, even when he didn't have to go there.

Another good example would be Alex Murtha, who was an older brother. He was a senior when I was a freshman. Didn't have to get involved with me, didn't have to know the freshmen. He had a job lined up for after college and could have not met or cared about any of us. But, instead, he decided to meet all of us. He's a pretty good guitar player and I told him, "Hey, I want to learn guitar. I'm not very good. I have a basic understanding, but I don't know any music theory." And he would FaceTime me every Sunday, even after he graduated, just to teach me music theory while he was busy with his rocket science NASA job in Huntsville, Alabama.

Those are just two examples, and I could keep going. It's guys that care about each other and want each other to succeed the way that you would want your biological brother to succeed. You want to promote your family, and these guys are our family.

Q. What does silence mean at Alpha Sig?

That's our first value. There's a quote: "To develop the strength to embrace silence." Strength is emphasized, implying that strength is required to embrace silence. What I mean is that embodying the idea of silence is difficult, and it does require strength. It's easier to run your mouth, say whatever you want, talk to trash, belittle others, whatever it might be, than to be silent. But the value of silence leads a brother to be more intentional with everything that he's saying. I think it was Plato who said, "Wise men speak because they have something to say. Fools speak because they have to say something."

And the values are also open for some level of personal interpretation. Some people believe that the less you speak, the more powerful your voice is. When there's chaos going on in a room, they're probably going to look to whoever's sitting confidently, silently, and they'll ask for his opinion. What is interesting about silences is that it's the opposite of what you expect fraternities to be promoting. Fraternities are associated with noise, loud music, yelling, chanting. But embodying and respecting the value of silence calls a brother to be introspective, be reflective; a certain degree of self-reliance and independence when you're not sharing absolutely everything about you to everyone all the time comes from that. Silence is also being conscientious about what you say.

I spoke a little bit about how being in Alpha Sig will make you a better leader. I think part of what good leaders have in common is that they're usually great orators. They're good at speaking. It's a social advantage to be able to know when to use silence and know when to use your voice, and that's something that pledges learn pretty early on.

If someone's talking trash to you, your instinct is to talk back. But you might end up in trouble, get in a fight, get arrested, whatever it might be. It's more difficult to say nothing than it is to say something. The older brothers have the responsibility to say, "Hey, calm down. You have to be stronger than whatever this guy is telling you."

When you're silent, you have more time to listen. When you're talking, you can't listen. It makes our guys better listeners and everyone loves a good listener. I think it's Albert Einstein who said, "The world will not be destroyed by those who do evil, but through those who watch them without saying anything." That's not us, that's not what we mean by silence. We mean don't say anything ridiculous. There's no reason to talk just for the sake of talking. But this shouldn't be confused with looking on as a bystander, not using your voice when you need to.

Q. What does purity mean at Alpha Sig?

One of the quotes that we're told from maternity is that brothers should consistently strive for purity of mind, body, and soul. I give that one a modern interpretation. There's a lot of mental, moral, spiritual pollution out there. Social media is an obvious one. You can pollute your mind with these kinds of things, or you can have a pure mind where you're reflective and you use your own thoughts, come to your own opinions and you don't allow others to influence them negatively.

Somebody who's pure of mind is someone who knows the direction that they are headed, and using that mindset puts himself in the best situation to get there. I think you need a direction and a destination to be able to end up where you want to go, and our values provide that direction. And because we have values, we're able to understand the direction we want to go.

Q. What does "honor" mean to Alpha Sig?

We believe that every action should be governed with a high sense of honor. Everything you do should never be slimy, nothing like that. You should always be thinking of this value and understanding the importance of it. I would describe a man of honor as someone with personal integrity, and the type of guy who, when he says he is going to do something, that means he's going to do it. Personal integrity would be a pretty easy trait to associate with heroic masculinity, because there seems to be a lack of integrity. If you watch the news, whatever side you agree with, you can see a lack of integrity on both sides in politics and the business world, whatever it might be. Personal integrity is something that the world needs more of.

An honorable man is also someone who lives up to the promises that he's made to himself and others. If he says he's going to do something, he's going to do it. That includes sacrificing on behalf of others. I believe that someone with honor understands that they're not here for themselves alone. Their personal honor does matter, but they also have to honor those who went before them, those who will come after them, and the fraternity that gave them the platform, the ability to succeed, and opportunities. A man of honor is someone who's ethical, honest, trustworthy, and has a great deal of personal integrity. And like I kind of mentioned with silence, it's on every brother to hold every other brother accountable.

Q. What advantages does diversity provide?

We're don't think, "Oh, this kid is from a state that we don't know anyone from yet. Let's give him a bid." It happens pretty naturally, and it's just that people from different areas happen to like the brotherhood and are willing to join. We don't bid based on: "Oh, this kid's from Chicago. We don't have a Chicago kid yet. Let's get him in here." It's along the lines of, "No, this kid likes us. We like him. He's a good individual. Doesn't really matter where he is from. We're going to bring him in if we think that he can do a good job and promote this fraternity."

The reason I think geographic diversity benefits the brotherhood is because of the diversity of thought that it exposes brothers to, as well as the opportunity that it provides each of us. For instance, if I had come to Clemson, joined a fraternity of only Maryland kids or only DMV-area kids, only kids from north of South Carolina, I would've had far fewer perspectives to hear since we all live similar lifestyles, would've gotten in less disagreements, and learned a lot less.[1] But because of Alpha Sig, I know someone from Wyoming, I know someone in Georgia, South Carolina, North Carolina, Illinois, Michigan, Boston. And I probably could have gone my whole life without meeting anyone from wherever, the Midwest, Wyoming. But now I have friends there, and it gives me a reason to go there and see other parts of the country, which is something that I've always wanted to do, and now I have an excuse to do it.

I also mentioned the opportunities that it provides us. I had never even heard of the city of Charlotte, North Carolina. I knew about Raleigh, Durham, Wilmington, but there are so many guys in our fraternity from Charlotte. I went and visited Charlotte and loved it, and it's a place that I could see myself going and living after college. I wouldn't have had that opportunity had I not known someone from North Carolina who had lived there.

It's important to be in a group that isn't homogenous, and a reason for that is because it promotes you identifying yourself as an individual and proving yourself as an individual. You can't just be a DMV kid forever, a Southern kid forever, Northern kid forever. You have to distinguish yourself as an individual. I believe that having people who are unlike you does that already. We have one kid from Wyoming. Yes, it's cool that he is from Wyoming, but he also has to distinguish who he is as someone beyond that.

Q. Why do fraternities have a bad reputation?

The primary reason would probably be the media. *Animal House* is a bunch of raucous guys trying to one-up the administration. As well as movies like *American Pie*. I also think that people are sometimes looking for someone to get mad at, or to assign blame to. A pretty easy target is what is perceived to be a bunch of daddy's money, pretty boys gelling their hair, living carefree lives and then not having to worry about it because it won't ever catch up to them. And I think it's easy to be envious of people like that, and I definitely

---

1. "DMV" is an acronym for the District of Columbia, Maryland, Virginia. It's used to refer to the Greater Washington D.C. area.

understand that, but once again, guys like that are the outliers. I mentioned the silent majority before, and they don't make up the silent majority. I'd say the media and then the few loud in-your-face people are problematically enforcing that stereotype, or reinforcing that stereotype.

Q. *What should people think when they hear "Alpha Sig?"*

What currently happens if I mention to someone or someone asks and I tell them that I'm an Alpha Sig, they'll ask, "Oh, do you know this person?" And they'll be excited that I also know them. It's funny because obviously we all know each other, so it's always, "Yes, I know them." If you think of the Clemson football team, maybe you'll associate it with success, but more likely you'll probably think of a good memory that you had at a football game or watching it. What I really want with Alpha Sig is that when someone hears the name Alpha Sig or meets someone who is an Alpha Sig, they'll be able to tell a story and share a good memory that they have about Alpha Sig.

Q. *What's the pitch for Alpha Sig? What kind of guys are you looking for?*

It's those four competitive advantages: geographic diversity, community and campus involvement, leadership, and a culture of self-improvement. The type of guys that we're looking for, if you are ambitious, courageous, a young man that's interested and committed to developing himself and self-improvement, then you should definitely join Alpha Sig because you're looking for us and we're looking for you. If you are a leader or you want to become one, Alpha Sig is definitely the place for you.

We're looking for guys who give a damn. What I mean by that is everyone thinks it's cool to not care. We want guys who care, and we want guys who give a damn about themselves, about us, about the school, about the community, about the country, about the world, and we want people who are going to make the world better. We have a lot of them here, and of course we want more. Future leaders of America, that's who are looking for; young men who are looking to get it more than they take.

One thing that my pledge brother Anthony Donato told me is, "If you get 1 percent better every day, it'll only take a hundred days for you to be twice as good." We're looking for guys who are willing to do that, and if you want to do that, we'll be able to help you do that.

Q. What will you remember after graduation?

I'll have so many stories to share. So much fun was had, and so much growing was done. In terms of the impact that it had on me, I believe that anything of consequence or of importance that I accomplish, and any good that I might put into the world, will be a result of what I learned from Alpha Sig. And presumably, I don't want to be doing it alone. I want to be successful in creating good in the world with my brothers. I think that that's what Alpha Sig has really allowed me to do, and will allow me to do in the future.

10

Alpha Phi Alpha, Clemson University

J amison Taylor was elected Alpha Phi Alpha president in 2021. A native of Washington, D.C. and a second-generation Alpha Phi, he majored in operations management at Clemson. He thinks fraternities can be inspiring. "When you think of some of the most notable leaders, particularly within the black community, a lot of them are members of Greek organizations. You think of Dr. King, you think of Thurgood Marshall, who both are brothers of Alpha Phi Alpha," he says. "When you come here to campus," he adds, "one of the brothers in a fraternity might be one of the next civil rights leaders or want to be the next big activist."

Q. What drew you to Clemson?

I came to Clemson after my father took me on a college tour. I fell in love with the school and felt like I could make an impact. I looked at Hampton, I looked at Virginia Tech, UVA, UNC, all on the East Coast. But I really loved Clemson.

There's a family atmosphere. Despite some of the things you might hear about the South and some of the stigmas and conflict that there is, I felt like I belonged at Clemson. I felt like I could make a change and impact here on this campus. I was excited to come here.

Q. Why join a fraternity?

My father, he's a member of the fraternity as well, so I would always see his stuff around the house and I'd ask him what it is. And he said, "When you get old enough, I'll tell you." It wasn't until I actually got on campus and I saw the Alphas that I realized, "That's my dad's fraternity." That's how I got interested.

I don't even think I recall knowing anything about fraternities, just that my father was a member of one. All of his close friends joined the same fraternity. That's the extent of what I knew. I didn't know what Greek life was in college.

Q. How do your high school friendships compare to your Alpha Phi Alpha friendships?

I think when you make friends in high school, most of the time guys are in the same circle. I went to DeMatha Catholic High School and played on the football team. Pretty much all of my friends were on the football team; they were the guys I spent time with. I had my friends from back when I was younger, and I spent more time with them than I spent with my friends in high school. But the fraternity is a more diverse subgroup and brotherhood of men. We all have these commonalities, we're all members of Alpha Phi Alpha, we all have a brotherly bond, but then also we have a chance to be exposed to different things. One of my brothers, he might be more into fishing, whereas myself, I'm from a city, I'm more of a city boy; I like to go out. I think it's more of a diverse group of men you surround yourself with in the fraternity.

Q. Why are fraternities good for college men?

I believe that fraternities are good because it gives the members a chance to develop both as an individual, and to develop the campus or community. I think one of the beautiful things that fraternities have is the opportunity to save the campus. When you think of some of the most notable leaders, particularly within the black community, a lot of them are members of Greek organizations. You think of Dr. King, you think of Thurgood Marshall, who both are brothers of Alpha Phi Alpha. When you come here to campus, one of the brothers in a fraternity might be one of the next civil rights leaders or want to be the next big activist. They have small beginnings from being on a campus and trying to save the campus and make it a better place for all people.

I think, not only does being a part of a fraternity shape the service aspect and community aspect of college life, but also the social aspect. A lot of the social events put on campus, not just parties, but in general, are by fraternities. And when the president of the campus wants to meet with a group of minorities to get some feedback, he's meeting with members of the Divine Nine, black Greek letter organizations.

They're coming to you to get your feedback from these other organizations, whether it be CUSG, other fraternities, or campus administration. They're coming to you to get your feedback a lot of times. There'll be meetings I have with President Clements, dinners or I'll meet with different student affairs leaders. I'll be one of the first to meet with these leaders about certain issues. Or if there's a project, I'll be asked to be a part of it and give feedback.

Q. What is the NPHC?

The National Pan-Hellenic Council. That's the governing council of all of "The Divine Nine" organizations you find on campuses. At Clemson, there are eight out of that nine right now. We have Alphas, of course, AKA, Deltas, Omega Psi Phi, Kappa Alpha Psi, Sigmas, Sigma Gamma Rho, and Zetas.

"The Divine Nine" is a group of the intercollegiate black Greek global organizations around the world. We have nine organizations around the world. When you think of prominent black leaders in black culture, a lot of them were members of our organizations. Currently the Vice President of the United States is a member of AKA, which is a first in a black collegiate sorority.

The way NPHC orientation works here at Clemson is they have a presentation held by the NPHC president. He'll lead the presentation, then he'll go through each of the organizations. Either the president or a number representative of a chapter will come give a brief synopsis of the chapter here at Clemson, the criteria, how to join and some of the aims and mission statement of the organization. Then there'll be a bigger room where it will be almost like a social setting where the different organizations will have tabling. You have a chance to talk to the brothers of the organization and learn about them in a more social setting, more open session.

Q. What is the rush process like?

Particularly at Clemson, one of the first things you have to do is go to the NPHC orientation. That way you get a chance to engage with all the organizations and learn about them, because you want to make sure you find the right fit for you, if that's something you're interested in. You want to make sure you're surrounded by a group of men that push you and challenge you or a group of women that push you and challenge you. Following that, once you make your decision after doing research, then you attend the interest meeting or awareness seminars, where you learn about the application process, the requirements, the criteria, as well as basic information about the fraternity nationally, as a whole, as well as the chapter.

Following that, you're going the organizations online portal to apply. You do the application. You need a recommender as well as a sponsor from the chapter, who have to write you letters. You also have to take a test, which you have to score a 90 percent or you can't apply again for a whole year. Then you submit all of your information and documentation, which is within this application. Then once accepted, you move into a three-week membership intake process that takes place later on throughout that semester. During the process you study the material with the brothers in the chapter and then you get tested at the end of each week, so forth and so on. Finally, you'll be initiated once you've passed all the tests with a 90 percent or above.

Q. Why Alpha Phi Alpha?

I did talk to the other organizations, but I knew right off the bat Alpha was one of the things I wanted to do. No question. Not because of the pressure from my father, but when I was younger, a lot of lessons he would instill with me were based off of the things he learned from Alpha. He always used to recite the last two lines of *Invictus,* and I used to hate it whenever he would use them. Becoming a member of the fraternity, I was able to truly learn the meaning of the last lines of that poem.

Particularly it's our ambition; not only were we the first black Greek organization in the collegiate realm to be founded, but when you think about leadership, Alpha is one the first to be leaders in most endeavors, if not all endeavors. There's always an Alpha being the first to do this, being the first to do that. Even now, the brothers we have in our chapter are always one of the first or they're leaders in whatever organization. You continue to see that trend. I think that's what makes us distinct from other organizations. We're the first to lead.

Q. What part of Alpha Phi Alpha's mission is your favorite?

One of the things that means the most from that motto is the servants of all standpoint. During my time as president what Alpha meant to me was being a servant, providing community service to others on campus, or the whole greater community. At the end of the day, that's what our organizations are founded upon and that's why we're here. Alpha originally started as a social state club to create a community where brothers or men of color can come study together. And now, thinking about the work we do, one of the things I always want to be able to do and say is, "I served, I gave back to the community."

We do it in a variety of different ways. We do mentoring for little children at the Little John Community Center, we've done highway pickups, we've done food kitchens. I think one of the most notable things we did this past year (we worked with Alpha Tau Omega, which is another IFC fraternity on campus) was to help repair a slave cemetery and support the woman whose family owns the slave cemetery, as well as the church. We sold fish fries every third Saturday to help raise money to pay off the church. There's a story, if you look up Clemson fraternities come together, and you'll hear about the story we had together. It made national headlines, it made the news.

That was so important to me because it knocked out a lot of things when you think about service. For one, it brought unity to our campus because a lot of times you don't see our two different councils work together, IFC and PHC. Then when you think about the work we did in the slave cemetery, you think about how slaves have proper burial rights and there were sticks and stones just laying there. Being able to clean that up and then have the brothers of ATO get to see that, as well as getting national attention on that. And then also supporting this woman's fundraiser for the church and bringing more attention to that so she could pay off the debt on the church.

Q. How do you stimulate each other's ambition?

As a president of the chapter at the time, one of things I wanted to do is empower the brothers in my chapter to be leaders on campus or wherever they see fit. I think of two examples in particular. One of my younger neophytes, who crossed in spring 2021, was a member of this organization called CODA, the Council on Diversity Affairs. They work hand in hand with student affairs. At the time it was during elections, so he was considering being president. There was no one else running for it or not too many. However, he was hesitant to do so. He didn't think he had the capabilities or was afraid of the workload, but I encouraged him to apply for the position, which he ended up getting. He's currently the president right now. I thought it would be a growing experience for him, having that leadership opportunity as well and working with different diverse organizations on campus. Having the experience of being a leader can help you transcend throughout the rest of your life. Regardless of how you perform, it's still a learning experience.

One of the other times I stimulated the ambitions of our members was with the vice president at the time, Gavin Vasquez. The president of student government-elect wanted to visit our Chapter and was looking to establish a Greek affairs vice president on his own council. I recommended that our Vice President be part of it, that way we have a member of our chapter be in those meetings with the student government to make decisions.

That's how these fraternities save that college experience, you have them be leaders all across campus. Currently, one of our brothers, Malik Balogun, is the president-elect for student government next year. We're able to make an impact and make changes on our campus that we want to see to bring the campus together and help all people.

Q. How do you prepare for "the greatest usefulness in humanity, freedom, and dignity of the individual"?

That means educating our members and giving them valuable experiences in life. Oftentimes when I thought about my leadership, particularly as it came towards its end, I wanted to prepare them to lead. That means allowing them to lead themselves and experience things firsthand. One of the greatest teachers in life is failure. Instead of being on top of them and almost being a helicopter person, allow them to take control and if they miss something or don't see something and it backfires, it's just a learning opportunity for them. At the end of the day, this is all a learning experience to prepare you for later in life. You get to learn, "How does the organization run? How do you plan an event?" Lead a project, work with a budget. Give them that valuable experience, that way they can take that into the real world and carry that with them.

Q. How do you encourage "the highest and noblest form of manhood"?[1]

From a fraternity standpoint, encouraging the highest and noblest form of manhood means making sure that the brothers in our chapter carry high character or high standards. This is the way you carry yourself as well as how you want to do business. Particularly around engaging with women. We're not going to have brothers who are inappropriately touching women

---

1. Alpha Phi Alpha website, https://apa1906.net/.

or disrespecting women in any way, as well as other people on campus in general. Respecting our members, respecting our differences, being open minded, and always being willing to learn how we can improve. That comes with holding each other accountable.

We have bylaws. When you have that brotherly relationship as our chapter does, we're able to come to each other one on one and say, "Hey bro, that really wasn't cool," or, "You shouldn't really do that," and brothers aren't necessarily going to take it personally. Obviously, we are young adults and we're all humans, so we have challenges. But I can constantly say that regardless, if it was my line of brothers or the chapter as a whole, I was able to work on our differences for the betterment of ourselves.

Q. How do you "aide downtrodden humanity in its efforts to achieve higher social, economic and intellectual status"?

For us that comes down to service and uplifting our campus. We do that through a variety of ways. As I mentioned before, we have leadership in different organizations. We have brothers everywhere, all across campus, leading in some shape or form or fashion. Oftentimes president, but in other ways too, whether it be on the exec board or a general member. When you think about, particularly as an undergraduate chapter, there's still problems that exist on our campus. Social justice wise or whatever you want to say. We want to be able to combat these with more members of our chapter here at Clemson, and oftentimes that means being in these rooms. These people are making the decisions, organizing protests, however they see fit. And also bringing campus together, uniting the campus and working with different organizations on campus.

Q. Why do fraternities have a bad reputation?

I think there's negative stigmas around fraternities, particularly when you think of undergraduate college life. And when you think about black fraternities, a lot of people from outside the community don't realize these are lifetime commitments. Once you become an Alpha you're going to be an Alpha until you go into Omega Chapter. When you think about it from that standpoint, that's often overlooked. Also, the work that we do as fraternities is often overlooked. Not just by the world as a whole, but also by the college community in some standpoint. You might get recognized from student affairs, but you don't see the university as a whole publicizing it as much. They might publicize the football team winning a game against a sucky team.

That's some of the reason why we have those stigmas, but then also some of those are true. There are some bad chapters, some bad apples, as you might say, that have issues or have challenges. And they need to be held accountable as such. There's no excuse for why they are doing some of the things that they do. But that isn't a representation of the fraternity, that goes completely against what the fraternity stands for. That can fall in line for a number of things, where the brothers in the chapter don't hold each other accountable, nationals doesn't hold them accountable. The brothers you decide to bring into your chapter is one thing to keep in mind too. One of our founders once said is, "Quality, not quantity." Bringing quality brothers versus quantity. It's better to have one good brother versus seven bad brothers. That can also play well as to why we have these stigmas and these issues in Greek life.

Q. What should people think when they hear "Alpha Phi Alpha"?

During my time as president, I wanted our legacy and reputation to be that we ran the campus. We were running it from the standpoint of service. We have the most service hours. We have 600 community service hours done. We have leaders across campus fighting, advocating for the student members of campus. Literally running the campus, being in the rooms that are with the president of Clemson University, the Vice Presidents. We want brothers to be there helping make those decisions or advocating for or representing the students. And then we're degrees above the rest. On Mondays, we would have brothers dress up and wear suits, just to make ourselves more distinguishable and give the perception that we are about our business and about the real work. Oftentimes, you might see fraternities or other organizations that say they are this and that, but you don't really see them working. I want our chapter to be the brothers where, you see us working, you know what we're about.

Q. What's the pitch for Alpha Phi Alpha?
What kind of guys are you looking for?

I would tell that young man that if he wants to enhance his college experience, if he wants to grow around like-minded men who have the ambition to be leaders in this world, who want to give back to community, who actually want to do the work and provide the service and advocacy for our communities, then he should be a member of Alpha Phi Alpha. Particularly here at Clemson, we are a diverse group of men; you see us everywhere, you often see us leading. At least for me, I wouldn't be the person I am today without the experience I had at Alpha Phi Alpha, through the leadership experiences, the bonds I've built through the brotherhood, even outside of fraternity. I met a lot of my friends from other brothers that were in the fraternity even before I was in the fraternity. Seeing the work we've done for this campus and the surrounding communities and the work we'll continue to do, if you have any ambition aligned with that, you should be a member of our fraternity.

Our fraternity is diverse. It's good to have a diverse group of brothers in your organization because it helps with the innovation, creative projects and impacting community and also being representative of different kinds of people. There are general commonalities that we see in the brothers that are involved. Before you become Alpha, you're involved. You're a member of different organizations. Having some leadership experience helps, it adds to the Chapter. When you think about the spirit of fraternity, it's not what the fraternity can do for you. What can you do for us, as well? Having brothers who have leadership experience or skills helps. You may not have had an executive position, but you know how to make a flyer, you're sociable, you know how to unite people involved with different organizations regardless of the level.

Academics is important as well. We see that as your college drive. You want to make sure you're graduating and you're doing well in school. It's okay to have to switch. The reason I'm staying a year longer is because I had to switch, but I was able to push myself in my academic career and be a member of this organization. Being involved, being cultured and caring about your academics is important as well.

Q. What will you remember after graduation?

I'll be talking about the bonds I've made. The brothers I've met here are my lifelong friends and some of my closest friends. They've been there during my hard times as well as the times where I was prosperous. Definitely bonds the fraternal bonds that I've built. Having that support system has been helpful. And then the same things that my father learned, the life lessons that he instilled in me. The things I've learned and experienced becoming a member, being a member, being a leader of this chapter, and the challenges you face doing that.

There were some other things going on in chapter as well. I learned about myself: "I'm not really interested in this, but I'm more so interested in this." I think being a member of this fraternity helped me grow into the person I am today, mold me to who I am, in terms of my values, the characters, my principles, some of my tastes, etc. Being more comfortable with being myself. I hope that my experience in the chapter and the work I've done for this chapter via service or leadership left the legacy of ambition, overcoming obstacles, and never counting yourself out.

11

Chi Psi, Clemson University

K ent Carroll was elected to serve as Chi Psi president in 2022. A computer science major, with a minor in cybersecurity, he is a native of Charlotte, North Carolina. He describes how his pledge class reimagined their chapter, which at the time of his pledge had shrunk to only eight brothers. "I was recruited by a couple of national guys," he explains, "who came in to try to rebuild us." In an extraordinary turn of events for new pledge class, "We were all given leadership positions." Now that they are the ones recruiting, they seek candidates who want "to better themselves." He knows the fraternity will be life-changing for the next group of pledges "because I know I'm going to be there for my brothers for the rest of my life. And I also know that they'll be there for me."

Q. Why join a fraternity?

I wanted to join one for the wrong reasons at first. I thought it was going to be fun, like a lot of partying, getting to meet girls. But it really didn't turn out to be like that for me at all, and that was really cool for me.

Definitely from the media. The media always is talking about fraternities because they're always on the news about bad things happening, and that's all you really hear about. You hear about the partying and all the drinking.

Q. How would you compare your friendships in high school to the ones you have at Chi Psi?

I'm very close to my friends in high school, I still am to this day. But my Chi Psi brothers are really like my family. It's really awesome because any Chi Psi meet that's not at Clemson, they also treat me like their brother, which is a really cool experience to have.

Q. Why are fraternities good for college men?

It's probably the best thing I think someone could be a part of in their time in college. We're giving men these leadership roles that can teach them so many skills that you wouldn't have gotten without joining a fraternity. It's pretty much like running a company, except we're all volunteers and we're all working really, really hard to further this. And it's awesome to be a part of.

Everyone's there for me. We're not just all about parties. Every guy that I have made a connection with cares about me and I care about them more than anything. We really put each other above ourselves.

Q. What is the rush process like?

At Clemson, it's a week-long process. It starts off the week with something called Smokers, where every fraternity sets up their tent outside, and anyone who's rushing can go to the tents they're interested in to meet some of the brothers. Once the Smokers is over, the fraternity will then go back and vote for the next round, for the rushees that they liked. And this round will be either at a bar or restaurant. And once again, you'll just be meeting brothers. The fraternity will then go back again and vote for the final round, which is at the fraternity house usually. And then brothers will then vote on who gets bids, and they're given out at the end of the week, so it's a very short process.

The rushees will then be able to accept or decline the bids that they're given. And then once you join a fraternity, pledging is an eight week long process of learning about the fraternity and getting to know brothers better.

Pledges are given leadership opportunities right from the start, whether that be with social events, being a part of our social committee, philanthropy committee, or brotherhood committee. They can help plan events along with us, so when they hop into positions, when they're a little bit older, they'll know how to run the fraternity. And when they're doing that, they really get to know brothers because it's like a job. It's like we're their co-workers.

We've had guys in the past who don't really have the time to do it, their time management skills aren't great, so they'll just ask to back out. And we always have great connections with them afterwards and we still talk to them to this day for the most part.

Q. Why Chi Psi?

When I first looked at Chi Psi, there were only eight active brothers. We got down to a very small number, and my pledge class was around 13 guys. And I was recruited by a couple of national guys who came in to try to rebuild us. Along with my pledge class, we all saw a lot of potential in really making a name for ourselves in Clemson because of how small we got. It was crazy how much we could do with this. And we were all given leadership positions as pledges, which is not normal for most fraternities to do. One of our vice presidents was actually a pledge at the time. I was given the Wellness chair. So we were really treated like brothers and not pledges, which is something I've never really heard of. I would just hear about the hazing. So I really saw an opportunity.

We're really distinct because of the genuine personal relationships that you make with others. And when you're being recruited, we're not trying to sell you the fraternity. We show you the incredible opportunity of lifelong friends that you'll make with our group and any Chi Psi around the nation.

Q. What's the pitch for Chi Psi? What kind of guys are you looking for?

I think anyone who's interested in rushing us should because there's no other fraternity that will give you the support and encouragement, not just through college, but also life. We are looking for any guys who are wanting to better themselves through intellectual, moral and social lives. And it will make a difference in their lives because I know I'm going to be there for my brothers for the rest of my life. And I also know that they'll be there for me.

Q. How do pledges get connected?

We have a lot of different brotherhood events, whether it's corn hole, a cook-out; we give them all these opportunities to be as close with these guys as they can be.

We definitely like for the pledges to go eat with brothers who are active in the fraternity so they get to know them better. We also encourage them to go hang out with a couple brothers a couple times a week, just to get to know them better.

Q. What's the mission of Chi Psi?

Our exact mission is to create and maintain an enduring society, which encourages the sharing of traditions and values, respect for one's self and others, and responsibility to the university and community.

One of the first things that we talk about is the values that we have at Chi Psi and how they need to be using those values every single day.

We hold each other accountable for everything that we're doing to try to make ourselves better men. And that's what our main goal is of Chi Psi, is to make better men. And if we hold each other accountable, then it's hard to mess up.

We have a culture here at Clemson Chi Psi of putting brothers above ourselves. If a brother is ever in need any time of the day or night, we are always all there for them. If they put in the group chat, "Hey, I'm really not doing well, guys," you will be flooded with texts to make sure he is okay and he's getting the help that he needs.

Q. Who needs this kind of support?

I think every guy needs some sort of support system like we have, but I don't think there is one in the world right now. And mostly, it's just fraternities or these organizations that have mental health help and stuff like that.

A pledge should . . . know he's in great hands with us, and that we're a fraternity that really cares about his college experience and his friendship, his academics, and even establishing alumni connections.

In high school, I had friends who struggled a lot with mental health, and I really saw how much it affected them. And when I first came to college, I had very similar experiences with my mental health and I saw how big of a problem it was that men don't really talk about that.

A lot of it we don't know. But we do know that men tend to have higher suicide rates and substance abuses that women don't usually have. Especially in this time at college, we're the most vulnerable to that. It's a problem that not a lot of people are trying to have initiative on or fix.

Q. What is the Gentleman's Club like?

The Gentleman's club started two years ago when I was pledging and I was the Wellness chair. We started having Gentleman's club once a week, where everyone was just welcome to talk about what's on their mind. And it really was an open space where guys can get out what's bothering them in their life socially, academically, or even physically. The wellness chair has mental health resources from our national office and from Clemson. They can be anywhere from CAPS, which is the mental health initiative on campus, or Talkspace, which is where nationals has its website where you go on anonymously and chat with someone about your mental health. And the mental health or Wellness chair's job is not to exactly give advice, but it's more to just listen and give advice if it's asked for. And it's really a place where brothers help each other and talk about their mental health.

We usually meet on Wednesday nights after everyone's done with class. It's around 8:00 PM, so everyone should've done most of their work by then. The Wellness chair will open up saying, "Does anyone have anything they really want to talk about?" Sometimes it takes a while for guys to start talking. It doesn't just have to be negative things. Some guys will talk about how they're having a great week mentally, like how they aced a test. And we really support them and cheer them on, encourage them more. But sometimes there will be guys who are struggling mentally. They can take a long time to talk, and we will all sit there and listen. There have been some meetings that went on for two hours for some guys to just talk through everything.

When I first became the Wellness chair, coincidentally, I was not doing great mentally, and no one really knew that; and I was still given the job for the Wellness chair. I was unhappy with everything. I was lonely. I was isolating myself from everyone and it was really not helping me. And I was on the verge of transferring from Clemson. I was about to start applying to other schools. And after going to Gentleman's Club for the first few weeks, I started to really get support from guys who had very similar experiences before joining Chi Psi. And we shared how we've all gone through the same thing. Because of that, it's the reason I'm still in Clemson today.

Q. What should people think when they hear "Chi Psi"?

I really want us to be a fraternity that goes beyond that negative stigma against most fraternities, and I want to be considered a welcoming environment of quality men where girls feel safe around. And that's what we love, is when girls say, "I really feel safe at Chi Psi." That really makes us feel great.

And we want our pledges to know that when they come in and graduate four years later, they'll be a better man than if he had not joined Chi Psi.

Q. What will you remember after graduation?

When I first came into Clemson, I was extremely shy and reserved, and I even had some brothers thinking I was going to drop the fraternity when I was pledging because I was just so quiet. And once I joined Chi Psi and became a leader, my social skills and my confidence skyrocketed. I would never have thought four years ago that I'd be a fraternity president. And I can honestly say that I would still be the kid too afraid to talk if it wasn't for Chi Psi.

12

Triangle, The Ohio State University

S teve Egnaczyk was elected to serve as president of Triangle in 2022. He's pursuing a double major in computer science and engineering. The Buckeye son of a Buckeye, Steve grew up in Downington, Pennsylvania. The youngest in his family and the only boy, Steve first joined Triangle because "It was just a bunch of guys having fun. That's what I really liked about it, because it reminded me of my friends back home." A special interest fraternity, Triangle is "exclusively composed of engineers, architects, and scientists. Essentially, it's a bunch of STEM majors who are academically and professionally minded. The way I like to advertise it to people is that it doesn't really feel like a fraternity; it feels like a group of STEM majors stacked in a trench coat, pretending to be a fraternity, which is what I love about it."

Q. *What drew you to Ohio?*

I've actually been a Buckeye my entire life. My dad went to Ohio State when he was going to college, and so I grew up rooting for the Buckeyes. But I never actually planned on going to college here. I applied just because my dad went here and I wanted to carry on that family tradition of at least applying. But as I went further and further into the admissions process, I chose Ohio State over a school like Penn State or Clemson, just because you can never go wrong with a big school. I knew I wanted to go out of state because I didn't want to go to the same college as everybody else from my high school.

Ohio State provides a lot of opportunities as I'm sure any of the Big Ten schools do in terms of having a lot of people there, having a lot of ideas, circulating a lot of stuff. "You can never go wrong with a big school," is what my dad said.

My dad was super concealing of his true intentions, which were him wanting me to go to Ohio State. He stayed silent throughout the entire decision process. But I remember when I sat down at the kitchen table and told him that I wanted to go to Ohio State, he was so happy. It was a cool moment.

Q. Why join a fraternity?

I think if you talk to any of the guys in Triangle, one of the common things that unites us all is that none of us were really thinking about Greek life. I never considered myself to be a fraternity guy, even though everyone else in my family was in Greek life. I have three older sisters and a mom who were all in sororities. So I was always exposed to the Greek life system, but I never really thought of myself as a fraternity guy.

The reason I rushed was honestly because of the unique experience that Triangle provided. I got DMed by somebody from the fraternity, who's been a great mentor to me. He showed me that Greek life wasn't all that I had seen on TVs and movies, and that it could actually provide a lot more than what is typically shown in those things.

I'm actually quite new to the fraternity. I rushed last spring in January, and then I was elected president this December, so I've only been in the fraternity for a little over a year.

Q. How would your friendships in high school compare to the ones you have at Triangle?

I would say that a lot of the friendships that I've made in terms of the banter is similar in comparison to my high school friendships. That's what I really liked about Triangle. When I joined the first rush event, it just seemed like a bunch of guys who were having fun. It didn't seem like some very serious fraternities which I had seen on TV and movies. It was just a bunch of guys having fun. That's what I really liked about it, because it reminded me of my friends back home.

When I came to college, it was during the COVID-19 pandemic, so we really didn't go outside very much. I remember leaving my dorm twice a day, once to go to the gym and once to get food. Besides that, you were just held up inside. Once I got exposed to that fraternal life and I started making friends through Zoom and through the rush events, it opened my eyes to a whole new college experience.

Q. Why are fraternities good for college men?

There certainly is that stigma. If you watch any of the movies or TV shows, you get a really bad image of what fraternal life is. I think the main reason is that it's not showing you the actual good side of fraternal life. It's not talking about philanthropy, or the brotherhood, or any of the good stuff that goes on in terms of professional or academic development. It's just all of the social aspects blown up to a massive caricature, which doesn't encompass a lot of the Greek life on campus here, or at any of the other schools, I'm sure. It's a really good thing for men because of the opportunities that it provides you.

There's a reason that in fraternities we call each other brother. It provides a lot of people who didn't have that experience growing up, me included. I grew up with three older sisters, I never had any brothers. When I came to college and I got inducted into a fraternity where I had thirty of them, it was life changing in terms of how my collision experience has progressed through so far.

Q. What is the rush process like?

The rush process at Ohio State starts about two weeks after everyone gets to campus and usually lasts around two weeks. Triangle will specifically have around five different rush events over those two weeks. We've done events such as Meet The Brothers, where people come by, they learn about Triangle and eat pizza. We'll do STEM games where you do the classic egg drop or build spaghetti towers. We have a professional development event where all the freshmen or sophomores bring their resumes and we go over interview prep, resume review, stuff like that. After those two weeks, we have an invite-only event, which is where the bids are given out.

From there, they'll go through the new member education process, where they learn about the fraternity, its inner workings, and how it actually runs as an entity. Six weeks after that they're initiated and become full brothers of the fraternity. From start to finish, it's about two months, from when you first meet someone to when they get initiated into the fraternity.

One thing to note about Ohio State specifically is that it's on what's known as a "Delayed Rush." Any freshman that comes to campus their fall semester won't be allowed to rush because OSU wants to provide them with a welcoming experience where they're not immediately rushing into a fraternal life, which will take up a lot of their time. They want them to get accustomed to campus, so you need at least twelve credit hours in order to rush a fraternity. That usually puts off people until their second semester of freshman year in order to rush.

Rush was actually in-person this year, which was super nice. We were able to meet the potential new members in-person, both this semester and last semester. We did offer some Zoom options for people who weren't comfortable coming in-person.

Q. Why Triangle?

My rush was a little bit different because it was over Zoom. But I specifically remember that the first moment I joined the Zoom call, it was completely different to anything that I had ever seen at any of the other rush events. It was a group of men bantering with each other and having a good time before the event started. It reminded me of my friends back at home. Everyone was engaging with each other and having a good time. On the outside, looking in, it was an experience where I went, "Wow, those guys seem like a lot of fun. I've never seen anything like this before and I'd like to be a part of them."

Once the sanctions lifted and I was able to meet a lot of them in-person, it was pretty much the same. Any event, social events, philanthropy events, brotherhood events, it was the same. They were finding ways to have a good time and banter with each other in a way that made me want to join the fraternity even more.

Triangle is unique in a lot of ways. We're one of the three fraternities that don't have any Greek letters. Our name is just Triangle. We get jokes all the time about people saying, "Oh, it's Delta, right? You're the Delta fraternity." But no, it's Triangle. It's exclusively composed of engineers, architects, and scientists. Essentially, it's a bunch of STEM majors who are academically and professionally minded. The way I like to advertise it to people is that it doesn't really feel like a fraternity; it feels like a group of STEM majors stacked in a trench coat, pretending to be a fraternity, which is what I love about it.

The reason that Triangle is so distinctive is that it's unlike any other fraternity or club that you can get on campus. You'll have professionally and academically minded clubs that you can join, but they don't have that social or brotherhood aspect to it. You can join other fraternities here on campus, but they don't have that professional and academic focus like Triangle does. I like to say it's the best of both worlds. Wherever you lie on that spectrum of wanting to be academically or professionally inclined and wanting to be socially inclined, Triangle offers you an opportunity for that.

It's all about making a big school seem small. Triangle is not one of the bigger fraternities on campus. We have around twenty-eight active members now and a pledge class of fifteen, so it's a really small percentage of the sixty thousand OSU student population. But it's the quality of those men that sets Triangle and Greek life apart. I think there's a statistic where the average GPA of somebody in a fraternity is higher than that of someone who's not in a fraternity, which just goes to show that connections and brotherhood help you succeed, as opposed to bringing you down.

Q. What's the pitch for Triangle? What kind of guys are you looking for?

Triangle is a social STEM fraternity here on campus which focuses on social, academic, and professional help. It's going to provide you with social opportunities that you're not going to get anywhere on campus, and it's going to provide you professional and academic opportunities that you're not going to get at any other fraternity. That usually sparks some more questions such as, "Oh, you guys are a STEM frat, but you have social gatherings, what's that like?" Or, "Oh, so you guys are a fraternity? I'm a little bit hesitant about Greek life. Can you tell me more about those professional or academic opportunities?"

In terms of what men Triangle is looking for, in the past it's been well-rounded individuals; people who are able to have that balance of a social life, as well as focusing heavily on their academics, because it's not an easy thing to do. I think a lot of people get caught up, especially in their first semester. It's why I think OSU has a delayed rush for those coming into college who have all that freedom and don't know what to do with it. That's where I think some people can get down the wrong road. We want well-rounded individuals who are able to make that balance and have both aspects of their life turned up to the max.

Q. What part of Triangle's mission is your favorite?

The part about balanced men. Triangle tries to focus on four main factors: the social aspect of a college experience, the brotherhood aspect of a college experience, and the professional and academic sides as well. You have guys who are all over the spectrum on that. You have guys who joined a fraternity because they wanted a social aspect. You have guys who joined a fraternity and weren't really socially inclined, but wanted to have that academic and professional balance. You have guys who are just looking for a group of friends to hang out with on the weekends.

Trying to provide events and things to do for all four types of those people is my job as president and is what me and my executive board work on for most of the time, trying to offer a balance between that. Like I said, the great part about Triangle is that it offers you the best of both worlds. But at the same time, that means you have to provide events for both of those types of people. We're always thinking about new ideas and new ways that we can get people involved.

Q. How do you "develop high standards of personal integrity and character"?

I'd say the best example of that is our code of ethics. Triangle has a list of ten ethic codes, which serve as rules to follow as a Triangle brother. It'll encompass everything from maintaining a creditable scholastic effort to helping ensure that you create a positive environment in your chapter home; doing your full share of any task however menial it is in maintaining a chapter home. It's our rules of being a Triangle brother. If we had a rule set that people had to follow, it would be the code of ethics. We're all about building better men here at Triangle. That's our unofficial official slogan. When you're coming in, you're following those codes of conduct and you are becoming an outstanding member of society, in my opinion.

It bleeds into every one of those four aspects that I talked about previously. In terms of specific examples, the most common one that I can think of is our Extra Life fraternity. Every fall, we have a twenty-four-hour gaming live stream on Twitch where we spend time and raise money for Nationwide Children's Hospital. It's an example of upholding high moral character and taking time out of your day to give back to a cause which is greater than yourself. We'll have events that go on throughout the livestream. We'll have donation goals that people hit to have stuff done in order to spark more people donating. It's a really good time, and I think it's a great example of Triangle character.

Q. How do you "foster an environment of intellectual maturity and companionship"?

If you put thirty STEM majors in a room together, you're going to get a lot of great ideas, and you're definitely getting a lot of professional and academic help. We have older brothers who have taken all of the STEM classes that the younger guys are taking. We often have them help out with tutoring or studying for exams. We set super high standards for academic and professional development. We have a lot of resources available for our students.

One example I can think of is our "Resume Review" chat. We use Slack, which is a communication software that allows people to chat and make different channels. One of the channels is Resume Review. I can remember a specific instance where I got added to the Slack and immediately joined the Resume Review channel because I thought it might be interesting later down the road when I'm working on a resume. The first thing I saw was that two of my pledge brothers, Sammy and Teddy, had already thrown their resumes in there and were getting feedback from the older brothers. I thought, "Wow, I am behind the ball on this." So I went home that night, wrote up a resume, threw it in the chat, and tried to compete with them.

That's the thing, you're always being pushed by your brothers. The one thing I always tell potential new members is that in college, you become exactly like the people you surround yourself with. I don't think you can find a better group of men on campus to start surrounding yourself with than Triangle brothers. Everyone here is super academically focused and professionally inclined to the point where if you're not, you're thinking, "Wow, I should really get on top of this. I should get help from some of my brothers in some of my classes."

Another example I can think of is that when internship season rolled around, everyone immediately started applying to internships. We have a "Good News" section of our chapter where people can share their good news. And week after week, I kept hearing about brothers getting internship opportunities and internship offers. I thought, "Wow, that's really great for them, but I should probably get on top of this too." So I applied to over seventy-five internships over the next two weeks so that I could get my spot in the Good News talking about how I accepted my internship position.

There've been so many instances that I can think of where somebody has a question about a class or somebody has a question about, "Hey, I have this interview on Friday, can anybody help me out with mock interviews?" Or, "Can somebody just please look over my resume?" Brothers are so quick to help each other out because a lot of them have been through the ringer. A lot of them have had high quality internships, been through the process, and have been through the hard classes. What you get is a lot of brothers who are ready, willing, and able to help each other out in order to help everyone succeed at the highest level, which I think is an amazing aspect of Triangle.

Q. How do you "provide for social and moral challenges and responsibilities"?[1]

I'd say in terms of Triangle, or Greek life in general, it's learning how to lead and execute events. For a lot of people, this is their first experience, especially on an executive board, learning how to plan and carry out events, learning how to deal with the fact that things aren't always going to go as you plan them to. People aren't always going to like the events that you put on. It becomes even more challenging when these people are your good friends, trying to have hard conversations with people about responsibilities and getting things done.

The one thing I've learned as president for at least my first two month term is that if you're not organized, you're going to get caught up immediately. My Google Calendar looks like a mosaic. I'm always checking emails and making sure that I'm staying on top of things, and my executive board is doing the exact same thing.

A specific example of this I can think of is Block. In the fall we and a lot of other fraternities do an event called "Block," which is a pre-game to the football games. You'll section off part of your backyard and you'll hang out with a bunch of people before the game and pre-game. This past fall was the first time that Triangle had done it in a few years, and the lessons that we learned in terms of responsibility and accountability were insane. We had a bunch of problems, including managing the guest list and getting people to show up for the cleanups that they signed up for. But if people aren't pulling their weight, not having accountability for the actions that they signed up for, then you have to sit them down and talk about those moral responsibilities and social challenges. Not just for the individual, but also for the Chapter as well. And that was a super hard conversation to have because they're your friends.

1. Ibid.

Q. How do you "bridge the gap between undergraduate study and the vocation of industry/academic world/government"?[2]

On the professional development side of things, learning in college how I can better prepare myself for the computer science industry or the mechanical engineering industry. A lot of that goes hand in hand with the resume review and interview prep stuff that we do, but it also has to do with other things that we put on. One of our older members, Joey Hughes, who's a computer science major, is one of the smartest guys I know. This past semester he set up something called Code School, which is where all the computer science majors will come to the House on Wednesday and do something programming related. And it's open to everyone. We've had a few ECE majors show up.

The events range from doing interview prep to working on practice coding interview questions. We had one of the alumni come in and talk about what he does in terms of his job as a software engineer. We prepare people for that real world experience that you might not get in a class where everything is project based and you're worried about grades and stuff like that. It's a really good way to get people ready for the real world.

One thing I've noticed is that if you wanted to go the route of getting a lot of professional development help, a lot of the strain would be on you to go out and look for opportunities and things that you could do in order to help improve your professional development skills. But Triangle is there to provide those opportunities for you.

Q. What's been done to not make stereotypes a reality in your fraternity's chapter and culture?

It makes the case for why someone would want to be in Triangle in the first place, if that's something that they want. It's really cool that when guys are interested in building each other up. You want each other to succeed, but that's not what people think about when they hear the word "fraternity."

I wonder, "How would you say that you guys are working against some of those stereotypes on purpose, trying to be something different and better that builds?" It looks like for guys saying, "You know what, we're not a bunch of drunk and rambunctious men who do nothing but take advantage of girls and things like that. We want to be better men." We are better men and we have created a culture in our fraternity that puts that on display.

2. Ibid.

A lot of the stuff that gets mentioned about fraternities is negative because those are the big stories. No one wants to hear about how Triangle's holding a mental health seminar. It's just not as interesting as the big stories. But one thing that we try to push is that our actions speak louder than words. The more involved we get in the community, volunteering for places like Star House (a homeless shelter here in Columbus that helps at-risk youth) by sorting through donations and helping them out, we try to push that on our social media as much as we can.

We try to do shout-outs for brothers who are exceeding academically or professionally. Anything we can to get the word out that Triangle is not like those other fraternities that are ruining the reputation of Greek life around the country. Triangle works to build people up instead of putting them down. Every week we have our Good News section in our Chapter where people can share good news. We also have a section called Brother Shout-Outs, which is where you can shout out brothers for doing something for you that they didn't have to do.

That will always be my favorite part of the Chapter. After everybody says anything, it could be something as small as, "Yesterday I learned how to cook a burger," or, "Yesterday I made a really good burger," everyone goes buck-wild and claps and cheers. It's really amazing to see.

Q. What do you guys do to spend time together?

One thing is the "Big-Little" system, which is where every member will get their big brother. We push that a lot. Recently, we had a big-little game night where we came to the House and played some board games, and that was a really good time. We even had a small get together where somebody put it on the chat that they were going to be coming by the House to watch a movie and order some pizza. We hold brotherhood events. We're trying to get a paint-balling session. We planned trips for spring break and fall break.

There's so many events that are like that. One thing that we've recently started up again is "Taste of Columbus." One of the older members will pick a restaurant that's in downtown Columbus and we'll all drive down there on a Sunday afternoon and check out some weird or fun restaurant that none of us have ever been to before. That's always a great time.

Q. What should people think when they hear "Triangle"?

I think it's fun when I ask people if they've ever heard about Triangle. Their immediate gut reaction is to stereotype us as the nerd frat, which I don't think is a bad thing. But we push the idea that Triangle is a rare opportunity on campus where you can have that mix of academic and professional development that a club or extracurricular involvement would give you with the social aspect of it too. A lot of people think that because we are a STEM major fraternity only, we don't have social events. But that couldn't be farther from the truth. A lot of people have come up to me after themed gatherings or events and said, "Wow, I really did not expect the STEM majors to have this much fun."

In terms of what I would like people to think about Triangle, I'd say it's everything I've been talking about. It's a place on campus that provides opportunities for any type of architecture, engineering, or STEM major student. I'd like us to be known as the frat that gets everyone good job offers when they graduate, and also has a good time here at college.

Q. What will you remember after graduation?

The biggest thing that I am going to take away is the memories that I've made and the friends that I made them with. I haven't been in Triangle that long. I've only been in the fraternity for over a year, but I can already name countless memories that I've made and people who, as crazy as it sounds, are the people that I would consider to be brothers at this point. The people that I pledge with, Sammy, Teddy, and my friends, Telmo, Aiden, I've made so many countless memories with them. I can talk for hours on end about the outer bank summer trip that I had, because so many crazy and fun things happened, as well as all the TGS and events that we've had so far. Even the little things I think of a lot.

What I'll remember about Triangle is not really knowing what to do. I'm a little bored on Sunday afternoons, so I'll text my friends and say, "Do you guys want to go down to the Triangle House?" We'll always find something to do there because there's always people in and around the House. And the conversations with people about how to help me with coding interviews; any of the late night conversations that I've had with my pledge class are always great. And even shooting with my CS buddies. The people in the fraternity that are in CS will always talk about how crazy the field has become and our plans for the future because Triangle is very CS focused.

The CSE majors definitely dominate the population here, which we like to have a superiority complex about. We'll always talk about what internships we have lined up and what we're planning for the future. And I can't wait to see where those guys go because they're going to be really high places.

13

Phi Delta Theta, University of Arkansas

Joe Huett served as Phi Delta Theta president in 2021. A marketing major from Springdale, Arkansas, he explains the bad rap fraternities with a sales analogy. "Any bad apple you get is the apple that's put on the stand right out front." Religion is an important factor in his life and in his chapter. "If I say I'm a Christian and I believe that Jesus is the way," he says, "Why would I not share that with my fraternity brothers whom I am supposed to love? One man is no man. I can't leave anybody behind. Love is to stand up and say, 'Hey, I love you. This is the right way to go, and I'm an idiot. I'm doing this wrong. Let's work together, because this is real.' I think that's super important. What's given me strength is that guys have been receptive to that."

Q. What drew you to Arkansas?

I didn't really look at any other schools in the region. I looked at the Naval Academy in Arizona state. I know, super random on either side of the U.S. But really what brought me to Arkansas is that my three older brothers all went to the University of Arkansas and were in fraternities. Two of them were in Beta Theta Pi here. One of them was in Bucks, which technically isn't a fraternity. That's initially what drew me, and it's home and I love Arkansas. It's the best kept secret in the world, and I'd like to keep it that way. But it's home, and it's beautiful and I love it. And that's ultimately what made me decide to go here.

Being so close to the university, having friends and even my own brothers who were involved in the IFC at University of Arkansas drew me here. One of my best friends has a brother was in Lambda Chi, and we would come down and play Xbox at the house and hang out with them Thursday, Friday, Saturday. That was never a weird thing, which was nice. Coming to college, it was really normal to be on stadium drive, which is where Phi Delt is and Lambda Chi's right next door. It was a really cool experience.

Q. How did you maintain your faith while being in a fraternity?

Part of it is that in high school, I was training up my faith, whether that be surrounding myself with good community, knowledge of the scriptures, a real relationship with Christ. A lot of the South is, "Yeah, I'm a Christian," but I don't think a lot of people necessarily have a true, committed relationship. And I didn't. I know I didn't. I said I was a Christian for a long time and just never meant anything to me. It was just a word that I said, because we were in the South. And so through that in high school, having a real, true relationship with the Father, producing fruit and pouring into other people younger than myself and having older people pour into me, I wanted that in college, too. And there's not a better place to do that than in a fraternity.

I spent so much time as a freshman in this house and had people pour into me as a freshman when everyone was telling me that I was a piece of crap and lower than dirt. When you're a pledge, hearing that is kind of tough. You'll think, "Maybe this kind of sucks." But you'll have guys that are leaders in the fraternity saying, "Hey, I love you. I did this. The Lord loves you. Think about the impact that you can make with guys in our fraternity that can be eternal." If I say I'm a Christian and I believe that Jesus is the way, why would I not share that to my fraternity brothers who I am supposed to love? One man is no man. I can't leave anybody behind. Love is to stand up and say, "Hey, I love you. This is the right way to go, and I'm an idiot. I'm doing this wrong. Let's work together, because this is real." I think that's super important.

What's given me strength is that guys have been receptive to that. And I have a great group of friends that were around me when I was a freshman, when it's not just about not drinking, it's not just about not smoking. It's about being a light and every day guys noticing, "I don't know why Joe's different, but he's different. And I love that about him." And conversations of, "Why are you different? Why are you happy?" Even COVID has brought up a lot of depression and depravity. It showed me the depravity of man without Christ as a savior, which I got to see even before COVID with drinking and partying and smoking. It's all good and fun, but ultimately it leaves me empty at the end of the day. I'm not a stick in the mud. I love to party. I like to have a drink and that's not bad, but it leaves me empty when I put my faith in that. Christ is the only thing I put my faith in to be fulfilled and satisfied.

My friends there really helped during pledgeship of freshman year and sophomore year when we were living in-house. The temptation there for me was never gone. As an eighteen-year old and nineteen-year old kid, I wanted to go drink and get drunk with everybody else. But having friends there and being in the Word was how I was successful at fighting that.

Q. How would your friendships in high school compare to the ones you have at Phi Delt?

I rushed with about four guys that I was super close with in high school. These guys were my squad. We all rushed Phi Delt. And we had some guys that came into our friend group freshman year that we met through Phi Delt. I think friendships are very synonymous from high school to college. But I think the speed of what college did was greater than high school.

With my high school friends, it seemed like a longer period of time to get closer. The school I went to was K through 12. It was a small private school. Some of them I knew in fifth grade, but for some of them, it was ninth grade. We had a long time to get close. When I got to college, the friendship with the guys that I became friends grew like that. It was super close, really quick. I think it was because we had like-values, and it was us encouraging one another to keep on doing this. We're doing a good thing, this is a just cause. This is how we gather strength from each other and through the Word. We're reading together and all of that. There's maturity that plays in being a freshman in college. That's what I'd say is the most different between my high school friends and the friends that I made in college.

Q. Why are fraternities good for college men?

I think everything you hear about fraternities is so damning. It makes you want to not wear letters or do stuff around campus. But the only evidence I can give to why that's all wrong is because with any organization you have (especially now in the culture that we live in) is that any bad apple you get is the apple that's put on the stand right out front. But my fraternity brothers are some of the greatest men that I've ever met in my life. I can confidently say that about each and every one of these guys in that house. I've known them for a long time. And for a lot of them, I was very involved with their upbringing. As their pledge trainer, on exec, and now for a lot of them I'm their president.

But I think there's something special about when you get an immature kid, which I know I was when I was a freshman, and you put him in a room. Most eighteen-year-old men are douches regardless of where they came from. I probably didn't think I was a douche, but looking back, I totally was. I don't think you could find a group of guys on campus outside of the engineering school that wouldn't be. That's just the truth. But there's something really special about when you get that and all these high-testosterone, high sense of self freshmen in a room and present them with something like our manual: "One man is no man, and you're going to leave this place better than when you found it." Seeing how they, through that of a good pledge trainer, then begin through that process of learning why we have three pillars. This is why our six founding fathers are important. They wanted our three pillars to be drilled in every single man in this fraternity.

Friendship, sound learning, and moral rectitude is what we want, and that's what we do at Phi Delt. It's crazy because most people don't know what goes into a fraternity. I, as president, am running a three-quarter million-dollar business. We make that much money through dues and stuff just because we have so many people. And then you're managing fifty-six eighteen-year-olds that left their parents' home so that they could go rebel. It's really hard to control those people because you don't pay them. They don't necessarily have any reason to listen to you other than you possibly giving them social probation. But sometimes even that's not a huge deterrent.

The challenge is great, so of course you're going to have bad apples. Big boy decisions have big boy consequences. This is the part of time when you are a big boy. And there have been some people in our house that have made big boy decisions who probably weren't ready for it because the consequences were very big. But I don't think that's necessarily a reason to shine so much bad light on a fraternity. I know that not only Phi Delt, but for every fraternity that's outside my window, they are great for the community, great for building men. I hope my son gets the opportunity to go through some fraternity organization, because I do think it helps. Pledgeship is a sucky time, but it's also why you grow close with friends quickly. "Hey, remember when we did that at 3:00 in the morning? That was dumb, but it's fun now." You get to build stuff like that, so it's great for friendship.

You have to have a goal to get into the fraternity. You have to have a 2.75 or 3.0, or whichever one it is for any fraternity. You have goals set up for these freshmen. If I wasn't in a fraternity, I don't know what my GPA or outlook as a freshman would've been like. I would've just been alone. It was great to have sophomores, even juniors and seniors help me and care about me. I don't know why a junior or senior would care about you if you weren't in the same house and seeing them every day.

Q. What is unique about the fraternity experience?

I think, number one, it's just fun. It's more fun to be in a fraternity in college because I get to go to functions and tailgates. That was huge. It's probably more fun than any VBS or anything like that you can go to.[1] The second thing is that the problems, the hurt, the hang-ups, and habits that you encounter while being in a fraternity are very great. There are people who are really hurting and have serious struggles and issues that don't just go away after college. And for me to even have an influence in someone's life, just one, even just to plant a seed. I'm sure half of my fraternity brothers think I'm crazy, but I love them so much whether they think I'm crazy or not. I love getting to sit and listen to them when they are struggling. I don't think I would've gotten that if I was doing dorm stuff.

The problems and the hang-ups and the hurts are so real. It helps me so much to be reminded that, one, the Lord's very gracious and, two, I'm a sinner. I'm really messed up. I'm not better than any of my fraternity brothers. I struggle with the same thing they do. It's really beautiful to walk through that with them, because they might think, "Oh, Joe's just a goody two-shoes." No, I'm not a great person. It's also been great for me to walk through that line of, "How do I show grace to people?" It's been great for my relationship with the Lord to understand him more and understand his heart, and how he deals gently and lowly with us.

We didn't have a lot of IFC push for a mental health share to be added in, but our whole exec team was there for our guys. It was great to have that already built in, actively sitting and listening to our guys whenever they want to talk to us. I don't think I would've got that anywhere else other than a fraternity.

Q. What is the rush process like?

So there's a big range at the U of A. I think for me, it was multiple years I was on campus. From junior year, there were people rushing my group of friends from high school.

---

1. "VBS" often refers to Vacation Bible School.

That's the cool thing about being from Northwest Arkansas. We start-ed rushing in an informal way junior year. From going to houses, going to fraternity houses and hanging out with guys, and guys' older brothers would take us around and meet people. That's something that you get as a plus from living in Northwest Arkansas or close. Texas is huge. Texas kids coming to Arkansas is huge. You get in-state tuition if you're from Texas. We have a ton of Texas kids, which is a little bit harder for them to do, but still we kind of go around that. When you're a senior in high school, you gradu-ate in April. As a fraternity, we'll start rush trips in the summer.

We have a big golf tournament in Little Rock, Arkansas. It's three hours south, and a lot of our guys come from Little Rock and we have a big Little Rock pool. Then we do a lake day event in Hot Springs. And then we'll do some Texas events, whether it's in Dallas or Austin. Some years, it's just determined on who is the Texas rush chair. We elect rush chairs, and we'll elect three upperclassmen. We'll have a Northwest Arkansas rush, which is Bentonville, Rogers, Springdale, Fayetteville. Those are like the four big towns in Northwest Arkansas. This year, we have two Northwest Arkansas, which is a big deal. Two Little Rock. One's an upperclassmen, one's a fresh-man. And then we'll do a Texas rush chair.

A lot of people do pre-bids. Basically, you hang out the whole summer with a guy who'll say, "Hey, I like you. You've got a bid to Phi Delt." And people will say, "Yeah, I want that," or, "No, I don't want that." Some kids who are awesome have pre-bids to every place. They have a big decision coming on pref night. I didn't have that decision. I just had Phi Delt. Some guys in our pledge class had big decisions to make. That's a huge decision for where you're going to spend the next four years. That's essentially the sum-mer rush. It's usually big events all throughout the summer, with smaller events as well. It's a lot of meeting people. If you can meet people, then you're doing good. And if people like you, it's really good.

Then they move back onto campus. Then there's about two weeks where nothing goes on. Sorority rush happens in those two weeks, and your rush parties just become sausage fests. It's dudes everywhere. The girls are rushing. And then formal recruitment starts for IFC. They go around from house to house. You've got parties. I think there's fourteen allotted parties throughout the day. And you've got small groups with Rho Chi's.[2] They're rush leaders from every fraternity. You get placed in one. And then your Rho Chi's will be your guide through the rush process, and they'll take you from house to house. Then the parties get longer each day: fifteen-minute house tour, thirty-minute philanthropy day, forty-five-minute something,

2. A Rho Chi is a recruitment counselor.

an hour-and-a-half preference night. Then you'll only have three parties on preference night. So you get dwindled down as you go to year three. Then you have preference night, and you go to the union and fill out your bid card. The next day is bid day, and we all meet in the Greek theater.

You get a bid card on a piece of paper. I think maybe the rush chairs text them the results. I know I was texted by a rush chair, and then went back to Phi Delt and hung out. The bid day wasn't as big of a deal.

We would usually initiate them in February of that next year. From September, they would go until February. Now the university's put limits on that. I think they will have to be initiated November 14th if they're in the fall.

Q. Why Phi Delta Theta?

It was all about the guys. The rush chair my year, his name's Jay Young, was just a big influence in my life that summer, and he was a believer. Another older guy, his name's Chase Arnold, I had met a couple times and really liked him. And my pledge brothers were awesome. They're the best. I love them so much. Even my group of friends said, "Dang, we love Phi Delt. This is the place. You're going here? I like it, too."

We didn't care what the letters were. I don't care. My brothers were Betas. They're not the greatest at the U of A, but I didn't care. I knew some guys there that said, "Hey, I'd go Beta." It wasn't the letters for me. It was all about the people that I met. I thought, "Man, I can get poured into here, and I love the people here, and I can pour into them as well." Which, again, could happen at any house. I just loved the people at Phi Delt. They weren't in a box. There's some fraternities that are like, you got to be super country or super hip or super this or this. What I love most about Phi Delts is that we've got everything across the board. You name it, it's probably in the house somewhere. We currently have two hundred to two hundred and sixty in our chapter, or somewhere around there.

I think that we are good at not putting people in a box. I think that's a lot of what has made us successful. In the Southeastern Conference SEC, there are people hesitant to take people of color, whether it be black, Asian, Hispanic. What I loved about my pledge class is that Jung Hon from Fayetteville was in it. And there are some houses that probably won't take Jung. But I love Jung so much, and I'm so glad he is in my pledge class. That's why Phi Delt has consistently been at the top. We're looking for the quality of men, and that's what we go after and seek after. It's not the sixties at Phi Delt still, and I don't think a lot of houses can necessarily say that. A lot of alumni still feel that way. But I know that our alumni don't, which helps because it's never, "Are you going to take him because he's black?" I don't ever feel that pressure. "Hey, is he a good guy? Yeah. Let's take him."

Q. What's the pitch for Phi Delt? What kind of guys are you looking for?

Something that we have to our advantages is a sense of alumni. The whole spiel is that these are the best guys on campus, grades, heart, stature, everything. These are the guys on campus you want to be around. And our alumni prove that in the fact that we've got tons of alumni who are extremely successful and also still active. It's not just a four-year thing and you're done. I think guys like to see that. Also the brotherhood that we have during rush. You look around in a room and there's fifty, maybe forty potential new members, and there's a room full of one hundred and eighty guys. That's overwhelming. Some guys say, "Wow, this is actually a brotherhood." It's plain and simple. It is, "Hey, this is what we're about. We're the best men on campus, here's why. It's because we have great friendships. We're smart, and we're kind. And that's what we're doing. That's what you get when you come here."

I think the beauty of what we do is that we look for a base in personality. Something that I loved about our pledgeship and what our pledge trainers did well and what I hope to do well as a pledge trainer was to influence people's characters. If you've got a making of character, you're confident and you are excited, you could really mold someone. And that's what we're looking for. And that's why it's great, because not every Phi Delt looks the same. It's kind of a hodgepodge, but we're the best. We're the best hodgepodge. It's not based on the outside, but the inside. Are we aligned? Can you do basic things like look me in the eyes, shake my hand, and not have a weird conversation with me, but a conversation about everything? If somebody's wearing a Star Wars tie, can we talk about that? If somebody's wearing a Hunter Henry jersey, can we talk about Hunter Henry moving to the Patriots? Can we do that? Can we do random things that help me understand that you are good conversationally, that you're not extremely awkward and that you're confident?

Q. What part of Phi Delt's mission is your favorite?

Friendship sticks out to me because I think friendship is most important for college students. It's something that might be hard for guys to even admit.

Friendship seems to be a soft characteristic, and obviously there are college guys that maybe don't want to be seen as soft. Something I think we do extremely well is that our fraternity builds friendships, not cliques. The Little Rock guys hang out with Little Rock guys. But some of my best friends are from Austin and Dallas, Texas. That's weird. Some are from Little Rock. A lot of fraternities can't say that. I think that's something that we do really well through our Phi Chi program, our pledge program. That's something I'm interested to see if that lasts four, ten years from now. It's something that we do really well, and I think that's one of the most, if not the most important thing from one of those pillars.

Q. How do you develop close friendships with your members?

I think it's been in part to our long pledge program. The university probably hates that, but it's something that I believe in. I was a pledge trainer, so I care a lot about my pledges. And I'm the youngest of four, so I never got the chance to be an older brother. I took my time as a pledge trainer, being fifty-six guys' older brother, which was super special. Those connections I made through that pledge class have been crazy. But I think it's the length of time that we do it that makes it so good. And having challenges through college, such as, "Man, this test week's going to suck. I don't want to do it." I got forty people that are going to take the same B-law test as me. And we're all studying in a basement with Walton College in January. And we've been doing it forever. We've been studying for the same tests.

A lot of people cut off, and I understand why the university wants to do that. Obviously, it's to mitigate risk, which I completely understand. Even if you get a great pledge trainer, there are guys in the house that don't care. But I think that's something that we've done really well. It makes our friendships last and makes the friendship valuable.

Q. What should a pledge expect to help him become academically excellent?

I think this semester was the first semester that we didn't get top in grades out of the whole time I've been on exec. We got second this year, Sigma Nu beat us out. That's some of our bread and butter; we spend time on the front end combing through guys as we build a base. These guys are going to do well in school. To give credit to everybody, the thing that all fraternities help with is that you get younger guys surrounded by sophomores who took their classes previously. They're say, "Hey, don't take him, or don't take her, or here's how you study for this." And then we have resources. We have a budget built for the scholarship chair. We don't buy Scantrons.[3] There's that weight lifted off. I've never had to buy a Scantron, which is great. And tutoring as well. We have guys in house to tutor, and we have a budget to pay for tutoring if you need it. If, say, you're a chemical engineer, and we don't have one of those, we can help you there, which I think has been nice. I think it's paid off for our chapter.

*Q. How do you keep each other accountable
with your moral virtue?*

It's hard. I think it's hard because for all of our alumni, accountability is their main topic. Back in the day, their parents necessarily didn't pick up the check for a lot, and so fines were heavy-handed. That's something that we've been working through, and this new exec team's going to have to make sure that they're good about fulfilling their duty to fine and make big- time decisions. We had to pull pins on seven members last year. That catches eyes and everybody kind of perks up a little bit, and that really sucked.

*Q. What does suspension mean? How do guys get
out of it? What are some lessons learned?*

We had some bumps in the road of spring 2021. We had to let some members go, kick them out, "excommunicate," because they had some pretty heavy-handed actions. That led us to a suspension from our nationals to get some things done. Essentially, that was just a Zoom call with people on our general headquarters team. They were asked a lot about the three principles, "Do you still believe this, what we're doing?" Everybody who's back said "yes."

And we got off our general counsel probation sometime in October. This was our first taste of regular since whenever COVID happened. We had one incident of a halfway semi-registered function, which was a miscommunication on our social chair and the university's part. This last one, we had just initiated and members and the ambulance was called to our house for a medical evac. Obviously, the police came and it was a big deal. That's why we are on social probation. We're on social probation, and we didn't take a spring pledge class.

3. "Scantrons" refers to the machine-readable multiple choice tests created by Scantron Corporation.

I think as this is my last rodeo, essentially this last suspension, it's always good to focus on Phi Delt, not other people. I know a huge excuse is that the people in the chapter, and even some alumni, understand that all across the university, there's people partying and all that good stuff. We still can't, even if they are. That's been something that we've been hounded on. Even something as little as a party, it could turn into an ambulance getting called to the house. It's things like a party in of itself that's pretty innocent. But there's big things that come with it. It's not just the fact that you're having a party. It's the fact that an ambulance comes, etc. We had an incident where someone stuck a pool cue at 2:00 AM in a fire extinguisher, and it blew up. It's not just that those things happen. There's some stupid things that some people are doing that could be avoided: "Let's just not walk by the fire extinguisher. Let's be smart about some of these things." I think that's been a big learning point; we have to focus on ourselves. We can't focus on other people.

Then you got to listen to people who know more than you. If I'm being honest, I think that it's clearly communicated not to do anything. I think some people just kind of thought, "It's just a little party." It wasn't very big, but still, an ambulance came. It's been on me to over-communicate on some of those things. "Hey, really? We're not doing anything tonight." Not, "Hey, don't do this or it's not happening," from my end. Those were the biggest things to learn.

Q. How do you help each other be the best version of yourselves?

I think that means growing up. I think the great part about college is that you come in maybe a little green, and you have the opportunity to put yourself around people who are maybe a little more seasoned than you. I think that phrase, "the best version of yourself," is you with experience. Maybe not the best version of yourself screams perfection, but it's that lack that really makes you the best version. How people learn best is through failures most of the time. It sucks because you get eighteen-year-olds, fifty-six of them, and they tend to play off failure sometimes. But they are learning. There's been no point in time in our history where there's been problems pushed under the rug. If they're stubborn and hardheaded, that's tough for me to handle, because I'm just here for a year, and they're here for three. But they have the opportunity and they have the reprimand that a fraternity offers, and that gives them seasoning.

They come in green, and then we help them whether that's giving them a helpful hand up or dragging them along against their will on some things; "Hey, you're going to be on social probation, or you got forty community service hours to do, or else you're out of here." Things like that really help you become the best version of yourself, because you learn from your mistakes.

Q. What's been done to not make stereotypes a reality in your fraternity's chapter and culture?

I think there's a couple ways we've done it. We do have some of those people in our fraternity. The contrary though, is that we have leaders throughout the university. And I think that's where we set ourselves apart. And I think that's what a lot of fraternities at the U of A are doing well. And a lot of people see that at SAE, Lambda Chi, Phi Delt, Sigma Nu, Sigma Chi, PIKE, Kappa Sig. They've got people in ASG.[4] They've got people leading teams in the engineering buildings. They have people in IFC leadership. There's people leading in the community. They're on the football team. So they're not cracked-out bums. It's not, "I'm a Phi Delt. I'm cool in this house." No, these Phi Delts are leaders in IFC. There's Phi Delts that are leaders on ASG. We've had one ASG president in this last five year stretch. I know we had a couple more older ones.

A guy from Sigma Nu is the president of the whole school right now. He's a great guy. That's how you abolish those stereotypes. And it's probably because we're in the SEC. I think that's a big reason why there's not so much of that here. A lot of our guys aren't just fraternity-focused necessarily. Our identity might not just be found in the fraternity, but it's found in other things, Walton College, or the engineering school, or whatever it may be.

Q. What should people think when they hear "Phi Delt"?

Friendly. I think what we do well is we talk to you. It doesn't matter who you are. I want people to say that about Phi Delt. I want people to say that about every one of our men. I think that's a good character trait to have. To be strong in stature. I would like us to walk around with a puff in our chest. I don't think that's a bad thing either. I think confidence is great. I want to instill in every one of our members that we're not confident because we're tools. We're confident because we're Phi Delt men, and we know what we're

---

4. Associated Student Government.

doing. We know what direction we're going, and we're going to go do it. That's what I want. And smart, but our academics do speak for themselves. If someone came to me and said, "Hey man, this guy, he had no clue who I was, but he treated me like I was king for the day. And he wasn't pouty or weird, sad. But he was confident in who he was. He didn't come up to me timid or shy. He was confident that he was about to make a friend." That's what I would want from meeting our guys on campus.

Q. What will you remember after graduation?

I would say leadership is hard, especially when there's not a lot of motivating factors. I don't pay any of these guys to be here, and they don't necessarily work for me. They do in a weird way, but I don't really pay them to be here. They oddly pay to stay in Phi Delt. It's almost kind of backwards. It's a different leadership than a corporate side of leadership. It's really unique, because it's peers and younger.

This might not sound like I learned a lot, but I learned that asking for forgiveness and admitting wrong takes the stick out of people's hands. When you sit in a chapter room in front of sixty-eight guys, and you say, "Hey guys, I didn't communicate this well. I should have done this, I should have done this, and I should have done this. And I'm really sorry, and I'm not going to do that again," it takes this mob and turns it into brotherhood. That's when we come back to brotherhood and say, "I love you. Thank you for that." It really does that. And I think nobody likes to admit that they're wrong. I hate doing it more than anybody. I hate to admit that I'm wrong. I will go to my grave thinking that I'm right. I'm just really stubborn. I don't like saying I'm wrong. And that was a big learning curve for me this last year. "Who cares if you're wrong?" You have to admit that at some point, or more problems come from burying that.

It's harder to get people to be on your side when they don't apologize for anything. When no one takes blame for what was done, you just look like a bad leader, period. Then you don't get the chance for people to say, "Hey, he apologized. He knew what he did wasn't good or right." If you don't do that, then they'll say, "This guy sucks, and I hate him." Most of the time, people might say about me, "Hey, this guy sucks, but I still like him with an apology," which is nice. But that's probably the biggest thing I've learned. That'd be the thing I'd tell them about. That's been my biggest lesson and maybe it's just because it's hit me all as I'm leaving this year. But I think my time here would've been a lot easier if I would've just said, "Hey, I did that. I did do that wrong, and I'm really sorry. And I won't do that again."

14

Kappa Alpha, University of Arkansas

C onnor Kilgore was elected to serve as president of Kappa Alpha in 2022. A supply chain major from Argyle, Texas, he doesn't drink or smoke, and shortly before his freshman year, he decided that "I wanted to pursue my faith fully, I wanted to be all in. . . . At that point, I felt called to go into this darker place of fraternities." Pledges find it surprising when he tells them about the fraternity's weekly Bible study. But he thinks it's important to tell pledges that fraternity life can include many things pledges might not expect, including, in the case of Kappa Alpha, a chaplain. In Kilgore's words, "Hey, we value this."

Q. How do your high school friendships compare with your Kappa Alpha friendships?

In high school, I think your friends are decided based on what you do. For example, if you play football and that's your main sport, most of your friends are probably going to be other football players, or someone who does similar things as you. And so they're created for you, in a way. I think in fraternity, the relationships I've been able to see are because we came here and we wanted a more intimate relationship with each other, a deeper relationship with each other. And so I think that's how I've been able to see that play out in a fraternity, is these guys all came here wanting more of a deeper relationship, rather than just friends that were going to be created for them, in a way.

Q. Why join a fraternity?

During pretty much all of high school, I had two thoughts in my head. One of them was, I will never go to the University of Arkansas, and the other one was, I will never join a fraternity, because I knew, at least from what I had heard, Arkansas was this big party school. From what I knew at the time I didn't want to be in that environment. That's never been me. So I told myself, "You will never see me in those two places." Yet, here I am.

It was a pretty last-minute decision, towards the end of summer, going into my freshman year. I actually had just surrendered my life completely over to Jesus, and decided that I wanted to pursue my faith fully, I wanted to be all in. And so at this point, I was already committed to the University of Arkansas, and I thought, "Okay. Well, my life just changed a lot. I'm making this decision to pursue Jesus fully. What is next? What is this going to look like?" At that point, I felt called to go into this darker place of fraternities. There's not a lot of guys who have that vision in their mind, and have that faith. I thought, "Okay, I want to join this fraternity, and I want to be a light to the people that I surround myself with, and just share some truth with those guys."

When I was going through rush, it was during COVID. So our entire rush was virtual, it was on Zoom calls. There was no going into the houses, meeting guys in person, it was all virtual, which was very weird. But from all of those Zoom calls that I attended for KA, I could tell they were much more organized and set up in that way that was different from other houses. And then also, the night before pref night, I got invited to go to just a small dinner, and then go bowling, just so they could get to know me a little better. I went to that, got to know some of those guys better and went bowling, had a good time, and got to talk to them more. They were guys that I definitely wanted to surround myself with.

Q. Why are fraternities good for college men?

I think we should be giving insights as to what fraternity life actually embodies, not just this view of what we think it's been growing up, and seeing in films and TV shows, but actually giving a point of view being inside the fraternity. "Hey, there are other things that are within a fraternity." It's especially the reason that I joined, and what I've been trying to do in my fraternity. A lot of guys when I talk to them say, "Hey, we've been doing a Bible study, and we have guys that are coming, and this is something that we're trying to build up a little bit." A lot of them are like, "Wow, that's not something I was expecting or didn't think I was going to hear." That's something I'm honestly interested in. Essentially allowing prospects to know that there are a lot of things that they probably didn't know would be in a fraternity.

Q. Why be a light for Christ? How did you distinguish yourself? Do others respect that?

I think the biggest thing was the heartbeat for that. I think when I made that decision to fully give my life over and to pursue God, he gave me the heartbeat for that environment and to be in that environment. When you think of the purpose behind a Christian, and what our purpose is, it's to go and share the good news of Jesus and the gospel of Jesus. Yes, these on-campus ministries are great for that, but there's a place within fraternities, where there isn't anyone really doing that, and they're not receiving that truth in their life. Simply being able to come here and give these guys the opportunity to at least receive that truth and see what it truly means to be in an environment where you probably think you can't pursue that life.

It's really establishing yourself early on as that person. So for me, when I first joined the chapter, letting my pledge brothers know, and the guys in the fraternity know, just by the way I live, "Hey, here's what my life looks like." So early on, they realized that I don't drink, I don't smoke, I'm not doing these things. Being able to establish that early on, you'll start to have guys come up to you and ask. "Why? Why don't you do this?" And it gives you the opportunity to tell them why, and the purpose behind it.

At that point, there's a lot of respect behind it, which was cool for me. A lot of people probably have been very persecuted because of that. I've been blessed, not necessarily to be extremely persecuted, but have more respect behind it. Guys say, "Okay, I don't agree with that. However, I respect what you're doing." Because I was able to establish that respect, it made it easier on me going forward, because guys know I'm not going to live that life because of this.

They don't try to force me, but there is still a running joke where guys are always coming up to me, "Kilgore, let's go do this, let's go do that." Obviously, they know my answer, what it's going to be every time. It's not so much them trying to force me to do this, but more just friendly conversation.

Being able to establish yourself for who you are, that's how you're going to end up in the place where guys are actually going to accept you for who you are. Guys don't want to see this fake face while you're trying to rush, and then you join, and you're someone else. That's not what guys want to see. If you establish yourself early on with your belief and what you want to pursue, and you also are getting into that fraternity because you were being honest in yourself, then you already have that advantage moving forward, of what you want to do, and those guys know that.

Q. What is the rush process like?

On a Friday night, Saturday morning, and pretty much all of Sunday is our formal rush round one and round two. As a person rushing, you go to every house. When you come in, the chapter will give a speech, not a super long speech, but give a speech about who they are, what their values are, and what they're looking for. Then you'll start meeting guys at the house, and then that'll be about twenty to twenty-five minutes each, and then you move on to the next house. That's how the first two days work. And then you come back again on Sunday for around two, and you've made cuts to where you're down to a maximum of seven houses.

You do a similar process, maybe have a little bit more time. And then we have this whole week off, up until Friday, and Friday is the last round, which is called preference night, and you're down to your final three houses. Those are the longest parties, about an hour long at each house. You come to the house, try and talk to whatever guys you can one more time, make sure that relationship has been established and built up. At that night the final cuts are made, and the chapters decide who they want and who they don't want. And the next day you find out what chapter you've been accepted to.

After bids For us, it's typically around eight weeks, on average. Around two months. We currently have about two hundred and forty members in our chapter, give or take.

Q. Why Kappa Alpha?

When I was going through rush, it was during COVID. So our entire rush was virtual on Zoom calls. There was no going into the houses, meeting guys in person; it was all virtual, which was very weird. But from all of those Zoom calls that I attended for KA, I could tell they were much more organized and set up in that way that was different from other houses. Also, the night before pref night, I got invited to go to a small dinner and then go bowling, just so they could get to know me a little better. I went to that, got to know some of those guys better, went bowling, had a good time, and got to talk to them more. They were guys that I definitely wanted to surround myself with.

I think a very big thing is the reputation that we have on campus. It's very good. I'd say if you go ask anyone on campus, "What's the reputation like at KA? What are the good things? What are the bad things?" Almost everyone's going to tell you, "I have nothing bad to say about KA. They're respectful guys, they're good dudes." Honestly, that's what a lot of the rushees have told me this weekend when they come in, "Honestly I've asked a lot of people about KA, and they've had nothing bad to say." That's awesome when you have that reputation established. I think that's a very big thing that we have going for us.

Our motto, *Dieu et Les Dames*, means "God and woman." Even if you're not necessarily a Christian, all of our members believe that there's a higher being, that there's someone above them, and that we have respect towards that being. We know that there's a higher being, and that God is above us. Also the woman. We have a very high respect for women and they are also above us. We're putting them before ourselves, and I think that's where the whole reputation comes into play. We have a great reputation because of this value that establishes we have high respect for this being, for God, and also for ladies, and also for others on campus.

I see my brothers in action respecting others, not only guys in our chapter, but on campus. You're never going to see one of our guys be disrespectful to someone else. Also, just for the fact that not a lot of fraternities have the position of chaplain. And so we have that position which informs the members of that value, and to hold Bible studies once a week. So that's what I did last year as a freshman. I held Bible studies once a week, again, establishing my purpose and beliefs and values, and being able to have that and say, "Hey, we value this." This is something that means a lot to us. Once a week, we have this. I think those are two things that show that value in place.

I think most guys honor that and respect that, and want to see that in a chapter. I think that's something that helps set us apart. Guys see that value and want that reputation, want to be that gentleman, and want to establish themselves as that. It goes hand in hand with reverence, just being that gentleman. We don't really see a whole lot of that anymore these days. You go on campus, and you're going to hold the door for someone coming behind you. Whether or not they're going to tell you thank you, whether or not they were respectful of that, you're still going to go do that every time. That's just an example of what that value means for us.

Q. What's the pitch for Kappa Alpha? What kind of guys are you looking for?

We ultimately run through our past, give them a little bit of history on our chapter, and talk about, "Yes, you can have a fun time here," and then wrap it up with, "However, is that why we're here? The answer is "No, we're not here for that." That's a benefit that we can have, but we're here to surround ourselves with leaders and successful guys who are going to put academics first, their degree first, and others first. Everything else is just another benefit of joining. We want guys who already align with the values that we have. We're not trying to take a guy who may or may not embody a value and then try and shape them into this person we want them to be. We want to take the guys who already embody that and build off of that.

Q. How can Kappa Alpha's mission be practiced?

I wouldn't necessarily say we've had too many programs to go off for that value. However, my whole goal is to show guys those values by the way that I live, and how I treat others. I think being in the role of president, you always have eyes looking towards you. If I'm always with my exec team, I'm putting them first, I'm putting their needs before mine, I understand that their jobs are just as hard, and they have tasks to do, and if I can help them, and also just have the idea of, my door's always open. So if someone in the chapter needs something for me, or needs to talk to me, they know that they can come knock on my door, and they can have a one-on-one conversation with me, and not worry about anything. I think just setting that up as a leader of a chapter, and leading by example, really can establish a lot for every member.

It's been a process over the year of establishing that value. I keep going back to that, but it's so important, because those guys that have now seen me and see what I live for and the values that I embody are now comfortable coming to me and talking to me about personal things in their life, and things that they may not go to other people about. I have multiple guys that'll text me and say, "hey, are you in your room? Can I come talk to you?" Or whatever that may be. Yeah. I've definitely seen that.

I think it starts with the guys that we want to recruit here. So it starts with us, and it starts with, okay, let's look for those values now in the guys that are coming to join a fraternity, because those are all going to ultimately be the guys that carry on this chapter. So we really want to focus on those guys that embody those values already. I think as they go through the recruitment process, and they see those values, and they have those conversations with us, they can see that we all want and do hold each other accountable for our actions, and I think that is one of the biggest things that comes into play with that brotherhood.

Ultimately, we're all here because we know that KA has a good reputation, and we want to be seen as those gentlemen, and we don't want to ruin that. Because who doesn't want to be seen as a gentleman and embody those values? And so we establish that accountability with each other, so we can keep that reputation and keep us to make sure we are gentlemen, and we are embodying the values that we say we do.

Q. Why do fraternities have a bad reputation? How do you combat that?

Honestly, I think from what people see as they grow up in films and TV shows. I know that probably seems like a generic answer. When I was joining a fraternity and had decided that's what I was going to do, I still didn't know exactly what that was going to look like. Even just a couple days ago, I was texting a guy who's coming to the University of Arkansas in the fall and thinking about rushing, and even he was saying, "Honestly, I'm interested in joining a fraternity, but all I know is what they look like on shows and movies." And I said, "Yeah, I know how you feel." That was me coming in. I didn't know a lot about it outside of what was shown in movies. So I think that's where it starts, what culture has built.

I think that's something that can be difficult. It's good to have conversations and say, "Hey, I was right where you stood. I didn't know much about it, I thought the same thing. But I was welcomed by these guys in KA to the point where I saw out of that, and I saw through that. I knew that these guys were going to hold me accountable, they were going to respect me for who I was, and they were going to welcome me into the chapter, despite who I was." I think that was the biggest thing that allowed me to see, okay, there's way more to a fraternity than just what is shown on those shows and movies.

None of my parents were in a fraternity or in Greek life, but they were actually encouraging of it. When I brought up the idea, they thought, "Go do it." They knew what fraternities and Greek life actually embodied, and they knew it was going to be a great opportunity for me and great networking. I think that helped, as well.

Q. When does accountability matter?

I think first of all, accountability matters in pretty much every aspect of your life. But I think somewhere that we can start is how guys are going to act in the house. Are they damaging property? Are they messing up things in the house? If so, we're going to handle that appropriately. If we see someone damage the house, we're going to sit down and say, "Hey, you did this. Here's what this is going to look like. You're going to have to help pay for those damages, and we're not going to do that again." Those sorts of things. By establishing that accountability, even in the smaller things, I think it sets up the bigger picture of, okay, if I'm going to be held accountable for this, then I'm most certainly going to be held accountable for this over here.

I think, again, it all starts with the rush process, and first being able to establish that we do have that, and then showing that as they become new members. "Hey, we're not just saying this is one of our values, this is actually important. We're not going to invite girls over, and then get a better reputation, or do things that we shouldn't be doing. We're going to respect them, we're going to show them the respect that they deserve and that they need." Ultimately, over the years, as we've done that, here we are with this great reputation, and girls have nothing bad to say about our chapter. They do know that yes, guys like to have a good time, but they're also going to respect us, and they're going to take us home or walk us back to wherever we need to be, if it comes to that point.

Q. What should Kappa Alpha's reputation look like?

I think the biggest thing that comes to mind is respect. That word, "respect." I think that is so huge for our reputation, not only now, but in the future, that people here KA, and they can ultimately associate that with respect. Whatever that looks like, whatever they want to associate any situation with, it's going to come back down to respect. I think that's the most important thing. I'm pretty confident that we embody that right now, and we have in the past, and I think that's something that I would love for us to be able to say that we embody in the future.

Q. What will you remember after graduation?

I honestly think I will talk about the relationships I was able to build. I think that's going to be my number one talking point, my number one thing that I enjoyed most, was starting fresh, from high school to college, joining a fraternity, building these relationships within this time at KA, growing as a person and as a leader to the point where these guys had not only respect for me, but they wanted to get to know me more, they wanted to know my values more, and they became open and comfortable talking about personal issues, personal things in their life that they may not have been able to talk about with anyone else. So I think it would be really cool to just talk about how, man, these guys really opened up to me, they became comfortable with me, and became really good friends with me, and were able to talk about all of these things.

15

Epilogue

I followed over two thousand and two hundred fraternity chapters on Instagram during the writing of this book.[1] It was extraordinary to see the everyday brotherhood across America. On 12 December 2021, I saw a post on Grand Valley State University's Alpha Tau Omega account: their brother Quinn Campbell had tragically lost his life.

His story ultimately reshaped the direction of the book. His loss confirmed that many fraternity critics don't understand the real challenges that young men face. In the months following, I saw many more posts about young fraternity men who had also lost heartbreaking battles with anxiety, depression, hopelessness, and substance abuse. They eventually gave this project new meaning, underscoring why I care so much about fraternities.

What critics fail to understand is that men in fraternities have the same struggles as college-aged men everywhere. In my view, universities should be spending significant resources on all their young men, including those in fraternities. One of my dreams is to go from campus to campus, gathering all of the fraternity men in an arena in each one, just to tell them how important they are and how much the world needs them. Too many college-aged men don't know how desperately the world needs what they have to offer. Too many men don't understand their own excellence.

I was particularly inspired by Tami Campbell's courage. After she lost Quinn, she actively began to encourage other college men struggling with depression to get help. She even invited those who were struggling to contact her directly. I eventually contacted her as well, and she reported how

1. The address is abradley@heroicfraternities.com.

impressed she was by the outpouring of love and support from the Alpha Tau Omega fraternity at Grand Valley State. Quinn was their brother, which made his mother family too. The brothers did a heroic job of checking in on her and making her feel cared for during the most difficult time of her life. This is what heroic masculinity looks like. That is what the critics don't see.

If a fraternity man is reading this book, and *you* are struggling with depression or hopelessness, please talk to someone. Sometimes it's easier to talk to a stranger, like a counselor. But whatever you do, let someone help you. You are more than worth it, and the world needs you, even if you can't see it right now. You can even contact me, and I'll help you get some help.

I would like to offer a special dedication of this book, and the entire heroic fraternity project, to the heroism of the brothers of Alpha Tau Omega at Grand Valley State University, and to the memory of Quinten "Quinn" Campbell (2002–2021). May his memory be eternal.

Bibliography

@badgerbarstool. "This girl was an inch away from death @5thyear." Instagram video, June 30, 2018. https://www.instagram.com/p/BkqzxcYhxGD/?utm_source=ig_embed&utm_campaign=embed_video_watch_again.

ABC13 Houston. "SMU Fraternity Suspended for Hazing Allegations." *ABC13.com*, October 5, 2017. Accessed January 24, 2019. https://abc13.com/smu-fraternity-suspended-for-hazing-allegations/2492276/.

Abelson, Max, and Zeke Faux. "Secret Handshakes Greet Frat Brothers on Wall Street." *Bloomberg.com*, December 23, 2013. Accessed August 15, 2019. https://www.bloomberg.com/news/articles/2013-12-23/secret-handshakes-greet-frat-brothers-on-wall-street.

Adams, Stephen, and Kurtis Quillin, and Brandon Gray. "Baylor Suspends Fraternity Following 'Racist' Mexican-themed Party." *9News.com*, May 1, 2017. Accessed January 17, 2019. https://www.9news.com/article/news/local/baylor-suspends-fraternity-following-racist-mexican-themed-party/435707064.

Arnold, Patrick. *Wildmen, Warriors, and Kings: Masculine Spirituality and the Bible* New York: Crossroad, 1992.

Assalone, Amanda E., Meghan M. Grace, and J. Patrick Biddix. "Mental Health Study FFE Research Grant Report (2020)." Accessed June 17, 2022. https://foundationfe.org/wp-content/uploads/2021/01/PERC_Mental-Health-Study-2020.pdf.

Associated Press. "California University Suspends Fraternities, Sororities over Photos." *The Seattle Times*, April 18, 2018. Accessed January 12, 2019. https://www.seattletimes.com/nation-world/cal-poly-slo-suspends-all-fraternities-and-sororities/.

———. "Clemson Suspends Fraternity Social Events after Sex Assault Report." *Post and Courier*, January 29, 2018. Accessed January 12, 2019. https://www.postandcourier.com/news/clemson-suspends-fraternity-social-events-after-sex-assault-report/article_79e1b7ec-04fd-11e8-afd3-539bd3afa2e5.html.

———. "Frat Suspended after LeBron James White Powder Stunt." *AP News*, March 3, 2018. Accessed February 15, 2019. https://www.apnews.com/9e9f82ebeadd432faf415f481cc52afd.

———. "Penn State Sorority Pledges Forced to Lick Members' Toes, Hazing Report Finds." *New York Post*, January 16, 2019. Accessed March 01, 2019. https://nypost.com/2019/01/16/penn-state-sorority-pledges-forced-to-lick-members-toes-hazing-report-finds/.

————. "Police: Cold Likely Contributed to Death of College Student." *AP News,* February 3, 2019. Accessed May 5, 2022. https://apnews.com/article/c50997e8e6dc417e816ad824f3d7503d.

————. "University of Central Arkansas suspends Kappa Sigma chapter." *AP News,* December 17, 2018. Accessed May 5, 2022. https://apnews.com/article/c669485d f6b94b53b582d1379a1d75cc.

Atkins, Tony. "Fraternity Suspended after Sexual Assault Claim at Rhodes College." *Fox13,* February 21, 2019. Accessed February 26, 2019. https://www.fox13memphis.com/top-stories/fraternity-suspended-after-sexual-assault-claim-at-rhodes-college/923933146.

Baier, John L., and Edward G. Whipple. "Greek Values and Attitudes." *NASPA Journal* 28.1 (1990) 43–53.

Baker, Wayne. "Miami University Suspends All Frat Activity after Reports of Hazing." *Journal-news,* February 21, 2018. Accessed January 5, 2019. https://www.journal-news.com/news/miami-university-suspends-all-frat-activity-after-reports-hazing/ljtZuChxhIM8zrRDhUx2MO/.

Baldasare, Angela. "Why Fewer Men Are Attending College and What Should Be Done." *Insidehighered.com,* November 22, 2021. Accessed February 6, 2022. https://www.insidehighered.com/views/2021/11/22/why-fewer-men-are-attending-college-and-what-should-be-done-opinion.

Barstool Sports. "The Science Behind a Frat Party." YouTube video, 7:23. November 30, 2019. Accessed July 20, 2022. https://www.youtube.com/watch?v=_PHbluQ6Hcc.

Bartnett, William. "Fraternities aren't going away: Here's what UR can do to fix them." *The Collegian,* January 16, 2022. Accessed on June 21, 2022. https://www.thecollegianur.com/article/2022/01/opinion-fraternities-arent-going-away-heres-what-ur-can-do-to-fix-them.

Bass, Robert, Jr. "What It's like Being the Only Black Guy in a White Fraternity." *The Tab.* University of Miami, May 4, 2016. Accessed July 20, 2022. https://thetab.com/us/umiami/2016/05/04/like-black-guy-white-fraternity-1405.

Bauman, Anna. "OU Beta Theta Pi Fraternity Suspends Member after 'completely Unacceptable' Rhetoric in Alleged Campus Corner Incident." *OU Daily,* August 24, 2018. Accessed January 5, 2019. http://www.oudaily.com/news/ou-beta-theta-pi-fraternity-suspends-member-after-completely-unacceptable/article_0d08b1c4-a7b5–11e8-a32c-7f3134ab8f6d.html.

Blade Staff, The. "BGSU Students Suspended from Fraternity after Mocking Mexican-Americans." *The Blade,* December 1, 2018. Accessed January 5, 2019. https://www.toledoblade.com/sports/bgsu/2018/11/30/bowling-green-students-suspended-from-fraternity-after-mocking-mexican/stories/20181130131.

Bookwalter, Genevieve. "Fraternity Will Return to Northwestern after It Was Suspended for Serving Minors, Subject of Sexual Assault Allegations." *Chicago Tribune,* September 22, 2018. Accessed January 22, 2019. https://www.chicagotribune.com/suburbs/evanston/news/ct-evr-sae-fraternct-evr-sae-fraternity-returns-northwestern-university-tl-0927-ity-return-northwestern-tl-0927-story.html.

Braucher, David. "The Pandemic of Male Loneliness: The Hidden Reason Men Struggle with Social Distancing." *Psychology Today,* February 24, 2022. Accessed on June 29, 2022. https://www.psychologytoday.com/us/blog/life-smarts/202102/the-pandemic-male-loneliness.

Breaux, Aimee. "A Month before the Out-of-state Party Ban, This UI Fraternity Damaged $107K worth of Property in Illinois." *Iowa City Press-Citizen*, October 23, 2018. Accessed January 25, 2019. https://www.press-citizen.com/story/news/education/university-of-iowa/2018/10/23/university-iowa-fraternity-caused-107-k-damages-illinois/1740248002/.

———. "Suspended Fraternity Presidents Line up for Interviews about Possible Alcohol-related Violations." *Iowa City Press-Citizen*, October 11, 2018. Accessed December 22, 2018. https://www.press-citizen.com/story/news/education/university-of-iowa/2018/10/11/suspended-university-iowa-fraternities-questioned-investigation/1601095002/.

Breunlin, Erica. "University of Tennessee Sorority Says It Has Suspended Member over Racist Comment." *Knoxville News Sentinel*, January 4, 2019. Accessed January 25, 2019. https://www.knoxnews.com/story/news/education/2019/01/04/ut-sorority-suspends-member-over-racist-comment/2480460002/.

Brown, Elisha. "AKA Sorority in Georgia Under Investigation for Sexual Misconduct." *Daily Beast*, May 1, 2018. Accessed February 7, 2019. https://www.thedailybeast.com/aka-sorority-in-georgia-under-investigation-for-sexual-misconduct.

Brown, Patrick T. "Opioids and the Unattached Male." *City Journal*, January 13, 2022. Accessed July 11, 2022. https://www.city-journal.org/opioids-and-the-unattached-male.

Brumley, Ben. "Impact of the Change in the 18-Year-Old Drinking Age on College Students." NIC Research, April 2021. Accessed June 17, 2022. https://nicfraternity.org/wp-content/uploads/2022/06/Impact-of-the-Change-in-the-18-Year-Old-Drinking-Age-on-College-Students-Citations.pdf

Burke, Minyvonne. "Two Swarthmore fraternities disband after leaked documents refer to 'rape attic.'" *NBC News*, May 1, 2019. Accessed July 24, 2022. https://www.nbcnews.com/news/us-news/two-swarthmore-fraternities-disband-after-leaked-documents-refer-rape-attic-n1000551

Burke, Peter. "University of Miami Sorority Suspended amid Investigation of Hazing Allegations." *Local10.com*, February 28, 2018. Accessed February 5, 2019. https://www.local10.com/education/university-of-miami-sorority-suspended-amid-investigation-of-hazing-allegations.

Burkhard, Brian and Kimberley Timpf. "New Perspectives on Fraternity and Sorority Life." NIC Research. Accessed June 17, 2022. https://nicfraternity.org/wp-content/uploads/2022/04/2021-EverFi-NIC-Research-Report-Final.pdf

Cacioppo, John T., and William Patrick. *Loneliness: Human Nature and the Need for Social Connection*. New York: W.W. Norton, 2008. 119, 126–27, 183, 215–17, 237, 240.

Capelouto, J.D. "Fraternity Closes at Ga. College; Student Taken to Hospital after Drinking Too Much." *The Atlanta Journal-Constitution*, February 13, 2019. Accessed February 19, 2019. https://www.ajc.com/news/crime—law/fraternity-closes-college-student-taken-hospital-after-drinking-too-much/zAkXEqjaOo42iIs2z9ok6L/.

Cardona, Claire Z. "SMU's Pi Kappa Alpha Fraternity Suspended after Hazing Investigation." *Dallas News*, March 26, 2018. Accessed January 12, 2019. https://www.dallasnews.com/news/higher-education/2018/03/26/smus-pi-kappa-alpha-fraternity-suspended-after-hazing-investigation.

CBS News. "The Delinquents." *CBS News—Breaking News, 24/7 Live Streaming News & Top Stories*, August 22, 2000. Accessed 25 July 2022. https://www.cbsnews.com/news/the-delinquents/.

CDC: National Center for Health Statistics. Vital Statistics Online Data Portal. Accessed June 8, 2022. https://www.cdc.gov/nchs/data_access/vitalstatsonline.htm.

Chess, Richard. "AEPi Suspended After Possible Hazing." *The Emory Wheel*, February 19, 2019. Accessed February 26, 2019. https://emorywheel.com/aepi-suspended-after-possible-hazing-2-19-19/.

Chira, Susan. 2016. "The Crisis of Men in America." *The New York Times*, October 25, 2016, sec. Opinion. Accessed July 12, 2022. https://www.nytimes.com/2016/10/25/opinion/the-crisis-of-men-in-america.html.

Chiu, Allyson. "Syracuse Fraternity: Second Video Shows Mock Sexual Assault of Disabled Person." *Washington Post*, April 23, 2018. Accessed January 25, 2019. https://www.washingtonpost.com/news/morning-mix/wp/2018/04/23/second-syracuse-fraternity-video-shows-mock-sexual-assault-of-disabled-person-members-disciplined/.

Cianfrance, Derek, dir. *The Place Beyond the Pines*. Universal City, CA: Focus Features, 2012.

Cills, Hazel. "Women Sue Yale For Allowing Social Scene Dominated By Gross Fraternities." *Jezebel*, February 13, 2019. Accessed February 15, 2019. https://jezebel.com/women-sue-yale-for-allowing-social-scene-dominated-by-g-1832587616.

Ciurczak, Ellen. "'Ritual in Progress:' Hazing, Drugs, Weapons Found at USM Sigma Chi House, Reports Show." *Hattiesburg American*, February 6, 2019. Accessed February 15, 2019. https://www.hattiesburgamerican.com/story/news/education/usm/2019/02/06/university-southern-miss-police-reports-violations-sigma-chi-hazing-drugs-alcohol-weapons-usm/2730501002/.

Cohen, Howard. "UF Suspends Fraternity for Four Years over Alleged Alcohol and Drug Use." *The Miami Herald*, January 10, 2018. Accessed January 13, 2019. https://www.miamiherald.com/news/local/education/article194020969.html.

Cohen, Kate. "It's Time to Abolish College Fraternities." *The Washington Post*, April 7, 2021. Accessed 25 July 2022. https://www.washingtonpost.com/opinions/2021/11/01/its-time-abolish-college-fraternities/.

Cutway, Adrienne. "UCF Suspends Frat after Woman Says She Was Gang-raped at Party, Deputies Say." *True Crime Daily*, April 25, 2018. Accessed May 5, 2022. https://truecrimedaily.com/2018/04/25/ucf-frat-suspended-after-woman-claims-men-raped-her-officials-say/.

Daley, Suzanne. "Troublemakers: Teen-Agers, Tusked." *The New York Times*, December 28, 1996. Accessed 25 July, 2022. https://www.nytimes.com/1996/12/28/world/troublemakers-teen-agers-tusked.html.

Daugherty, Owen. "Ohio State Tau Kappa Epsilon Chapter Suspended for 3 Years." *The Lantern*, January 8, 2018. Accessed January 4, 2019. https://www.thelantern.com/2018/01/ohio-state-tau-kappa-epsilon-chapter-suspended-for-three-years/.

Dockterman, Eliana. "Fraternity Sigma Alpha Epsilon Bans Initiations After Hazing Deaths." *Time*, March 7, 2014. https://time.com/16378/sigma-alpha-epsilon-frat-bans-initiations/.

Ducre, Gwendolyn. "ULM Suspends Its Kappa Sigma Fraternity Chapter." *KNOE 8 News*, October 12, 2017. Accessed January 25, 2019. https://www.knoe.com/content/news/ULM-suspends-Fraternity-450672133.html.

Dunker, Chris. "Woman Sues UNL Fraternity over Alleged Sex Assault." *JournalStar.com*, November 30, 2018. Accessed December 28, 2018. https://journalstar.com/news/local/education/woman-sues-unl-fraternity-over-alleged-sex-assault/article1a78d449-eca6-5ed2-9816-2a6a01e1fcof.html.

Emsi. "Demographic Drought." *Emsi*, 2021. Accessed August 3, 2021. https://www.economicmodeling.com/demographic-drought/.

Enfinger, Matthew. "Hazing, Assault and Threats: A Timeline of Kappa Sigma's Recent Investigation." *The George-Anne*, December 6, 2018. Accessed May 5, 2022. https://thegeorgeanne.com/2915/news/hazing-assault-and-threats-a-timeline-of-kappa-sigmas-recent-investigation/.

Etters, Karl. "Two More FSU Fraternities Banned from Campus for Alcohol, Hazing." Tallahassee Democrat, January 17, 2018. Accessed January 23, 2019. https://www.tallahassee.com/story/news/2018/01/17/two-fsu-fraternities-sanctioned-suspensions-campus-several-years/1042398001/.

Farrell, Warren, and John Gray. *The Boy Crisis: Why Our Boys Are Struggling and What We Can Do About It*. Dallas: BenBella, 2018, 15–39.

Farrell, Warren. "'Boy Crisis' Threatens America's Future with Economic, Health and Suicide Risks." *USA TODAY*, April 7, 2019. Accessed March 28, 2020. https://www.usatoday.com/story/opinion/2019/04/07/males-risk-boy-crisis-identity-america-future-addiction-suicide-column/3331366002/.

Federal Bureau of Prisons, "BOP Statistics: Inmate Gender." Federal Bureau of Prisons, August 03, 2019. Accessed August 06, 2019. https://www.bop.gov/about/statistics/statistics_inmate_gender.jsp.

Field, Carla. "Upstate University Suspends Fraternity Chapter for at Least 4 Years." *WYFF*, January 16, 2019. Accessed January 22, 2019. https://www.wyff4.com/article/upstate-university-suspends-fraternity-chapter-for-at-least-4-years/25906806.

Fight the New Drug. "What's the Average Age of a Kid's First Porn Exposure?" May 31, 2019. Accessed 12 August 2019. https://fightthenewdrug.org/real-average-age-of-first-exposure/.

Foubert, John D., Angela Clark-Taylor, and Andrew F. Wall. "Is Campus Rape Primarily a Serial or One-Time Problem? Evidence From a Multicampus Study." *Violence Against Women* 26.3–4 (2019) 296–311.

Gallup. "Fraternities and Sororities: Experiences and Outcomes in College, Work and Life." Partnership with Gallup, the North American Interfraternity Conference (NIC) and the National Panhellenic Council (NPC), 2021. Accessed June 17, 2022. https://www.newamerica.org/education-policy/highered-public-opinion-hub/fraternities-and-sororities-experiences-and-outcomes-in-college-work-and-life/.

Gibson, Marlon Ladell. "The Narrative Experiences of Black and Brown First-Generation Fraternity Men in Historically White Fraternities." PhD diss., the University of Georgia, 2021.

Graduate A from spring 2019. Furman University. Interview by Jackson Kane, New York City, May 23, 2019; Graduate B from spring 2019, Furman University. Interview by Jackson Kane, New York City, May 30, 2019.

Graduate from spring 1988. University of Delaware. Interview by Jackson Kane, New York City, June 10, 2019.

Greif, Geoffrey. *Buddy System: Understanding Male Friendships*. Oxford: Oxford University Press, 2008.

Hagerty, Patrick. "Break Them Down, Then Build Them Up." *The Fraternity Advisor: The Fraternity Pledge Program*, July 18, 2010. Accessed July 24, 2022. https://thefraternityadvisor.com/break-them-down-then-build-them-up/.

———. "Reasons Why Guys Join Fraternities." *The Fraternity Advisor: Fraternity Recruitment*, January 24, 2010. https://thefraternityadvisor.com/reasons-why-guys-join-a-fraternity/ Accessed July 24, 2022.

Harmon, Matt. "Interfraternity Council Suspends All Fraternity Social Activity in Midst of Hazing, Assault Allegations." *The Michigan Daily*, November 9, 2017. Accessed January 12, 2019. https://www.michigandaily.com/section/campus-life/interfraternity-council-suspends-all-fraternity-social-activity-midst-hazing.

Hemmer, Jeffery. *Man Up: The Quest For Masculinity.* St. Louis: Concordia, 2017.

Herman, Jeff. "Safe Swimming Water Temperatures." *Livestrong.com.* Accessed July 16, 2019. https://www.livestrong.com/article/361005-safe-swimming-water-temperatures/.

Hernandez, Lauren. "Sonoma State Bans Fraternity Chapter for 5 Years after Investigating a Hazing Incident." *San Francisco Chronicle*, February 1, 2019. Accessed February 20, 2019. https://www.sfchronicle.com/crime/article/Sonoma-State-bans-fraternity-chapter-for-5-years-13582766.php.

Herzog, Karen. "UW Suspends Kappa Sigma after Woman Nearly Hit by Falling Television at Party." *Milwaukee Journal Sentinel*, July 6, 2018. Accessed January 17, 2019. https://www.jsonline.com/story/news/education/2018/07/05/uw-madison-frat-suspended-after-tv-nearly-fell-woman-party/761694002/.

Higher Education Research Institute (HERI). "2014 Freshmen Survey." The Cooperative Institutional Research Program, 2014. Accessed August 05, 2019. https://heri.ucla.edu/cirp-freshman-survey/.

History.com. "Industrial Revolution: Definitions, Causes, & Inventions." *History.com.* Accessed July 22, 2022, https://www.history.com/topics/industrial-revolution/industrial-revolution.

Hopkins, Anna. "9 LSU Fraternity Members Arrested for Shocking Hazing Incidents." *Fox News*, February 16, 2019. Accessed February 17, 2019. https://www.foxnews.com/us/nine-lsu-fraternity-members-arrested-for-shocking-hazing-incidents.

Horney, Karen. *Neurosis and Human Growth.* New York, New York: W.W. Norton, 1950.

Iberdrola, "Generation Alpha Will Lead a 100% Digital World." Accessed July 24, 2022. https://www.iberdrola.com/talent/alpha-generation.

IMDb. "Ryan Reynolds: *Van Wilder.*" 2002 IMDb.com. Accessed July 24, 2022. https://www.imdb.com/title/tt0283111/characters/nm0005351?ref_=tt_cl_t1.

Itel, Dan. "Ocean Submersion and Bloody Knuckles: Cal Poly Fraternity Suspended over Hazing." *The Tribune*, October 20, 2018. Accessed December 27, 2018. https://www.sanluisobispo.com/news/local/education/article220371680.html

Johnson, Grant S., and Jena Serbu, dir. *Frat Star.* Cleveland, OH: Gravitas Ventures, 2017.

Jordan, Heather. "CMU drops fraternity after student's death, sex assault claims." *mlive*, October 11, 2018. Accessed May 5, 2022. https://www.mlive.com/news/saginaw/2018/10/cmu_removes_fraternity_in_resp.html#:~:text=MOUNT%20PLEASANT%2C%20MI%20%2D%2D%20Central,Sigma%20Phi%20gatherings%20and%20events.

Junger, Sebastian. *Tribe: On Homecoming and Belonging.* New York: Twelve, 2016.

KARK. "UA-Little Rock Suspends Sorority, Fraternity." *KARK.com*, April 19, 2018. Accessed January 12, 2019. https://www.kark.com/news/local-news/ua-little-rock-suspends-sorority-fraternity/1130079461.

Kast, Monica. "UT Fraternity under Investigation after 2 Students Report Being Drugged, Raped." *Knoxville News Sentinel*, December 7, 2018. Accessed December 28, 2018. https://www.knoxnews.com/story/news/education/2018/12/07/ut-rapes-frat-under-investigation-after-2-report-being-drugged/2191400002/.

Kelly, Dave. "PTypes—The Expansive Solution." 1998–2006. Accessed July 24, 2022. https://www.ptypes.com/expansive_solution.html.

———. "PTypes—The Self-Effacing Solution," 1998–2006. Accessed July 24, 2022. https://www.ptypes.com/self-effacing_solution.html.

KSNB Local 4. "UNK Frat Member Arrested for Sexual Assault." *KSNB Local4*, February 28, 2019. Accessed March 1, 2019. https://www.ksnblocal4.com/content/news/UNK-fraternity-suspended-506461781.html.

KWWL. "Banned UI Frat Linked to Hazing Allegations of Body Slamming, Hot Sauce in Eyes and Forced Drinking." *KWWL*, December 17, 2018. Accessed December 28, 2018. https://kwwl.com/homepage/2018/12/17/body-slamming-hot-sauce-in-eyes-part-of-hazing-allegations-against-banned-ui-frat/.

KXAN. "Texas State University President Suspends All Greek Activity following Pledge's Death." *KXAN.com*, November 14, 2017. Accessed May 5, 2022. https://www.kxan.com/news/local/hays/texas-state-university-president-suspends-all-greek-activity-following-pledges-death/

Landis, John, dir. *National Lampoon's Animal House*. Universal City, CA: Universal Pictures, 1978.

Lattanzio, Vince. "Temple Suspends AEPi Frat Amid Sex Assault Investigation." *NBC 10 Philadelphia*, April 20, 2018. Accessed January 12, 2019. https://www.nbcphiladelphia.com/news/local/Temple-University-Suspends-Alpha-Epsilon-Pi-Fraternity-Amid-Sexual-Assault-Investigation-480403593.html.

Lembke, Anna. *Dopamine Nation: Finding Balance in the Age of Indulgence*. New York: Dutton, 2021.

Leonard, Ben. "Fourth Fraternity Chapter Disciplined: New Member Activities Suspended at Kappa Alpha." *The Chronicle*, February 7, 2019. Accessed February 19, 2019. https://www.dukechronicle.com/article/2019/02/duke-university-fraternity-suspension-kappa-alpha-hazing-allegation.

Lewis, Michele K., "Loneliness Among Teens Has Increased Over the Years: Violence, Depression, and Radicalization Realities Are Telling." *Psychology Today*, May 30, 2022. Accessed on June 21, 2022. https://www.psychologytoday.com/us/blog/cultural-neuroscience/202205/loneliness-among-teens-has-increased-over-the-years

Lindo, Jason M., Peter Siminski, and Isaac D. Swensen. "College Party Culture and Sexual Assault." *American Economic Journal: Applied Economics* 10.1 (2018) 236–65.

Linnabary, Andrew. "Investigation Documents Shed Light on Beta Theta Pi Suspension." *The Sunflower*, February 4, 2019. Accessed February 27, 2019. https://thesunflower.com/35552/news/investigation-documents-shed-light-on-beta-theta-pi-suspension/.

Loftus, Sawyer. "Police Report Reveals Student's Final Hours." *The Vermont Cynic*, April 9, 2019. Accessed July 12, 2022. https://vtcynic.com/news/police-report-reveals-students-final-hours/.

Madeson, Melissa. "Seligman's PERMA+ Model Explained: A Theory of Wellbeing," *Positive Psychology.com*, February 24, 2017. Accessed on June 28, 2022. https://positivepsychology.com/perma-model/#emotion.

Martinez, David. "University of Arizona Expels Fraternity over Alcohol, Drugs and Threats of Violence." *Arizona Daily Star*, February 10, 2019. Accessed February 20, 2019. https://tucson.com/news/local/university-of-arizona-expels-fraternity-over-alcohol-drugs-and-threats/article_2e4f1321–8606-5239-8634-6eddb4e8ba69.html.

Marx, Jeffrey. *Season of Life: A Football Star, a Boy, and a Journey into Manhood*. Simon and Schuster: New York, 2003. 36.

Mayo Clinic Staff. "Alcohol Use Disorder." *Mayo Clinic*, July 11, 2018. Accessed June 25, 2019. https://www.mayoclinic.org/diseases-conditions/alcohol-use-disorder/symptoms-causes/syc-20369243.

McAndrew, Siobhan. "UNR Suspends Tau Kappa Epsilon, Investigates Frat's Songbook That Promotes Sexual Violence." *Reno Gazette Journal*, December 6, 2018. Accessed December 28, 2018. https://www.rgj.com/story/news/education/2018/12/06/unr-suspends-tke-after-songbook-sexually-violent-songs-surfaces/2227179002/.

Miller, Vanessa. "Another University of Iowa Fraternity Suspended, Accused of Hazing." *The Gazette*, November 20, 2018. Accessed December 27, 2018. https://www.thegazette.com/subject/news/education/another-university-of-iowa-fraternity-suspended-accused-of-hazing-20181120.

Murphy, Dean E. "South Africa Reins In Its Young Elephants." *Los Angeles Times*, September 18, 1998. Accessed 24 July 2022. https://www.latimes.com/archives/la-xpm-1998-sep-18-mn-24037-story.html.

Musto, Drew. "Two Fraternities Placed on Yearlong Probation After Suspensions." *The Cornell Daily Sun*, May 10, 2017. Accessed January 19, 2019. https://cornellsun.com/2017/05/10/pi-kappa-alpha-taken-off-interim-suspension-put-on-yearlong-probation/.

National Alliance on Mental Illness (NAMI). "Mental Health in College-Age Men," *NAMI*. Accessed on June 2, 2022. https://cdn.zephyrcms.com/5a6b09be-4dfa-46ab-854a-271f5f4da48e/-/inline/yes/mental-health-in-college-men.pdf.

National Institute on Alcohol Abuse and Alcoholism (NIAAA). "College Drinking," *NIAAA*, February 2020. Accessed July 11, 2022. https://www.niaaa.nih.gov/sites/default/files/Collegefactsheet.pdf.

Neel, Andrew, dir. *Goat*. Los Angeles, CA: The Film Arcade and Paramount Pictures, 2016.

Nguyen, Ryan, and Michael Tobin. "UO Phi Kappa Psi Chapter Temporarily Suspended after Derogatory Document Surfaces." *Emerald Media*, May 1, 2018. Accessed February 4, 2019. https://www.dailyemerald.com/news/fsl/uo-phi-kappa-psi-chapter-temporarily-suspended-after-derogatory-document-surfaces/article_9a14d923-980f-5be9-bffd-092004465bcf.html.

NIC Research. "Fraternity Stats At-a-glance." North American Interfraternity Conference, February 3, 2019. Accessed 15 July 2019. https://nicfraternity.org/fraternity-stats-at-a-glance/.

———. "Research Findings," North American Intrafraternity Conference. Accessed July 11, 2022. https://nicfraternity.org/research/.

———. "The Decrease in Drunk Driving from the 1970s to Present." North American Interfraternity Conference (NIC), April 2021. Accessed 17 June, 2022. https://nicfraternity.org/wp-content/uploads/2022/06/White-Paper-Drunk-Driving-Citations.pdf.

Okolie, Stefania. "Texas A&M Fraternity Phi Gamma Delta Suspended for Violating Alcohol and Hazing Rules before Houston Teen's Death." *ABC13 Houston*, November 14, 2018. Accessed December 27, 2018. https://abc13.com/texas-a-m-fraternity-suspended-after-houston-teens-death/4687513/.

PennState. "Two Penn State Fraternities Lose Recognition over Violations." Penn State University: Administration, October 28, 2017. Accessed February 18, 2019. https://news.psu.edu/story/490912/2017/10/28/administration/two-penn-state-fraternities-lose-recognition-over-violations.

PERC, The University of Tennessee Knoxville. Final Study Report by the Post-Secondary Education Research Center (PERC), 1–4. "The Benefits of Single Sex Fraternity Involvement," 2020. Accessed June 17, 2022. https://nicfraternity.org/wp-content/uploads/2022/06/NIC-Single-Sex-Final-Study-Report-1.pdf. https://foundationfe.org/wp-content/uploads/2021/01/PERC_Mental-Health-Study-2020.pdf.

Petropoulis, Ivan. "The Problem with Abolishing Greek Life." *The Chronicle*, April 7, 2021. Accessed July 24, 2022. https://www.dukechronicle.com/article/2021/04/the-problem-with-abolishing-greek-life.

Phillips, Todd, and Andrew Gurland, dir. *Old School*. Universal City, CA: DreamWorks Pictures, 2003.

Phillips, Todd, dir. *Frat House*. HBO Documentary (unaired). YouTube video, 58:27. Accessed Jun 6, 2021. https://www.youtube.com/watch?v=bPHFe8Z1NOo.

Pike, Gary R. "The Greek Experience Revisited: The Relationships between Fraternity/Sorority Membership and Student Engagement, Learning Outcomes, Grades, and Satisfaction with College." Bloomington, IN: Research Report prepared for the North American Interfraternity Conference, March 2020. Accessed June 17, 2022. https://drive.google.com/file/d/1VO32qZdHh9tu7nWbbFudAvLVMJ_uT5lj/view.

Porter, Tom. "A Cornell Frat Was Suspended after Members Competed in a 'pig roast' to See Who Could Sleep with the Heaviest Women." *Newsweek*, February 7, 2018. Accessed January 23, 2019. https://www.newsweek.com/cornell-frat-suspended-after-pig-roast-sex-contest-800777.

PRX. "Living on Earth: Delinquent Elephants." *Living on Earth*, World Media Foundation, April 18, 2005. Accessed 24 July 2022. https://www.loe.org/shows/segments.html?programID=00-P13–0050&segmentID=7.

Ratchford, Dan, and Nikki Krize. "Student Found Drunk, Penn State Fraternity Suspended." *WNEP.com*, October 4, 2017. Accessed January 25, 2019. https://wnep.com/2017/10/04/student-found-drunk-penn-state-fraternity-suspended/.

Rex, Kasai. "I Was the Black Guy in a White Frat." *Salon*, March 16, 2015. https://www.salon.com/2015/03/16/my_shucking_and_jiving_years_i_was_the_black_guy_in_a_white_frat

Robbins, Alexandra. *Fraternity: An Inside Look at a Year of College Boys Becoming Men*. New York: Dutton, 2019.

Rohr, Richard. *Adam's Return: The Five Promises of Male Initiation*. New York, New York: Crossroad Publishing, 2004.

Rosa, Amanda. "Delta Chi Fraternity Suspended from UF after Pledge Nearly Died." *The Independent Florida Alligator*, September 4, 2018. Accessed January 4, 2019. https://www.alligator.org/news/delta-chi-fraternity-suspended-from-uf-after-pledge-nearly-died/article_d9812b16-b0b9–11e8-b2cd-9b5123778d9b.html.

Sanchez, Mario. "College Releases Hazing Reports, Sanctions from Last Five Years." *The Lafayette*, February 8, 2019. Accessed February 27, 2019. https://www.lafayettestudentnews.com/blog/2019/02/08/pen-hazing-reports/.

Schiraldi, Glenn. *The Resilience Workbook: Essential Skills to Recover from Stress, Trauma, and Adversity*. Oakland, CA: New Harbinger, 2017.

Seligman, Martin. *Flourish: A Visionary New Understanding of Happiness and Well-being*. New York: Atria, 2011.

Senior, Cornell University. Interview by Jackson Kane, New York City, May 29, 2019.

Shaw, Rissa. "Baylor Bans Rap Song after Sorority Sanctioned over Racially-tinged Video." *KWTX | Waco*, January 18, 2019. Accessed January 24, 2019. https://www.kwtx.com/content/news/Baylor-sorority-sanctioned-over-racially-tinged-video-504568331.html.

Sheridan, Jack. "Seven fraternities disaffiliate from Duke IFC." *The Chronicle*, February 16, 2021. Accessed on June 29, 2022. https://www.dukechronicle.com/article/2021/02/duke-university-fraternities-disafilliated.

Silvy, Tyler. "Suspended Sigma Chi Fraternity at University of Northern Colorado Had 21 Complaints in 3 Years, including 18 in 2018." *Greeley Tribune*, November 7, 2018. Accessed December 27, 2018. https://www.greeleytribune.com/news/university-of-northern-colorado-wont-release-records-related-to-suspended-fraternity/.

Slagter, Martin. "'40-yard Dash' on Backs of Students Led to UM Fraternity's Removal." *MLive.com*, December 5, 2018. Accessed December 28, 2018. https://www.mlive.com/news/ann-arbor/index.ssf/2018/12/40-yard_dash_incident_led_to_u.html.

Snyder, Susan. "Drexel Suspends Frat for Five Years." *The Inquirer*, May 25, 2017. Accessed January 25, 2019. http://www.philly.com/philly/education/drexel-suspends-frat-for-five-years-20170525.html.

Sundby, Alex. "'Revenge Porn' Lawsuit Filed against University of Central Florida Fraternity." *CBS News*, June 15, 2018. Accessed February 5, 2019. https://www.cbsnews.com/news/ucf-revenge-porn-lawsuit-michael-avenatti-sues-delta-sigma-phi-fraternity-university-of-central-florida-sex-tape/.

Swan, Steve. Twitter direct message to author, June 27, 2022. https://twitter.com/SteveTundraSwan/status/1541562792804753410

Syrett, Nicholas L. *The Company He Keeps: A History of White College Fraternities*. Chapel Hill, NC: University of North Carolina Press, 2009.

Szalewski, Susan. "Creighton Suspends Phi Kappa Psi until 2025, Citing Reports of Underage Drinking, Drug Distribution and Hazing." *Omaha World-Herald*, March 21, 2017. Accessed January 17, 2019. https://www.omaha.com/news/education/creighton-suspends-phi-kappa-psi-until-citing-reports-of-underage/article_330845f6-0dd3-11e7-9ff9-7317d0299435.html.

Tallahassee News. "Man Charged in Battery Incident at Suspended FSU Fraternity's House." *WTXL-Tallahassee*, August 31, 2018. Accessed January 25, 2019. http://www.wtxl.com/news/man-charged-in-battery-incident-at-suspended-fsu-fraternity-s/article_e335a73e-fc61-11e7-bf35-63e974750497.html.

U.S. Bureau of Labor Statistics. "College Enrollment and Work Activity of Recent High School and College Graduates Summary." April 26 , 2019. Accessed August 05 2019. https://www.bls.gov/news.release/hsgec.nro.htm.

U.S. Department of Justice, Office of Justice Programs, Bureau of Justice Statistics. "Rape and Sexual Victimization Among College-Aged Females, 1995–2013." 2014. Accessed July 20, 2022. https://bjs.ojp.gov/content/pub/pdf/rsavcaf9513.pdf

United Press International. "CDC: Many Men with Depression, Anxiety Untreated." *United Press International*, June 12, 2015. Accessed July 12, 2022. http://www.upi.com/Health_News/2015/06/12/CDC-Many-men-with-depression-anxiety-untreated/7341434139241/.

UWgreek.com. "Fraternity Facts." Accessed August 20, 2019. http://www.uwgreek.com/frat/home.html.

Van Wyk, Rich, and Carlos Diaz. "IU Fraternities Suspend Social, New Member Activities." 13 WTHR Indianapolis, November 28, 2017. Accessed January 12, 2019. https://www.wthr.com/article/news/local/iu-fraternities-suspend-social-new-member-activities/531–113b03cb-38ab-433a-89df-0840ec2f11f8.

Vestal, Christine. "COVID Harmed Kids' Mental Health—and Schools Are Feeling It." The Pew Charitable Trusts, 2001. Accessed November 8, 2021. https://www.pewtrusts.org/en/research-and-analysis/blogs/stateline/2021/11/08/covid-harmed-kids-mental-health-and-schools-are-feeling-it.

Wade, Kim. "Univ. of North Georgia Suspends 1 Fraternity, 2 Sororities in Hazing Reports." WSAV, March 9, 2018. Accessed February 7, 2019. https://www.wsav.com/news/univ-of-north-georgia-suspends-1-fraternity-2-sororities-in-hazing-reports/1077874561.

Waller, Andrew, dir. American Pie Presents: Beta House. Universal City, CA: Universal Pictures Home Entertainment, 2007.

Weiss, Evan. "UVM Suspends All Fraternity Activities in Response to Connor Gage's Death." Burlington Free Press, February 5, 2019. Accessed May 5, 2022. https://www.burlingtonfreepress.com/story/news/2019/02/05/connor-gage-uvm-student-fraternity/2781917002/.

Whitford, Emma. "Fraternity Members Suspended for Racist, Homophobic Video." Inside Higher Ed, June 11, 2018. Accessed January 11, 2019. https://www.insidehighered.com/news/2018/06/11/syracuse-suspends-fraternity-students-after-racist-homophobic-anti-semitic-videos.

Wiese, Dawn. "Male Enrollment in College and What Can Be Done to Improve It: An Annotated Bibliography" North American Interfraternity Conference (NIC), April 2022. Accessed June 17, 2022. https://nicfraternity.org/wp-content/uploads/2022/06/Men-in-College.pdf.

WKOW. "UW-Madison Suspends Alpha Sigma Phi Fraternity." WKOW.com. February 23, 2019. Accessed February 25, 2019. https://wkow.com/news/top-stories/2019/02/22/uw-madison-suspends-alpha-sigma-phi-fraternity/.

Wolf, Colin. "UCF Fraternity Suspended after Claims of Sexual Assault and Hazing." Orlando Weekly, June 28, 2017. Accessed May 5, 2022. https://www.orlandoweekly.com/news/ucf-fraternity-suspended-after-claims-of-sexual-assault-and-hazing-5311405.

Wolf, Marin. "AKPsi's UNC Chapter Is under Investigation following Allegations of Hazing." The Daily Tar Heel, February 17, 2019. Accessed February 21, 2019. https://www.dailytarheel.com/article/2019/02/businees-fraternity-akpsi0218.

World Sea Temperature. "Morro Bay Sea Temperature October Average, United States: Sea Temperatures." Global Sea Temperature, 2019. Accessed July 16, 2019. https://www.seatemperature.org/north-america/united-states/morro-bay-october.htm.

Yee, Gregory. "Five College of Charleston Fraternities Shut down within a Year, Pi Kappa Phi Shutters Doors after Misconduct Investigation." Post and Courier, August 3, 2017. Accessed January 25, 2019. https://www.postandcourier.com/news/five-college-of-charleston-fraternities-shut-down-within-a-year/article_96e131f4–77c4-11e7-b4ff-6b74c68f5a30.html.

Index

Made in United States
Orlando, FL
08 March 2023

30827936R00122